Handbook
of the
Nautical Rules
of the Road

Handbook of the Nautical Rules of the Road

SECOND EDITION

Christopher B. Llana and
George P. Wisneskey

Naval Institute Press
Annapolis, Maryland

Library of Congress Cataloging-in-Publication Data

Llana, Christopher B.
    Handbook of the nautical rules of the road / Christopher B. Llana
and George P. Wisneskey. — 2nd ed.
      p.   cm.
    Includes index.
    ISBN 1-55750-504-7
    1. Rule of the road at sea—Handbooks, manuals, etc. 2. Inland
navigation—Law and legislation—United States—Handbooks,
manuals, etc.   I. Wisneskey, George P.   II. Title.
VK371.L58   1991
623.88'84—dc20   90-46486
                                            CIP

Printed in the United States of America on acid-free paper ∞

9 8 7 6 5 4 3 2

First printing

Acknowledgments

We wish to thank the following individuals from Coast Guard Headquarters in Washington, D.C., for their unstinting assistance in preparing this second edition (in alphabetical order): Joe Hersey, Ed LaRue, Tom Meyers, Peter Palmer, Bruce Riley, Mike Sollosi, and Chris Young.

Contents

Preface to the Second Edition

The International Rules have been amended three times since they were completely overhauled in 1972—twice since this book was originally published. Parallel amendments have also been made to the Inland Rules. Virtually all of these amendments can be described as fine-tuning rather than as basic changes. With the last set of amendments adopted, this "teething" process appears to be at an end, and we can look forward to a long period of stability before substantive changes are made again.

This edition of the *Handbook of the Nautical Rules of the Road* incorporates all of the amendments and other revisions to clarify and update the discussion of the Rules. We decided to present the Rules only in their latest form, without mention of "this recent amendment" or "last year's change" (with a couple of notable exceptions). We felt that such historical detours might confuse and not be of much significance to a mariner encountering another vessel. On the other hand, with the many recent changes and the long existence of the Rules, we felt that a short history would be useful to those who want to know when changes occurred or to those who are simply interested in the historical perspective.

To satisfy these purposes, this book now contains a short history of the Rules, starting from the beginnings of modern maritime commerce and proceeding up through the latest amendments. A new Appendix III has also been added, summarizing the new U.S. vessel traffic service regulations being proposed as this edition was going to press.

Preface to the First Edition

This book is intended as an explanatory text or reference work on both the International and Inland navigation rules and is aimed at those who earn their living operating vessels as well as at the serious recreational boater. In addition, designers and builders of vessels, maritime lawyers, and suppliers of nautical equipment will find much of the material, such as the technical lighting and signaling-appliance requirements, helpful.

The book follows the organization of the Rules themselves. The Rules are presented paragraph by paragraph, with the International Rule on the left of the page and the corresponding Inland Rule on the right. The succeeding discussion usually covers both the International and Inland requirements, pointing out similarities and differences. Where the requirements are wholly different, each version is discussed separately.

During our time at Coast Guard Headquarters, we saw the need for a book that would do more than simply restate the Rules in other language or analyze court decisions of historic significance. We saw the need for a book whose comments and interpretations would be applicable to real-life situations, a book that presented the Rules not as theoretical abstractions but as practical recommendations for behavior on the water. We have attempted to provide such a book. Using the expertise we developed through many years of providing, in response to letter and telephone inquiries, the "official" government interpretations of various Rules, we have striven to give as much specific advice here as possible. Specific advice, subject, of course, to whatever limitations apply, can be much more useful in assessing a real-life situation than can general comments. Also, we have cross-referenced the Rules and have attempted to make the interpretations consistent with each other.

A word of caution: If we say something is a "requirement," it is because the Rules say it is. Our own interpretations and advice can generally be distinguished by the use of the conditional term "should," rather than "shall" or "must."

Finally, this book is not a scholarly treatise for assigning legal responsibility for a collision after-the-fact; it is, rather, a reference guide for applying the Rules on the water.

Handbook
of the
Nautical Rules
of the Road

A Short History
of the Rules

Until the 1800s wooden sailing ships were so slow that there was no need for much in the way of navigation rules. With the advent of steel vessels propelled by machinery, collisions became more frequent; subsequent loss of life and cargo set the stage for the enactment of such rules.

In the United States the Act of 1838 required steamboats running between sunset and sunrise to carry one or more signal lights; color, visibility, and location were not addressed. Overseas an effort by London Trinity House prompted Parliament to enact the Steam Navigation Act of 1846, which required that steam vessels pass port-to-port, that crossing vessels make course alterations to the starboard, and that sailing vessels on the port tack give way to vessels on the starboard tack.

In 1848 the United Kingdom issued regulations requiring steam vessels to display red and green sidelights as well as a white masthead light. A year later the U.S. Congress extended the light requirements to sailing vessels on U.S. waters. In 1858, in separate actions, English and U.S. flag vessels were given procedures for the use of whistle and fog signals.

In 1863 the British, in consultation with the French, implemented new and more comprehensive navigation rules. These rules, known as the Articles, were sent to other maritime countries with the idea of establishing consistent and uniform regulations having the force of International Maritime Law. Along with over thirty other maritime countries, the U.S. Congress passed on these efforts and President Lincoln signed them into law in 1864. These new rules combined with previously adopted laws to give the U.S. mariner one set of unified rules covering all vessels in all waters.

Some provisions of these first international rules were that the overtaking vessel was required to stay out of the way of the overtaken vessel; the stand-on vessel was required to maintain its course only; and the only whistle signal prescribed was a one-minute-interval steam whistle signal for fog or poor visibility. In 1880 the "1863 Articles" were supplemented by whistle signals to indicate actions taken to avoid collisions.

In 1884 a new set of international regulations was implemented. There were not many changes to the sailing and steering rules, but their applicability was limited to the high seas and coastal waters. A distinction was now being made between inland rules and international rules.

In 1889 the United States convened the first International Maritime Conference to consider regulations for preventing collisions, held in Washington, D.C. The resulting Washington Conference rules were adopted by the United States in 1890 and became effective in 1897. Significant developments in this new body of rules included a requirement for stand-on vessels to maintain speed as well as course, for steamships to carry a second masthead light, for the give-way vessel not to cross ahead of the stand-on vessel, and for the use of whistle signals to indicate course changes.

In February of 1894 Congress enacted navigation rules for the Great Lakes. All previously enacted inland navigation and pilot rules were kept in force for waters other than the Great Lakes. The revision also provided the authority for lines to divide the high seas from rivers, harbors, and inland waters.

In June of 1897, just prior to the 1 July Washington Conference international rule effective date, Congress excepted the Great Lakes, the Red River of the North, and waters emptying into the Gulf of Mexico from inland waters rules. This meant that there were now four sets of statutory rules and three sets of pilot rules. Each governed a separate geographical area: inland, Great Lakes, western rivers, and international. Only the international rules were not supplemented by separate pilot rules.

Rule change activity slowed after the adoption of the Washington Conference rules. The 1910 Brussels Maritime Conference made some minor changes to the international rules. A 1929 International Conference on Safety of Life at Sea (SOLAS) proposed a few rule changes that were never ratified. The recommendation that the direction of a turn be referenced by the rudder rather than the direction of the helm or tiller was informally agreed upon by all maritime nations in 1935. Domestically, the Motorboat Act of 25 April 1940 specified the requirements for lights, whistles, and bells by powered vessels sixty-five feet in length or less, except tug-and towboats, on U.S. navigable waters. This act was revised in 1956. In 1948 Public Law 80–544 revised the inland and western rivers rules.

The international 1948 Safety of Life at Sea Conference recommended a mandatory second masthead light for power-driven vessels over 150 feet in length, a fixed sternlight for almost all vessels, the use of five short and rapid blasts as a wake-up signal, and formalized orders for the helmsman. The conference also recognized the use of radar but only to the extent that it did not relieve users from complying with any of the rules. It took four years for the participants to ratify the conference recommendations, and they became effective on 1 January 1954.

In 1960 another SOLAS meeting was held in London. Its recommendations (effective on 1 September 1965) included a paragraph requiring early and substantial action to avoid a close-quarters situation with a vessel detected forward of the beam in restricted visibility.

During this period the U.S. maritime authorities were making a concerted effort to unify our domestic navigation rules. A draft set of unified rules was sent to Congress in 1968; no action was taken, however, because by then preparatory conferences leading to a major revision of the international rules had begun.

The outcome of these conferences was a completely reorganized and substantially modified set of navigation rules. These new rules were called the 1972 International Regulations for the Prevention of Collisions at Sea (COLREGS). The drafters had, in one broad stroke, brought the navigation rules into the twentieth century, applying modern and evolving technology to the best of traditional practices.

During the same year a U.S. federal advisory committee of twenty members was created to unify and update the several sets of U.S. domestic navigation rules, and to bring them into the closest possible agreement with the new International Rules. With the entry into force of the 72 COLREGS on 15 July 1977, this activity increased. In working to find one set of rules that could be applied on high seas as well as in U.S. waters, the U.S. Coast Guard took an active role in seeking amendments to the COLREGS that would make the International Rules more acceptable for our own internal waters and the Great Lakes. Canadian authorities participated in our domestic unification efforts as well and were instrumental in "unifying" the navigation rules applying to the Great Lakes.

On 24 December 1980, the Inland Navigational Rules Act of 1980 was enacted and, a year later, fifty-six amendments to the 72 COLREGS were adopted. The Inland Navigational Rules Act superseded the old inland rules, western rivers rules, the Great Lakes rules, their respective pilot rules, and parts of the Motorboat Act of 1940. The new Inland Rules paralleled the International Rules, in great part word-for-word. The new unified rules became effective on all U.S. inland waters except the Great Lakes on 24 December 1981 and on the Great Lakes on 1 March 1983, to match the effective date of Canada's revised rules. The amendments to the 72 COLREGS became effective on 1 June 1983 and, with the exception of some small-craft lighting provisions, were mostly editorial. On 28 September 1988, an amendment (Public Law 100–448) to the U.S. Inland Rules was enacted that made Inland Rules 3(g)(v), 27(b), and 27(f) consistent with the first set of International Rule amendments.

Separate changes to the Inland Rules were made on 30 October 1984 by Public Law 98–557—primarily the addition of Rule 14(d), a fourth western rivers provision.

The 72 COLREGS were changed a second time by nine amendments that came into force on 19 November 1989. The major change was the addition of new International Rule 8(f) explaining rights and obligations between vessels in "shall not impede" situations. The Coast Guard issued regulatory amendments to the Inland Rule technical annexes early in 1990 to reflect the changes to the International Rule annex. Congress passed legislation later in 1990 amending Inland Rules 1(e) and 8(f) to match the International Rule changes. The other International Rule amendments (dealing with traffic separation schemes and vessels constrained by draft) had no direct counterpart in the Inland Rules.

In 1989 the International Maritime Organization adopted a third set of amendments to the International Rules. This time there was just one amendment—to Rule 10(d)—which clarified the use of inshore traffic zones. The amendment is scheduled to enter into force on 19 April 1991. Because International Rule 10 (Traffic Separation Schemes) is not directly reflected in the Inland Rules, there will be no corresponding amendment to the Inland Rules. The Inland Rule 10 is on vessel traffic services, incorporating by reference the Coast Guard's VTS regulations. The Coast Guard planned to begin a complete overhaul of the VTS regulations in 1990.

There appears to be a strong consensus in the international community of navigation authorities to oppose further amendments to the navigation rules, at least for as many years as possible. The three sets of amendments already adopted reflect the tuning process—first fifty-six amendments, then nine, and finally a single amendment. Any fine adjustments that are left presumably could be made through interpretations. Only time will tell.

PART A

General

Rule 1—Application

INTERNATIONAL
(a) These Rules shall apply to all vessels upon the high seas and in all waters connected therewith navigable by seagoing vessels.

INLAND
(a) These Rules apply to all vessels upon the inland waters of the United States, and to vessels of the United States on the Canadian waters of the Great Lakes to the extent that there is no conflict with Canadian law.

Where and when do the marine navigation rules, or "rules of the road," apply? Do the International Rules apply only on international waters (or the "high seas")? Do they apply only to large commercial ships, or to small boats as well? Rule 1 provides the answers.

First, notice that both the International and the Inland version apply to "all" vessels. If you're not sure what can be called a "vessel," you may be surprised to find out that Rule 3(a) gives a very broad definition, which includes large craft, small craft (even sailboards), seaplanes on the water, and military craft.

Older rules that allowed Navy and Coast Guard vessels to operate in violation of these Rules under some circumstances are no longer in effect. Navy and Coast Guard vessels do sometimes operate at night without navigation lights, but the commanding officers of those vessels assume full responsibility for avoiding collisions and are liable for damages resulting from their violation of the Rules.

Now, where do each of the two sets of Rules apply? The International Rules apply on the "high seas" and connecting waters. High seas waters are beyond the limits of a country's territorial sea. The U.S. territorial sea now extends twelve nautical miles beyond the baseline, which runs along the coast and across the mouths of rivers and bays. The width of the territorial sea varies from country to country, but twelve miles is now the internationally accepted standard.

Even though the actual language says that the International Rules also apply to connecting waters "navigable by seagoing vessels," that requirement is often overridden by the application of paragraph (b). In almost all cases the International Rules apply on territorial waters (lying between the coastline and the high seas) and also on some "internal waters" (inside the baseline). Rivers, harbors, bays, and so forth are examples of internal waters. The U.S. internal waters to which the International Rules apply include the rivers and bays of Alaska, Puget Sound, the rivers and bays of most of Maine, and some other waters.

There is no one rule describing the boundary marking the limit of application of the International Rules, but rather the line is set out in detail by regulation. The lines of "demarcation" dividing application of the International Rules and Inland Rules are described in Part 80 of Title 33 of the Code of Federal Regulations. In most cases the demarcation line follows the shoreline. Where it doesn't, the line is laid out as a series of straight lines connecting prominent points, such as lighthouses or the ends of jetties.

The Inland Rules apply on U.S. navigable waters inside the demarcation line and on the U.S. side of the Great Lakes. These waters are called "inland waters" and are formally defined in Rule 3. The Inland Rules also apply to U.S. vessels operating on the Canadian side of the Great Lakes except for those provisions that conflict with Canadian navigation rules for the Great Lakes. The U.S. and Canadian navigation rule drafters worked together to minimize the differences between the two countries' rules and to help ensure that the Great Lakes mariner would have little difficulty transiting from one side to the other.

INTERNATIONAL

(b) Nothing in these Rules shall interfere with the operation of special rules made by an appropriate authority for roadsteads, harbors, rivers, lakes or inland waterways connected to the high seas and navigable by seagoing vessels. Such special rules shall conform as closely as possible to these Rules.

INLAND

(b)(i) These Rules constitute special rules made by an appropriate authority within the meaning of Rule 1(b) of the International Regulations.

(ii) All vessels complying with the construction and equipment requirements of the International Regulations are considered to be in compliance with these Rules.

A legal relationship exists between the two sets of Rules, and that relationship is explained, after a fashion, in paragraph (b). The International Rules recognize the existence and usefulness of special (national) rules but admonish the navigation rules authorities to eliminate unnecessary differences between international and national rules. Consistency, of course, minimizes confusion, errors, and the potential for collisions.

Inland Rule 1(b) cites the International Rule 1(b) authority for special rules and incorporates the International Rule construction and equipment requirements as alternative provisions of the Inland Rules. This allows vessels complying with the International Rule requirements and operating on International Rule waters to enter U.S. inland waters without having to switch over to, for example, a different navigation light arrangement. Vessels operating only on inland waters may elect to comply with International Rule navigation light requirements instead of Inland Rule requirements. If they do, however, they must comply exclusively with all International Rule lights. You can't mix and match the International and Inland requirements to suit your individual style. An important caveat: all vessels entering U.S. inland waters must follow the Inland Rule Steering and Sailing Rules and use Inland Rule sound signals (or radiotelephone).

(c) Nothing in these Rules shall interfere with the operation of any special rules made by the Government of any State with respect to additional station or signal lights, shapes or whistle signals for ships of war and vessels proceeding under convoy, or with respect to additional station or signal lights or shapes for fishing vessels engaged in fishing as a fleet. These additional station or signal lights, shapes or whistle signals shall, so far as possible, be such that they cannot be mistaken for any light, shape or signal authorized elsewhere under these Rules.

(c) Nothing in these Rules shall interfere with the operation of any special rules made by the Secretary of the Navy with respect to additional station or signal lights and shapes or whistle signals for ships of war and vessels proceeding under convoy, or by the Secretary with respect to additional station or signal lights or shapes for fishing vessels engaged in fishing as a fleet. These additional station or signal lights and shapes or whistle signals shall, so far as possible, be such that they cannot be mistaken for any light, shape, or signal authorized elsewhere under these Rules. Notice of such special rules shall be published in the Federal Register and, after the effective date specified in such notice, they shall have effect as if they were a part of these Rules.

Special *additional* station or signal lights, shapes, or whistle signals are explicitly authorized by the International and Inland navigation rules for certain classes of warships, vessels in convoy, and vessels fishing in a fleet. These *supplement* the normal lights, shapes, and signals and are not to be used to replace them.

Additional optional lights for vessels fishing in close proximity (in a fleet) are separately permitted under Rule 26(d) and are listed in Annex II.

Special additional signals for Navy vessels are listed in Part 707 of Title 32 of the Code of Federal Regulations and include the following:

- §707.2 Man overboard lights (two pulsating all-round red lights in a vertical line)
- §707.3 Yardarm signaling lights (flashing all-round white lights)

- §707.4 Aircraft warning lights (one all-round red light)
- §707.5 Underway replenishment contour lights (red or blue lights)
- §707.6 Minesweeping station-keeping lights (two white limited-sector lights)
- §707.7 Submarine identification light (intermittent flashing amber beacon—three flashes, one per second, followed by three-second off period)
- §707.8 Special operations lights (revolving beam colored red, green, or amber)
- §707.9 Convoy operations sternlight (blue light in lieu of regular sternlight)
- §707.10 Wake illumination light (white spotlight)
- §707.11 Flight operations light (combinations of different colored lights)
- §707.12 Amphibious operations lights (various combinations of colored lights)

INTERNATIONAL	INLAND
(d) Traffic separation schemes may be adopted by the Organization for the purpose of these Rules.	(d) Vessel traffic service regulations may be in effect in certain areas.

Rule 10 of the International Rules applies to traffic separation schemes (TSS) "adopted by the Organization." The "Organization" is the International Maritime Organization (IMO), a body of the United Nations. Rule 1(d) authorizes IMO to adopt traffic separation schemes to which Rule 10 will apply.

Traffic separation schemes are used to keep apart ships that are proceeding in opposite directions (usually in well-traveled "sea lanes") and are most commonly found in the coastal approaches to busy ports around the world. The traffic separation schemes associated with U.S. ports lie, for the most part, in high seas waters where ships are mostly outside of U.S. jurisdictional control. International Rule 10 applies in those cases. This goes for traffic separation schemes off foreign coasts as well. Violations of Rule 10 are reported by the country off whose coast the traffic separation scheme is located to the flag state of the vessel involved. It is then up to the flag state (country of vessel registry) to adjudicate the violation and impose any penalties.

Vessel routing systems on *inland* waters can be regulated directly under U.S. laws—statutes and regulations. The inland waters counterpart to a traffic separation scheme is called a vessel traffic service (VTS). Inland Rule 1(d) merely calls attention to the fact that separate regulations may apply to certain heavily trafficked areas. A more complete discussion of this subject is contained under Rule 10.

INTERNATIONAL

(e) Whenever the Government concerned shall have determined that a vessel of special construction or purpose cannot comply fully with the provisions of any of these Rules with respect to the number, position, range or arc of visibility of lights or shapes, as well as to the disposition and characteristics of sound signaling appliances, such vessel shall comply with such other provisions in regard to the number, position, range or arc of visibility of lights and shapes, as well as to the disposition and characteristics of sound signaling appliances, as her Government shall have determined to be the closest possible compliance with these Rules in respect of that vessel.

INLAND

(e) Whenever the Secretary determines that a vessel or class of vessels of special construction or purpose cannot comply fully with the provisions of any of these Rules with respect to the number, position, range or arc of visibility of lights or shapes, as well as to the disposition and characteristics of sound signaling appliances, the vessel shall comply with such other provisions in regard to the number, position, range or arc of visibility of lights and shapes, as well as to the disposition and characteristics of sound signaling appliances, as the Secretary shall have determined to be the closest possible compliance with these Rules. The Secretary may issue a certificate of alternative compliance for a vessel or class of vessels specifying the closest possible compliance with these Rules. The Secretary of the Navy shall make these determinations and issue certificates of alternative compliance for vessels of the Navy.

The navigation rules have set up navigation light, shape, and sound-signal requirements that can readily be applied to almost all vessels used today. Occasionally, however, a vessel that has been designed or modified to perform a particular, perhaps unique function will not be able to comply fully without having its special function impaired. In those cases, Rule 1(e) permits a deviation from the navigation light, shape, or sound-signal requirements but only to the point of preventing interference with the special function. This permitted deviation from the Rules is called "alternative compliance," and the document granting that deviation is the Certificate of Alternative Compliance.

Vessels must fulfill two criteria before receiving a Certificate of Alternative Compliance. First, the vessel must be of special construction or purpose. Ordinary passenger, cargo, or recreational vessels do not meet this first criterion, but offshore oil and gas facility supply vessels and cable-laying vessels, for example, do.

Second, it must be shown that full compliance would interfere with the special function of the vessel. If this second criterion is also satisfied, the vessel must still comply *as closely as possible* with the requirement without interfering with its special function.

For example, full compliance by an offshore supply vessel over fifty meters long would require the placement of an after masthead light (and mast) in the middle of its long open cargo deck. However, doing this would interfere with the vessel's cargo-handling function. Instead, the after masthead light is placed at the forward end of the cargo deck and the forward masthead light is placed at the stem, thereby obtaining the maximum horizontal separation possible (although still less than specified by the Rules).

The secretary of the department in which the Coast Guard is operating makes alternative compliance determinations for Coast Guard and private vessels. This authority has been delegated to the Coast Guard. Procedures for obtaining Certificates of Alternative Compliance are found in Title 33 of the Code of Federal Regulations, Part 89 for the Inland Rules and Part 81 for the International Rules. The Secretary of the Navy makes alternative compliance determinations for Navy vessels.

INLAND

(f) The Secretary may accept a certificate of alternative compliance issued by a contracting party to the International Regulations if he determines that the alternative compliance standards of the contracting party are substantially the same as those of the United States.

Only the Inland Rules contain a paragraph (f) in Rule 1, which states that, in determining whether a foreign vessel in U.S. inland waters complies with the navigation rules, U.S. authorities may rely on the determinations of the flag state (the state in which the vessel is registered).

Rule 2—Responsibility

INTERNATIONAL

(a) Nothing in these Rules shall exonerate any vessel, or the owner, master or crew thereof, from the consequences of any neglect to comply with these Rules or of the neglect of any precaution which may be required by the ordinary practice of seamen, or by the special circumstances of the case.

(b) In construing and complying with these Rules due regard shall be had to all dangers of navigation and collision and to any special circumstances, including the limitations of the vessels involved, which may make a departure from these Rules necessary to avoid immediate danger.

INLAND

(a) Nothing in these Rules shall exonerate any vessel, or the owner, master or crew thereof, from the consequences of any neglect to comply with these Rules or of the neglect of any precaution which may be required by the ordinary practice of seamen, or by the special circumstances of the case.

(b) In construing and complying with these Rules due regard shall be had to all dangers of navigation and collision and to any special circumstances, including the limitations of the vessels involved, which may make a departure from these Rules necessary to avoid immediate danger.

Rule 2, worded identically in both the International and Inland versions, says when the Rules shall be followed, when supplemental action is required, and when the Rules are not to be followed. Although a statement warning against failure to comply with the Rules would not seem to be necessary (because the Rules are the law), Rule 2 emphasizes that the navigation rules are not merely statements of customary practice or recommended guidance.

Furthermore, Rule 2 holds the mariner responsible not only for complying with the Rules but for avoiding collisions. Merely complying with the Rules is not enough. If, in fact, strict compliance with the Rules would result in immediate danger, a *departure* from the Rules (to the extent necessary to avoid the danger) is *required*. A mariner who chooses to adhere strictly to the word of the Rules, and thereby causes or fails to avoid a collision that could have been prevented by other action, may not use compliance with the Rules as a defense to liability.

The basis for this apparent catch 22 is that the Rules cannot possibly cover every conceivable situation of vessel encounter. The Rules are written for usual or likely situations; atypical situations are termed "special circumstances." A complete list of special circumstances is, of course, impossible to provide. A number of examples should give some idea of the term's meaning.

During routine operations, almost all vessels engage in maneuvers that are not covered by the Rules. These maneuvers, which normally take a very short time, may occur near other vessels. Vessels entering or leaving a slip, for instance, do not follow the steady course needed for Rule applications. Likewise, vessels proceeding stern-first are considered to be in special circumstances.

Vessels not making way may be in special circumstances. First, a vessel should avoid stopping in a high-traffic area, and when a vessel decides to stop, it should make its intentions clear to other vessels in the area. As always, a proper lookout should be maintained. Risk-of-collision situations are a bit tricky. If good conditions exist, and if the stopped vessel can put on maneuvering speed quickly, and if one assumes that its steady course is that indicated by the point of its bow, and if then, by Rule 15, it would be the give-way vessel, then the Steering and Sailing Rules would apply and the stopped vessel would be obligated to keep out of the way of the other. But if the vessel is drifting, its course may not be obvious. If the stopped vessel is large, it may not be able to move out of the way of a fast oncoming vessel. Whatever the "if" of the situation, encounters with vessels not making way through the water merit extra caution.

Another special circumstance occurs when two vessels have managed to get themselves much too close to each other and are headed in unfortunate directions. Collisions about to happen are often called "extremis" situations. The vessels involved are said to be "in extremis."

An extremis situation occurs when a collision can be avoided only by the action of both vessels. Here Rule 17(b) requires the stand-on vessel to maneuver to avoid the collision. In general, however, an extremis situation is one in which a collision is *imminent*, in which there is an *immediate* danger of collision ("in the jaws of a collision"). The collision need not occur for an extremis situation to have existed.

In an extremis situation, the operators on one or both of the vessels have failed to take the first line of preventive actions prescribed by the Rules. The second line of defense comes into play; the parties in extremis are required to do *whatever* is necessary to avoid a collision or at least to minimize the damage.

The physical limitations of the vessels may also impose special circumstances. Draft limitations will prevent some give-way vessels from turning into shallow water; a sluggish craft may preclude a timely maneuver for others.

The presence of more than two vessels may preclude full compliance with the Rules; action required with respect to one vessel may conflict with the action required with respect to one or more of the others. Again, special circumstances exist.

Sometimes vessel masters find it more convenient (as opposed to necessary) to maneuver in conflict with the Rules. This is permitted only after all vessels involved agree to a departure from the Rules. The master proposing to depart must comply with the Rules until agreement is reached by all parties. This means that the master should not begin to line up his or her vessel for a maneuver in conflict with the Rules until *after* agreement on that maneuver has been reached—early planning is a must. The proposal is in no way binding on the other vessel's master until he or she agrees to it. Once agreement is reached, neither vessel is the stand-on vessel, and each should proceed with caution. Agreements to depart from the Rules should not be made under normal circumstances, and an agreement to depart should never be assumed from customary practice or prior agreements.

Rule 3—General Definitions

This rule provides definitions to terms that reappear throughout the Rules. Less frequently used terms are defined where they appear; see Rules 12(b), 13(b), 14(b), 21, and 32.

INTERNATIONAL	INLAND
For the purpose of these Rules, except where the context otherwise requires:	For the purpose of these Rules and this Act, except where the context otherwise requires:
(a) The word "vessel" includes every description of water craft, including non-displacement craft and seaplanes, used or capable of being used as a means of transportation on water.	(a) The word "vessel" includes every description of water craft, including non-displacement craft and seaplanes, used or capable of being used as a means of transportation on water;

All vehicles that operate on the water are vessels, including displacement craft (those that "float" or are supported by the static buoyancy derived from the water that their hulls displace), non-displacement craft (those that are supported by the dynamic lift of hydrofoils or other lifting surfaces), and seaplanes. The phrase "used or capable of being used as a means of transportation" implies the *practical* transportation of people or cargo. Inner tubes are not included, although sailboards are.

The "Act" in the Inland version refers to the Inland Navigational Rules Act of 1980, which contains the Inland Rules.

INTERNATIONAL	INLAND
(b) The term "power-driven vessel" means any vessel propelled by machinery.	(b) The term "power-driven vessel" means any vessel propelled by machinery;

Vessels propelled by oars, paddles, or other human- or animal-powered means are not included in this definition, nor are they covered in the Steering and Sailing Rules (Rules 4–19)—if you are in a rowboat, canoe, kayak, or the like you must use Rule 2 (in other words, common sense and good judgment). Vessels propelled by machinery *as well as* any other means of propulsion are considered to be power-driven vessels. A day shape is required for most vessels using *both* sails and machinery for propulsion. See Rule 25(e).

INTERNATIONAL

(c) The term "sailing vessel" means any vessel under sail provided that propelling machinery, if fitted, is not being used.

INLAND

(c) The term "sailing vessel" means any vessel under sail provided that propelling machinery, if fitted, is not being used;

Vessels using only their sails for propulsion are included, even though they may be fitted with an engine. Operation of the engine to generate electricity or to heat water, for example, does not make the sailing vessel a power-driven vessel, so long as the propeller (or paddle wheel) is not engaged. Rule 18 tells us what the responsibilities of sailing vessels are with respect to other types of vessels, and Rule 12 does the same with respect to other sailing vessels.

INTERNATIONAL

(d) The term "vessel engaged in fishing" means any vessel fishing with nets, lines, trawls or other fishing apparatus which restrict maneuverability, but does not include a vessel fishing with trolling lines or other fishing apparatus which do not restrict maneuverability.

INLAND

(d) The term "vessel engaged in fishing" means any vessel fishing with nets, lines, trawls or other fishing apparatus which restrict maneuverability, but does not include a vessel fishing with trolling lines or other fishing apparatus which do not restrict maneuverability;

As a general rule, this definition includes most commercial fishing vessels (while fishing) and excludes most recreational or sport fishing vessels. The term "lines" in the phrase "fishing with nets, lines, trawls" refers to lines such as long-lines which may be miles long and to which are attached at regular intervals many leaders and hooks. The term "trawls" refers to large open-mouthed nets that are towed through the water by one or two specially equipped fishing vessels (trawlers). Not included in the definition are vessels fishing with trolling lines (for example, a sport fisherman's rod and reel with the line towed astern), which do not restrict maneuverability.

The use of nets, lines, or trawls is presumed to restrict maneuverability while the use of trolling lines is presumed not to restrict maneuverability. The master determines whether the fishing apparatus restricts maneuverability; if a collision occurs, the court may subsequently make the determination. In any case, a master electing to take on vessel-engaged-in-fishing status is required to display the day shapes and lights prescribed by Rule 26.

Rule 18 assigns the privileges and obligations of vessels engaged in fishing with respect to other classes of vessels.

INTERNATIONAL	INLAND
(e) The word "seaplane" includes any aircraft designed to maneuver on the water.	(e) The word "seaplane" includes any aircraft designed to maneuver on the water;

When on the water a seaplane is a vessel. Rule 31 gives the navigation light and shape requirements for seaplanes.

INTERNATIONAL	INLAND
(f) The term "vessel not under command" means a vessel which through some exceptional circumstance is unable to maneuver as required by these Rules and is therefore unable to keep out of the way of another vessel.	(f) The term "vessel not under command" means a vessel which through some exceptional circumstance is unable to maneuver as required by these Rules and is therefore unable to keep out of the way of another vessel;

A vessel claiming not-under-command status must (1) find itself in exceptional circumstances, and (2) thereby be unable to maneuver as would ordinarily be required by the Rules. The following are examples of conditions that could result in not-under-command status:

- Vessel with anchor down but not holding
- Vessel riding on anchor chains
- Vessel with inoperative steering gear
- Sailing vessel becalmed or in irons
- Exceptionally bad weather (relative to vessel claiming status)

Vessels claiming not-under-command status are considered to be underway. That is, they are not considered to be at anchor, made fast to the shore, or aground.

Rule 18 assigns the privileges and obligations of not-under-command vessels with respect to other classes of vessels. Rule 27 prescribes the lights and shapes to be displayed by not-under-command vessels.

INTERNATIONAL	INLAND
(g) The term "vessel restricted in her ability to maneuver" means a vessel which from the nature of her work is restricted in her ability to maneuver as required by these Rules and is therefore unable to keep out of the way of another vessel.	(g) The term "vessel restricted in her ability to maneuver" means a vessel which from the nature of her work is restricted in her ability to maneuver as required by these Rules and is therefore unable to keep out of the way of another vessel; vessels restricted in their ability to maneuver include, but are not limited to:
The term "vessels restricted in their ability to maneuver" shall include but not be limited to:	
(i) a vessel engaged in laying, servicing or picking up a navigation mark, submarine cable or pipeline;	(i) a vessel engaged in laying, servicing or picking up a navigation mark, submarine cable or pipeline;
(ii) a vessel engaged in dredging, surveying or underwater operations;	(ii) a vessel engaged in dredging, surveying or underwater operations;
(iii) a vessel engaged in replenishment or transferring persons, provisions or cargo while underway;	(iii) a vessel engaged in replenishment or transferring persons, provisions or cargo while underway;

(iv) a vessel engaged in the launching or recovery of aircraft;

(v) a vessel engaged in mineclearance operations;

(vi) a vessel engaged in a towing operation such as severely restricts the towing vessel and her tow in their ability to deviate from their course.

(iv) a vessel engaged in the launching or recovery of aircraft;

(v) a vessel engaged in mineclearance operations; and

(vi) a vessel engaged in a towing operation such as severely restricts the towing vessel and her tow in their ability to deviate from their course.

Both the International and the Inland version carry the same message, despite slight variations in wording. A vessel restricted in ability to maneuver (1) must be unable to keep out of the way of other vessels (2) *because of the nature of its work.* The status does not apply to vessels that cannot maneuver because they are in a narrow channel or in shallow water or because of strong currents or bad weather.

The definition lists a number of vessel activities that entitle the vessel to restricted-in-ability-to-maneuver status. Note that vessel types are not named, but vessels engaged in certain activities are listed. The distinction: a cable-laying vessel is not necessarily entitled to status as a vessel restricted in ability to maneuver, but a vessel *engaged* in cable laying is. The cable-laying vessel may claim the special status only when it is actually laying cable.

A towing vessel with tow is under some circumstances less able to maneuver than a power-driven vessel alone. However, the master of a vessel engaged in a routine towing operation is not normally justified in claiming restricted-in-ability-to-maneuver status. This is emphasized in the definition by the words "*severely restricts.*" The master must make the determination, and the towing vessel and the tow are considered as a unit—"restricted in *their* ability to deviate from *their* course."

Vessels restricted in ability to maneuver may or may not be underway.

INTERNATIONAL

(h) The term "vessel constrained by her draft" means a power-driven vessel which, because of her draft

in relation to the available depth
and width of navigable water, is severely restricted in her ability to
deviate from the course she is following.

This term covers such cases as a large vessel passing between
islands or a vessel in a channel whose draft exceeds the water
depth outside the channel. The depth of water directly underneath
the vessel is not the determining factor; rather, the depth (or lack
of it) close to either side of the vessel determines the level of
constraint. International Rule 18(d) prescribes the action to be
taken by vessels constrained by draft and other vessels in the
vicinity. International Rule 28 gives the lights and shapes for vessels constrained by draft.

The Inland Rules do not contain a parallel definition for "vessel
constrained by draft" because that term is not used in the Inland
Rules. In inland waters almost all vessels will be limited in maneuverability by their drafts at one time or another.

INTERNATIONAL	INLAND
(i) The word "underway" means that a vessel is not at anchor, or made fast to the shore, or aground.	(h) The word "underway" means that a vessel is not at anchor, or made fast to the shore, or aground;

"Underway" should be distinguished from the phrases "making
way through the water" (used in Rules 26, 27, and 35) and "making
no way through the water" (used in Rule 35). A vessel that is
"underway" need not be moving through the water but may simply be not anchored, aground, or made fast to the shore. If a vessel
is making no way through the water, it is stopped and drifting,
unless it is not underway. If it is moving relative to the water, it
is making way. For example, if a ship is headed up a river, making
five knots through the water, and there is a five-knot current
against it, then it is making way through the water even though
it is making no progress relative to the shore. Another ship drifting
down the river is not making way, even though it is moving much
faster over the bottom.

It is fairly common for river towboats (pushing ahead) to hold their position by putting the head of their tow against the bank and applying some forward thrust to prevent movement. In this situation the tow is free to maneuver and not considered to be aground. Therefore, it is considered to be underway.

INTERNATIONAL	INLAND
(j) The words "length" and "breadth" of a vessel mean her length overall and greatest breadth.	(i) The words "length" and "breadth" of a vessel mean her length overall and greatest breadth;

Length overall can be visualized by bringing the bow (excluding the bowsprits and so forth) of the vessel's hull up against a vertical wall and then bringing another vertical wall up against the stern. Length overall will then be the distance between the two walls. Other lengths commonly referred to, though not in these Rules, include waterline length (measured between points where stem and stern enter the water) and length between perpendiculars (measured from the point the stem intersects the design waterline and the centerline of the rudderpost).

The greatest breadth does not always occur amidships.

INTERNATIONAL	INLAND
(k) Vessels shall be deemed to be in sight of one another only when one can be observed visually from the other.	(j) Vessels shall be deemed to be in sight of one another only when one can be observed visually from the other;

Rules 11 through 18 apply only to vessels in sight of one another. These Rules assign responsibilities as give-way or stand-on vessels for various situations. These eight rules do not apply to two vessels not "in sight of one another." Even though the vessels may know each other's exact course, speed, and position by means of automated radar plotting aids or other devices, Rules 11 through 18 apply only if visual contact is also made.

INTERNATIONAL	INLAND
(l) The term "restricted visibility" means any condition in which vis-	(k) The term "restricted visibility" means any condition in which vis-

INTERNATIONAL
ibility is restricted by fog, mist, falling snow, heavy rainstorms, sandstorms or any other similar causes.

INLAND
ibility is restricted by fog, mist, falling snow, heavy rainstorms, sandstorms or any other similar causes;

Rules 19 and 35 apply only to vessels in or near an area of restricted visibility. Restricted visibility may be due to any of the listed natural causes or to other factors such as smoke or smog. Visibility need not be restricted all around the vessel, nor does the vessel in question have to be in the fog, mist, or whatever. For example, a vessel must follow the Rules for restricted visibility if it is close to a fogbank, even though it may be in clear air and have clear air on three sides. The vessel in this example would, however, follow the Rules for vessels in sight of one another with respect to vessels also in clear air that it can see.

Rule 20(c) requires the display of navigation lights during periods of restricted visibility. As a guideline, lights should, if carried, be turned on whenever the visibility drops below the minimum visibility distance specified for your masthead light by Rule 22—six miles for the largest vessels, down to two miles for the smallest.

Rule 35 requires the use of sound signals in or near an area of restricted visibility. As a guideline, signals should be given when visibility in any direction falls below the minimum audibility range specified for the whistle on your vessel by Annex III—two miles for the largest vessels, down to one-half mile for the smallest.

INLAND

(l) "Western Rivers" means the Mississippi River, its tributaries, South Pass, and Southwest Pass, to the navigational demarcation lines dividing the high seas from harbors, rivers, and other inland waters of the United States, and Port Allen–Morgan City Alternate Route, and that part of the Atchafalaya River above its junction with the Port Allen–Morgan City Alter-

nate Route including the Old River
and the Red River;

Certain provisions in the Inland Rules apply only to vessels
operating on the western rivers or apply to the western rivers and
other specially designated waters. These special references to
western rivers waters appear in Rules 9(a)(ii), 14(d), 15(b), and
24(i). Supplemental regulations contained in Part 89 of Title 33
of the Code of Federal Regulations clarify the boundary for western
rivers waters in the New Orleans area.

The reference to the "navigational demarcation lines dividing
the high seas from harbors, rivers, and other inland waters" is a
misnomer. The navigational demarcation lines have no geopolitical significance and do not separate high seas waters from inland
waters. "Inland waters" is a term unique to the navigation rules;
"internal waters" would be the closest corresponding geopolitical
term. The "territorial sea," twelve miles wide, is adjacent to the
internal waters, and then outside of the territorial sea are "high
seas." The navigational demarcation lines only serve to divide the
waters where the International and the Inland navigation rules
apply.

INLAND

(m) "Great Lakes" means the Great
Lakes and their connecting and
tributary waters including the Calumet River as far as the Thomas J.
O'Brien Lock and Controlling
Works (between mile 326 and 327),
the Chicago River as far as the east
side of the Ashland Avenue Bridge
(between mile 321 and 322), and
the Saint Lawrence River as far east
as the lower exit of Saint Lambert
Lock;

Similarly, the Rules contain some special provisions applicable
to vessels operating on the Great Lakes. References to the Great
Lakes are made in Rules 9(a)(ii), 14(d), 15(b), and 23(d).

INLAND

(n) "Secretary" means the Secretary of the department in which the Coast Guard is operating;

The Coast Guard is now under the Department of Transportation, and in time of war it may be placed under the Secretary of Defense.

INLAND

(o) "Inland Waters" means the navigable waters of the United States shoreward of the navigational demarcation lines dividing the high seas from harbors, rivers, and other inland waters of the United States and the waters of the Great Lakes on the United States side of the International Boundary;

Non-navigable waters under sole-state jurisdiction are not included. The demarcation lines are set out in Title 33 of the Code of Federal Regulations, Part 80. These lines are used *only* to indicate whether the International Rules or the Inland Rules apply. They do *not* mark the boundary between U.S. territorial waters and the high seas (international waters). For a more complete discussion of this subject, see Rule 1(a).

INLAND

(p) "Inland Rules" or "Rules" mean the Inland Navigational Rules and the annexes thereto, which govern the conduct of vessels and specify the lights, shapes, and sound signals that apply on inland waters; and

There are five annexes to the Inland Rules. They are published as regulations and appear in Title 33 of the Code of Federal Regulations, Parts 84 through 88.

INLAND

(q) "International   Regulations"
means the International Regulations for Preventing Collisions at
Sea, 1972, including annexes currently in force for the United States.

These are also known commonly as the International Navigation
Rules, International Rules, 72 COLREGS, and COLREGS. The International Regulations for Preventing Collisions at Sea, 1972, is
the name of the treaty containing the Rules and is the responsibility of the International Maritime Organization (IMO). The treaty
became binding on the United States on 15 July 1977. The first
set of 56 amendments to the International Rules went into effect
on 1 June 1983, and the second set of nine on 19 November 1989.
Another amendment goes into effect on 19 April 1991, expected
to be the last for many years.

PART B

Steering and Sailing Rules

Of the five parts in the Rules, Part B is by far the most important. The very heart of the Rules, it prescribes precautions and duties the master should observe in detecting and assessing the risk of collision. It then mandates the action to be taken as soon as the risk materializes.

Because the visibility around a vessel is so critical in avoiding collision, the Steering and Sailing Rules contain different requirements for different conditions of visibility. Part B's Rules are divided into three sections (called "subparts" in the Inland Rules): the first applies to vessels in all conditions of visibility; the second only to vessels in sight of one another; and the third to vessels in or near areas of restricted visibility.

SECTION/SUBPART I—CONDUCT OF VESSELS IN ANY CONDITION OF VISIBILITY

Section (or Subpart) I contains general rules for lookout, safe speed, risk of collision, action to avoid collision, narrow channels, and traffic separation schemes (International) or vessel traffic services (Inland).

Rule 4—Application

INTERNATIONAL
Rules in this Section apply to any condition of visibility.

INLAND
Rules in this Subpart apply to any condition of visibility.

Rule 4 tells us that vessels operating under any and all conditions of visibility are required to follow Rules 5 through 10. In other words, these Rules apply all of the time.

Rule 5—Lookout

INTERNATIONAL
Every vessel shall at all times maintain a proper lookout by sight and hearing as well as by all available means appropriate in the prevailing circumstances and conditions so as to make a full appraisal of the situation and of the risk of collision.

INLAND
Every vessel shall at all times maintain a proper lookout by sight and hearing as well as by all available means appropriate in the prevailing circumstances and conditions so as to make a full appraisal of the situation and of the risk of collision.

Rule 5 is a short rule that places a large responsibility on the mariner. Rather than specific duties, equipment, places, times, and number of persons, Rule 5 requires the master to decide how best to maintain a proper lookout. Instead of giving us precise guidance on the adequacy of the lookout, the Rule uses vague terms such as "proper" and "appropriate." Only in this way could the Rules reasonably provide for all vessels at all times. Requirements covering even the most common situations would have been intolerably detailed and complex.

The lookout requirement of Rule 5 relies heavily on common sense and good seamanship. If you are able to comply with the Steering and Sailing Rules (Part B of the Rules) and with Rule 34—all of which depend on lookout information—you will no doubt have met the demands of Rule 5. A proper lookout, therefore, provides all the information needed to comply with those Rules. If the information collected by the lookout is insufficient, then the master must intensify his or her lookout efforts (for example, by turning on the radar) or reduce the need for information (for example, by slowing down a fogbound vessel).

The "information gap" that sometimes opens between the amount of information collected and the amount needed to comply with the other Rules is a leading cause of most collisions. Too often vessels collide because their masters have either ignored the gap or have filled it with assumptions. An appreciation of the lookout requirement will take the mariner halfway toward avoiding collisions.

Definition and Purpose of the Lookout

What is a "lookout"? Perhaps the most common image that leaps to mind is that of a lone seaman wearing yellow foul-weather gear and a navy watch cap, stationed at the very bow of a ship and peering out into the gloom to catch a flicker of light or the moan of a foghorn. This perception is misleading. The term, as used by the Rules, denotes not a person but rather the systematic collection of information.

Responsibility for maintaining a proper lookout lies with the vessel's operator, not with a subordinate designated as "lookout." The vessel's operator—(that is, master, watch officer, or person in charge)—is the lookout manager. If the operator can keep a lookout personally, then coordinating the collection and analysis of information is relatively straightforward. But if the operator, that is, the decision maker, must rely on others to gather the information, then management of a proper lookout becomes more complicated. The operator must ensure that information on the vessel's surroundings is detected in a timely manner and promptly communicated, so that he or she can correctly analyze the situation.

The purpose of a lookout is simple, so simple that it can easily be overlooked. As the purpose of the navigation rules is to prevent collisions, it follows that the purpose of the lookout is to collect the information needed to avoid collisions. This fundamental reason for maintaining a proper lookout is something to keep in mind.

Duty of the Lookout

Traditionally, the duty of the lookout was to watch out for vessels, lights, and other objects (such as reefs and shoals) by sight and hearing alone and to report their presence to the vessel's operator promptly. The lookout was allowed some discretion on what to report in crowded waters and would be assigned no other duties that would interfere with this important function.

Although the traditional principles of the lookout are still pertinent, today's mariner has tools available that greatly extend the distance over which information can be detected. Today, a proper lookout is a team effort. Yet the master of the vessel is the one held accountable. For this reason, the master must see to it that each member of the lookout team is competent in the use of equipment and diligent in the performance of duty.

The master, who knows the vessel's needs for information and who has the authority and the Rule 5 responsibility, should determine the duties of each member of the lookout team. It is the master's duty to ensure that a proper lookout is maintained at all times. That duty cannot be delegated.

Tools of the Lookout

Sight, hearing, and "all available means" are tools of the lookout. While not too long ago "all available means" was limited to the spyglass, modern mariners have a wealth of tools with which to extend the human senses.

Human sight and hearing have, of course, their limitations. Near sightedness may be uncorrected or poorly corrected. Even good eyesight is affected by environmental factors such as ambient light, weather conditions, water spray, or wind. Fatigue can also affect vision, as can moving between extremes of light. Similarly, hearing may be impaired. The noise of wind and wave and ship's machinery may mask the sound you want to hear. The blast from a ship's own whistle blocks out other noises and will temporarily, perhaps permanently, reduce the hearing of the lookout.

Fortunately, mechanical means for maintaining a lookout are available. "Available" to Rule 5 means "shall be used" in appropriate circumstances. Some of these "other means" are listed below:

- Binoculars
- Radar
- VHF bridge-to-bridge radiotelephone
- Automated radar plotting aids (sometimes called collision-avoidance radar)
- Vessel traffic services
- Navigation and piloting instruments

Radar has assumed such importance on modern vessels that Rule 6 (Safe Speed) and Rule 7 (Risk of Collision) discuss it specifically. Most commercial vessels are now fitted with radar, and probably anyone who has seriously ventured out on the water has some concept of what radar is and what it does. Why, then, are there so many radar-assisted collisions—collisions that occur even though the other vessel was observed on the radar screen? And why are there so many nighttime collisions when the radar was either not turned on or not observed? As with most tools, radar will not provide any benefit unless used, and used correctly.

A lookout may check an empty radar screen and believe nothing is there because he or she *can't see anything*. What may have happened, though, is that a weak contact with a small nearby vessel was lost when the radar operator twisted the sensitivity knob to reduce sea-surface clutter. Collisions occur because radar observers rely on capabilities the radar does not have.

A lookout may observe a contact on radar, begin to form a mental picture of the other vessel, and possibly make a course change. A few minutes later, upon checking the screen, the observer "confirms" the other vessel's imagined course and speed as not leading to a collision. In making this "confirmation," the radar observer has incorporated a string of assumptions into the process. If the observer had taken the time to plot the tracks, rather than rely on assumptions, he or she would have seen that the vessels were in fact on a collision course. We cannot emphasize enough how important it is to distinguish between assumption and fact in your decision making. Consciously seek out, do not unconsciously suppress, conflicting evidence. It is very difficult to calculate mentally another vessel's relative course and speed after observing a radar blip two or three times—difficult to the point of impossibility. Assumption making is not one of the "other means" referenced in Rule 5.

Some mariners believe that radar is not necessary on clear nights, yet collisions continue to happen in those conditions. In one such instance, a ship not using its radar ran into a large, newly constructed oil platform in the Gulf of Mexico. The platform was inadequately lighted, but so are many other vessels and objects. Just because you can't see something at night in good visibility doesn't mean it isn't there.

Rules 5 does not require the installation of radar, but if radar is installed it must be used whenever it would contribute to the quality of the lookout. What are your obligations if radar is installed on your craft but is not working properly? Rule 5 does not require that malfunctioning radar be used. If the problem is temporary, such as a signal blockage caused by a heavy rainstorm, the use of radar can be suspended but not abandoned.

Radar can be carried one step further by incorporating a computer to calculate the courses and speeds of other vessels the radar detects. The computer then relates that information to the vessel's own course and speed. The automated radar plotting aid (ARPA) displays position, course, and speed for each target and signals when it detects risk of collision. Some ARPAs will also display the projected future track of each vessel, all against the background of an electronic chart of the area.

Because all of its information on the vessels comes from radar, ARPA's technical limitations are the same as radar's. However easy it is to become overdependent on radar, it is much easier to relinquish the lookout function, including decision making, to the magic-box ARPA. A poor understanding of this very useful tool may lead the unwary mariner into extremis.

In many situations the best way to find out if other vessels are in the area is to ask. A blind call on the radiotelephone may elicit an answer from an undetected vessel, or a call about traffic to a known vessel may produce useful information. In a number of heavily trafficked areas the mariner can call a vessel traffic service

(VTS) for advisory information. The VTS operators keep track of all major vessels' positions, course, and speeds, as well as accumulate information on navigation hazards. This service will be discussed in more detail with Rule 10.

The tools available to aid the mariner in maintaining a lookout will continue to develop. The use of shipboard coded radar transponders in conjunction with ARPAs and radiotelephones, for example, is being explored. The rapid development in microprocessor technology and accompanying decreases in costs will make available new means for maintaining a proper lookout. Whatever changes the future will bring, Rule 5 will continue to require that the person directing the movement of a vessel know the benefits and limitations of any new devices and be able to use them. Continuing education is part of the navigation rules.

Prevailing Circumstances and Conditions

A proper lookout is that which is sufficient to prevent a collision, without any allowance for good luck, in the prevailing circumstances and conditions. To give substance to this definition, we offer more specific observations:

- A lookout in the open ocean can be less intense than one in coastal or inland waters. It cannot, however, be abandoned—midocean collisions do occur.
- A lookout on a vessel at anchor is required, with the level of effort depending upon the location of the anchorage, depth of water, type of ground tackle, wind, currents, waves, and so forth. The lookout should determine whether the anchor is dragging and should warn other vessels of the anchored vessel's presence.
- The means and methods for maintaining a lookout vary with night and day. At night, lookouts should make greater use of binoculars and radar. Masters should post observers away from the vessel's own lights so as not to impair the night vision of the lookout. During the day and in good visibility, a vessel can be seen at a much greater distance, as indicated by the fact that a masthead light for the largest vessel need be visible for only six miles and for the smallest vessel, only two miles. During

daylight, and under the most favorable conditions, the watch officer on a large vessel may perform the lookout alone.

- The size and arrangement of a vessel have a direct bearing on the effort required to maintain a proper lookout. On small vessels where there is an unobstructed all-around view and where there is no impairment of night vision, the craft's operator may both steer and keep the lookout. Unobstructed view, simple controls, and high maneuverability are important here.

- Visibility is generally the key factor in maintaining a proper lookout. As the visibility decreases, the level of effort to maintain a proper lookout increases tremendously. Sight needs to be augmented by hearing, radar, and radiotelephone. Unless you are in the open ocean, you should seek precise navigational information. In the case of low-lying fog, at least one person should be positioned high enough to see over the fog.

Full Appraisal of the Situation and Risk of Collision

These last words restate the purpose of Rule 5. It is this broad objective that you should keep in mind when managing the lookout. If there is not enough information to assess the situation, you should tap all your resources to gather more. If you are still unable to acquire all the information you need, then you should take steps immediately to reduce your requirement for information— for example, by slowing or stopping. Otherwise, you are violating Rule 5. This is not one of those circumstances where doing more with less is a virtue.

Although it is true that the determination of a proper lookout is left to the mariner, it is also true that courts of law assign as a contributory fault the lack of a proper lookout in a very large proportion of collision cases.

Rule 6—Safe Speed

INTERNATIONAL	INLAND
Every vessel shall at all times proceed at a safe speed so that she can take proper and effective action to avoid collision and be stopped	Every vessel shall at all times proceed at a safe speed so that she can take proper and effective action to avoid collision and be stopped

within a distance appropriate to the prevailing circumstances and conditions.

within a distance appropriate to the prevailing circumstances and conditions.

Like Rule 5, Rule 6 begins with the words "Every vessel shall at all times," indicating its universal application, in good visibility as well as poor, and like Rule 5, it places a great deal of responsibility on the good judgment of the mariner.

How much does speed affect safety? Even if excessive speed is not the most glaring cause of maritime accidents, there have been very few collisions between stopped vessels; vessels involved in a collision are apt to have been moving too fast.

Some mariners are reluctant to change speeds and so pay more attention to factors that support their cruising speed and less attention to factors that indicate a need to slow down. It is very important that you give due consideration to any factor suggesting a change in speed. Because a closing situation may develop rapidly, the person in charge should feel free to call for a reduction in speed without having first to notify another person (for example, the master or engineer). Some power plants are capable of quicker speed changes if certain preparatory steps are taken. If a speed change becomes likely, the person in charge should provide timely notification to the engineers so that they can prepare the engines. Rule 19(b) specifically requires that power-driven vessels have their engines ready for immediate maneuver when in an area of restricted visibility. (The engines on smaller power-driven vessels are normally controlled from the helm position and respond immediately.)

While not directly relevant to collisions between vessels, a vessel's speed also is roughly proportional to its wake. The vessel operator will be liable for damages caused by a wake that is excessively high (for the circumstances).

Safe Speed versus Moderate Speed

The safe-speed rule first came into effect in 1977 for the International Rules and was adopted for the Inland Rules in 1980. Older repealed rules called for "moderate speed," but only in *restricted visibility*. Rule 6 uses the term "safe speed" and applies in *all* conditions of visibility. The term "moderate speed" was replaced by "safe speed" because for many conditions the term "moderate" was too restrictive.

The Rules now recognize speed as an important factor in preventing collisions in good visibility as well as poor. Newer vessels are bigger and faster and may take longer to stop and maneuver. Smaller vessels are also much faster, some capable of speeds greater than 50 knots. A vessel's performance limit is often no longer the controlling factor in good visibility; other conditions must be considered.

Proper and Effective Action

The first objective of maintaining a safe speed is to permit the vessel "to take proper and effective action to avoid collision." To be able to maneuver as prescribed by the Rules, the vessel must be moving slowly enough to control its forward motion. In some cases, it must also be moving fast enough for the rudder to effect a turn promptly.

A vessel passing close to a bank (as in a channel) or close to another vessel generates hydrodynamic forces that can pull the vessel off its course. If the speed is great enough, these hydrodynamic forces can overpower the correcting forces of the rudder. Vessel operators are expected to be familiar with these effects and to reduce their speed sufficiently to maintain positive rudder control.

Even vessels to which the Rules assign a right-of-way must proceed at a safe speed, which sometimes involves planning for the unexpected. Because Rule 2 sometimes makes a departure from the Rules mandatory, and Rule 17(b) requires action by the stand-on vessel when the risk of collision becomes extreme, a fast-moving stand-on vessel may find the action it expected under the Rules not to be the "proper and effective" action needed to avoid a collision. Rule 17 requires a stand-on vessel to maintain its course and speed after risk of collision has been established. A too-high initial speed will therefore place the stand-on vessel in a dangerously awkward position.

Stopping Distance

The second objective of requiring a safe speed is to enable the vessel to be stopped "within a distance appropriate to the prevailing circumstances and conditions." In most cases where the risk of collision exists, a course change will be the most common action. However, if maneuvering room is limited or if visibility is poor, stopping the vessel (perhaps in conjunction with a turn) could be the best way to avoid or minimize damage.

Before radar was common, an old rule of thumb was that a vessel should be able to stop within half the range of visibility. Thus, two vessels on opposite courses would be able to stop before colliding. This rule of thumb was not widely accepted by the courts, which wisely decided that the many factors involved warranted a case-by-case consideration.

Older rules concerning *moderate* speed (applied only in restricted visibility) included a statement about stopping or maintaining bare steerageway. Although Rule 6 does not explicitly contain the same provision, Rule 8 requires vessels to slow or stop to avoid collision or to give more time to assess the situation. Rule 19 requires that vessels in areas of restricted visibility encountering vessels forward slow to the bare minimum needed for steering, or stop altogether.

INTERNATIONAL	INLAND
In determining a safe speed the following factors shall be among those taken into account.	In determining a safe speed the following factors shall be among those taken into account.

Most of Rule 6 presents factors that must be considered in determining safe speed. These factors are not necessarily listed in order of importance, and the list is not exhaustive. Paragraph (a) contains factors to be considered by all vessels; paragraph (b) contains factors that are to be considered by vessels with operational radar.

INTERNATIONAL	INLAND
(a) By all vessels:	(a) By all vessels:
(i) the state of visibility;	(i) the state of visibility;

Visibility has traditionally been the most important consideration in the setting of speed. Rule 19 (Conduct of Vessels in Restricted Visibility) restates the necessity for limiting speed and adds that power-driven vessels shall have their engines ready to maneuver. That Rule also mandates further precautions when another vessel is detected ahead.

INTERNATIONAL	INLAND
(ii) the traffic density including concentrations of fishing vessels or any other vessels;	(ii) the traffic density including concentrations of fishing vessels or any other vessels;

Traffic density is important because the probability of a collision increases with density and because the probability that three or more vessels will share risk of collision also increases. In this latter special circumstance (see Rule 2), some departure from the Rules may be required, leading to unusual and perhaps unexpected action. Areas containing many small vessels require extra caution since those vessels are often difficult to detect either by radar or by sight. In either case, slowing will give extra time to assess the situation. Rule 8(e), on slowing or stopping to avoid a collision or to assess the situation, will probably come into play in these conditions.

INTERNATIONAL	INLAND
(iii) the maneuverability of the vessel with special reference to stopping distance and turning ability in the prevailing conditions;	(iii) the maneuverability of the vessel with special reference to stopping distance and turning ability in the prevailing conditions;

The vessel's operator cannot establish a safe speed without knowing how far the vessel will travel before stopping, for any normal loading condition or speed. Stopping distances will vary substantially depending on whether the vessel is turning or proceeding in a straight line. Many vessels will stop most quickly when put into a sharp turn. Large tankers are a good example; because their great bulk dwarfs the propeller, turning their broadsides across the line of travel stops them more efficiently than would running their engines astern alone.

Tug- and towboat operators should be aware of their vessels' stopping characteristics both without barges and with different numbers of barges.

The maneuvering characteristics of most larger vessels are required to be posted on the bridge. Operators should learn the characteristics *before* the information is needed.

INTERNATIONAL

(iv) at night the presence of background light such as from shore lights or from backscatter of her own lights;

INLAND

(iv) at night the presence of background light such as from shore lights or from backscatter of her own lights;

Background lights and backscatter decrease the effectiveness of lookout by sight and therefore require a proportional decrease in speed. A small vessel has a particular problem because the vessel's own lights are close to the operator. Careful design of the navigation light arrangement will minimize backscatter and reflection from the vessel itself.

INTERNATIONAL

(v) the state of wind, sea and current, and the proximity of navigational hazards;

INLAND

(v) the state of wind, sea and current, and the proximity of navigational hazards;

The need to reduce speed in the face of mounting adversity is obvious (we hope).

INTERNATIONAL

(vi) the draft in relation to the available depth of water.

INLAND

(vi) the draft in relation to the available depth of water.

Draft restrictions relate to speed in several ways. If there is little underkeel clearance, it is likely that shallower water is nearby. It is easier to avoid running aground from a low speed, and if a grounding cannot be avoided, the damage will be less.

If a vessel's draft exceeds the depth outside a channel, the vessel will be limited to straight-line stopping, which is less effective than a combination of slowing or reversing engines and turning away. Hence a lower speed is usually required. Rule 9 gives further direction for vessels operating in narrow channels.

In shallower water, a vessel's speed introduces hydrodynamic forces that are not present in deeper water. As a vessel moves forward, the water in front moves away and then closes in after the stern passes. In shallow water, especially in channels, the water ahead of the vessel is squeezed quickly through the relatively small space around the hull to the stern, moving fastest where it is squeezed the most. That happens under the bottom of the vessel in shallow water, or, if the vessel is near a bank, then along that side. The fast flow of water creates lift, in the same manner that lift is created by a wing or sail. On an airplane, the lift is directed up; on a sailboat, to the side; and on a vessel moving through shallow water, the lift that is produced is directed down or toward the bank. The force on the moving vessel pushes it closer to whatever it is close to.

The effect on the vessel is called "squat," and it increases as the underkeel clearance decreases and as the vessel's speed increases. Thus, a vessel that has ample clearance when moving slowly through shallow water may at high speed scrape the bottom. The hydrodynamic effect of high speed through a channel may cause a vessel to be pulled toward or into the bank or may pull two vessels passing close together off course.

INTERNATIONAL	INLAND
(b) Additionally, by vessels with operational radar:	(b) Additionally, by vessels with operational radar:

Radar-equipped vessels are obligated to use their radar in restricted visibility unless there is a compelling reason not to. Rules 5, 6, 7, and 19 together place great emphasis on the effective use of radar.

Vessels using radar in restricted visibility are justified in going somewhat faster than vessels without radar, but not as fast as they would in good visibility. In open waters a ship using radar may proceed at a relatively high speed, providing the speed is adjusted appropriately upon detection of another vessel.

INTERNATIONAL

(i) the characteristics, efficiency and limitations of the radar equipment;

INLAND

(i) the characteristics, efficiency and limitations of the radar equipment;

Radar equipment varies greatly in power, sophistication, antenna installation, and so forth. The mariner needs to understand these qualities and limitations thoroughly. For instance, a vessel's course might be changed regularly to ensure that any vessel in a blind arc, which may be caused by a vessel's masts or other structures, could be detected early.

There are two basic types of marine radar—navigation and search. Navigation radars transmit short-wavelength radio frequencies, and search radars use long-wavelength transmissions.

Navigation radars send out short high-frequency pulses. These rapid and sharply defined pulses bounce back from surfaces facing the transmitter, yielding a very accurate and detailed image of the surrounding area. Because of their lower power and higher pulse repetition rate, these navigation radars—also called three-centimeter (3 cm), X-band, and high-frequency radars—have a limited range.

Search radars, on the other hand, pack a lot of power into their low-frequency, long-wavelength signals and consequently are able to look into and beyond weather. When they reflect off a target, the signal returns to the receiver with more power, and they can detect objects at farther ranges. These radars go by various names—search, ten-centimeter (10 cm), S-band, or low-frequency radars. The name used is a matter of personal preference and does not distinguish variations.

INTERNATIONAL

(ii) any constraints imposed by the radar range scale in use;

INLAND

(ii) any constraints imposed by the radar range scale in use;

No matter how good a radar set may be, the range scale selected determines the nature of the information available to the operator. Short range scales give good resolution and enable the detection of small targets; long range scales sacrifice detail to gain early detection. Radar equipment is most effective if the operator switches scales regularly, or if the operator has two or more sets and uses a different range scale on each. To the extent that different range scales are not available, speed should be reduced.

INTERNATIONAL

(iii) the effect on radar detection of the sea state, weather, and other sources of interference;

INLAND

(iii) the effect on radar detection of the sea state, weather, and other sources of interference;

Vessel speed should be reduced when interference (caused by large waves, heavy rain or snow, or the like) impairs the performance of the radar.

INTERNATIONAL

(iv) the possibility that small vessels, ice and other floating objects may not be detected by radar at an adequate range;

INLAND

(iv) the possibility that small vessels, ice and other floating objects may not be detected by radar at an adequate range;

The location of the vessel and the season of the year are important in judging whether undetected vessels or ice may be present.

INTERNATIONAL

(v) the number, location and movement of vessels detected by radar;

INLAND

(v) the number, location and movement of vessels detected by radar;

Accurate radar plotting becomes more difficult as the number of vessels increases. Automated radar plotting aids make this task easier.

INTERNATIONAL

(vi) the more exact assessment of the visibility that may be possible when radar is used to determine the range of vessels or other objects in the vicinity.

INLAND

(vi) the more exact assessment of the visibility that may be possible when radar is used to determine the range of vessels or other objects in the vicinity.

The observed radar range of a vessel can be correlated to visibility by noting when the vessel can first be sighted. At night, when the vessel's lights can first be seen, the radar range of the vessel equals the visibility (assuming that the visibility is not so good that masthead light intensity becomes the controlling factor).

Rule 7—Risk of Collision

INTERNATIONAL

(a) Every vessel shall use all available means appropriate to the prevailing circumstances and conditions to determine if risk of collision exists. If there is any doubt such risk shall be deemed to exist.

INLAND

(a) Every vessel shall use all available means appropriate to the prevailing circumstances and conditions to determine if risk of collision exists. If there is any doubt such risk shall be deemed to exist.

Nothing grips a mariner's attention so fast as a late determination of risk of collision. The principles commended by this Rule can be taken lightly only at the risk of some very unwanted exciting moments on the water. The determination of risk of collision, timely or otherwise, triggers a number of other Rules on which the mariner must then act.

Rule 12, for instance, requires action by one of two sailing vessels approaching each other on a collision course. Rule 14 requires action in the case of power-driven vessels approaching each other on reciprocal or near-reciprocal courses so as to involve the risk of collision. Rule 15 applies to power-driven vessels crossing so as to involve the risk of collision. Rule 19 prescribes action by vessels in restricted visibility when risk of collision exists and in certain cases when the degree of risk is unknown. The existence of risk of collision is implicit to the operation of other Rules: Rule 13 (Overtaking), Rule 16 (Action by Give-way Vessel), Rule 17 (Action by Stand-on Vessel), and Rule 18 (Responsibilities between Vessels).

It is not surprising, then, that Rule 7, like Rules 5 and 6, begins with the words "Every vessel shall". These three Rules set up the mariner to take the proper and effective action required by the remaining Steering and Sailing Rules. The full responsibility for Rules 5, 6, and 7 is not excused or lessened for any vessel.

Like Rule 5 (Lookout), Rule 7 is an information-collection and analysis rule, although the tracking function of Rule 7 may involve more analysis than does the detection function of Rule 5. Besides the beginning mandate "Every vessel shall," Rule 7 also shares with Rule 5 the phrase "all available means appropriate to the prevailing circumstances and conditions." Rule 5 requires the proper lookout "to make a full appraisal of the situation and of the risk of collision." The transition from Rule 5 detection to Rule 7 tracking is not a sharp one.

The taking of compass bearings is one of the most important means of determining risk of collision. This technique depends on good visibility, on the vessel being tracked maintaining a constant course, and on several observations. Observations may be taken with a simple hand-bearing compass, a pair of binoculars incorporating a magnetic compass in its optics, or, on larger vessels, a bearing or azimuth circle or an alidade on a fixed gyrocompass repeater. Compass bearings will be discussed more fully below.

In restricted visibility, the primary tracking instrument is radar, if fitted and operational. Radar should also be used to track a vessel in good visibility in open areas after the vessel has been sighted visually. Paragraph (b) of Rule 7 gives specific guidance on the use of radar.

Having sighted a vessel, you may contact it by radiotelephone to confirm its intentions. The radiotelephone is especially valuable on U.S. inland waters where several vessels may be involved, maneuvering room is limited, and courses are frequently changed. In the United States, the Vessel Bridge-to-Bridge Radiotelephone Act and implementing regulations require larger vessels to monitor channel 13 (VHF-FM), which is used for broadcasting and exchanging navigation information. The International Telecommunications Union's Radio Regulations, Appendix 18 (q), now designates channel 13 for use on a worldwide basis as a navigation safety communications channel, primarily for intership communications. The International Maritime Organization's Global Maritime Distress and Safety System (1988 amendments to SOLAS

Convention) includes a requirement for all passenger vessels and for cargo vessels 300 gross tons and above to be capable of transmitting bridge-to-bridge (channel 13) communications. No international requirement to guard the channel has been established. Channel 16 can be used if nobody answers on channel 13.

Once you have detected and tracked another vessel in your vicinity, how do you judge whether risk of collision exists? What, in fact, is "risk of collision"? The Rules do not say. Risk of collision certainly exists for two vessels whose paths would take them to the same spot in two minutes. On the other hand, risk of collision would *not* exist for two slow-moving vessels 20 miles apart headed for the same spot of water, nor would it practically exist for two vessels passing a half mile apart in a busy harbor. What might be risk of collision for two large ships would probably not be risk of collision for two small vessels in the same situation.

A number of factors are involved in such an assessment:

- Closest distance of approach
- Type of waterway
- Vessel size and maneuverability
- Speed
- Distance out from closest point of approach
- Relative bearings

The closest distance of approach is perhaps the prime element in the risk-of-collision formula. A collision occurs when the distance of closest approach goes to zero, but a risk of collision may exist when the distance of closest approach is somewhat greater than zero. A passing within one vessel length would certainly involve risk of collision, but how much space is necessary for risk of collision *not* to exist?

Rule 34 of the Inland (but not International) Rules prescribes whistle signals for power-driven vessels "meeting or crossing at a distance within half a mile of each other." Each vessel indicates whether it intends to leave the other on its port or starboard side. As a general rule, then, we can conclude that on inland waters risk of collision exists for vessels whose paths will take them within a half mile and which are within hearing range of each other. What is the hearing range? Annex III prescribes ranges for vessels' sound-signal appliances (horns): one-half mile for vessels less than 20 meters in length, up to two miles for vessels over 200 meters in length.

International Rule 34 prescribes different sorts of maneuvering signals and requires them when vessels are "in sight of one another," although there would be no sense in giving a signal when the nearest vessel in sight is ten miles away, since the sound signal will be very unlikely to travel as far as five miles. On the open ocean, large vessels traveling at full speed should probably consider that risk of collision exists if their projected paths would bring them within a mile of each other.

The type of waterway plays a part in the calculation of risk. On the open ocean the distance of closest approach triggering risk of collision is greater than in more confined waters because on the ocean it is easier to keep well clear.

Vessel size and maneuverability have a substantial impact on risk of collision. A small vessel that can stop or turn in its own length has a much smaller zone of risk than a large vessel that may need a mile or more to stop and only begins to turn after the rudder is put over.

Speed expands the zone in which risk of collision exists. Higher speeds give the mariner less time to refine the accuracy of vessel path predictions (remember Rule 6).

Vessels are at risk of collision when they come within a certain distance of their closest point of approach. For medium-size ships moving at average speeds in open water in good visibility, risk of collision would probably become a concern at about five miles out from the closest point of approach. Keep in mind that risk of collision does not arise suddenly, like the light from an on-off switch, but rather increases or decreases gradually, like the light from a dimmer switch. For small boats maneuvering in a boat basin the distance out from closest point of approach could be a stone's throw.

An analysis of the Rules themselves will tell us at what distance from closest point of approach a risk of collision arises. As we noted earlier, risk of collision triggers the operation of a number of other Rules. Specifically, the existence of risk of collision obligates certain actions. In crossing situations, for example, the duties are different for each vessel; in a meeting situation, on the other hand, the duties for each vessel are the same. In all cases, however, risk of collision must be discovered early enough for each vessel to be able to carry out its obligations under the Rules.

When one vessel (give-way vessel) is required to keep out of the way of another (stand-on vessel), the give-way vessel must take "early and substantial action to keep well clear" (Rule 16). That doesn't tell us much except that action should be taken soon after risk of collision is established.

Rule 17 is more helpful. It provides that the stand-on vessel may take action to avoid collision as soon as its operator realizes that the give-way vessel is not moving out of the way. Before the stand-on vessel does this, however, it must hold its course and speed long enough for the give-way vessel to predict its path and to maneuver clear. The mariner should have a good idea of how long these events will take for the circumstances and types of vessels involved. Remember that the master of the stand-on vessel probably will be more conservative in judging when the give-way vessel should begin taking action, since he or she must hold on and wait, while the master of the give-way vessel knows better what will happen (use your VHF-FM channel 13).

Finally, the relative bearings of two vessels affect the degree of risk. Two vessels meeting on near-reciprocal courses would close relatively rapidly, because their closing speed would be the sum of the two speeds. The risk of collision would arise while they were still relatively far apart. On the other hand, where one vessel is overtaking another on nearly the same course, the closing speed would be the difference between the individual speeds. Unless one is traveling a great deal faster than the other, it would take a long time for the overtaking vessel to draw abeam of the other. In the overtaking situation, the vessels would be relatively close together before risk of collision arose. Crossing situations would be somewhere between meeting and overtaking.

All of these factors are interdependent and must be considered as a whole and in the context of the circumstances. The above examples and distances are merely ballpark figures for good conditions.

Either vessel is, of course, free to act before risk of collision exists in order to avoid it altogether. Also, in some cases where risk of collision exists, the give-way vessel may not have to alter its course or speed to keep "well clear" (Rule 16) of the stand-on vessel, as long as its course and speed will "result in passing at a safe distance" (Rule 8). The closest point of approach may represent a safe passing distance while at the same time triggering a risk-of-collision situation. Two vessels passing in a narrow channel is an example. Risk of collision and the need to maneuver can be distinguished; risk of collision and the need for extra care cannot.

Our discussion so far has been based on the premise that each vessel involved knows where the other is and generally knows where it is going and how fast. Rule 7 states that if there is any doubt, if the information at hand is not accurate or complete, then risk of collision shall be deemed to exist.

Doubt commonly arises under conditions of restricted visibility. Rule 19(e) implies that in restricted visibility when another vessel is detected ahead, risk of collision shall be deemed to exist until the mariner can positively determine that it doesn't—a guilty-until-proven-innocent standard.

Doubt can also occur because of instrument and measurement errors in tracking another vessel. Know the limitations of your instruments and measurement techniques and include them in the assessment of the situation (much as celestial navigation positions are plotted as circles rather than points).

Many other factors can cause doubt—wind and currents, the movement of another vessel in a busy harbor, and the like. For answers, use your radiotelephone.

INTERNATIONAL	INLAND
(b) Proper use shall be made of radar equipment if fitted and operational, including long-range scanning to obtain early warning of risk of collision and radar plotting or equivalent systematic observation of detected objects.	(b) Proper use shall be made of radar equipment if fitted and operational, including long-range scanning to obtain early warning of risk of collision and radar plotting or equivalent systematic observation of detected objects.

The second paragraph of Rule 7 covers the use of radar in assessing risk of collision. The requirements extend Rule 5 and 6 to define further the use of properly operating radar in avoiding collision. Rule 5 introduced the idea of long-range scanning for maintaining lookout, and Rule 6 made specific mention of using different radar range scales.

The value of the radar in assessing risk of collision in poor visibility is obvious. Rule 19 (Conduct of Vessels in Restricted Visibility) requires that a vessel in restricted visibility determine whether risk of collision exists when it detects by radar alone the presence of another vessel. But radar is also valuable in clear weather after a target has been sighted visually, being better able than the human eye to measure range and other distances.

If the vessel's radar is capable of both true-motion/north-up display and relative-motion/head-up display, the operator must select the display better suited to the operating conditions. Because of the adoption of both national and international standards, the accuracy of both displays is the same. In general, true-motion (sea- or ground-stabilized) radars are preferred for navigation and piloting in confined waters as the position of the observer's own ship moves in accordance with its own path. On the other hand, relative-motion displays allow the observer to assess more quickly the movement of other vessels in relation to his or her own movement. All but the smallest vessels are required to have radars stabilized in azimuth (that is, in the horizontal plane). Radars without compass stabilization are almost useless for determining the actions of other vessels without highly accurate maneuvering board plotting or unless the vessel's heading does not vary by a degree or two at the very most.

Radar plotting (or equivalent systematic observation) is *required* by Rule 7. It is not enough just to *look* at the radar, unless plotting would not be helpful, as, for example, on meandering inland rivers where observations of the vessel's position relative to the channel or banks may be more informative. Plotting is usually appropriate in relatively open water.

Plotting is not required if "equivalent systematic observation" is used. These other observation techniques include manual and automatic (computerized) radar plotting aids or the listing of bearing, range, and time at regular intervals. Plotting by the vessel's operator in congested waters may take so much time that it becomes counterproductive. In such cases automated radar plotting aids (sometimes improperly called collision-avoidance systems) are especially appropriate.

INTERNATIONAL

(c) Assumptions shall not be made on the basis of scanty information, especially scanty radar information.

INLAND

(c) Assumptions shall not be made on the basis of scanty information, especially scanty radar information.

While Rule 7 requires the full and proper use of radar, it also warns against relying on radar for more information than it can realistically give. The mariner who assumes an approaching vessel will pass well clear after making a couple of long-range radar observations is inviting danger and violating Rule 7.

Distances magnify small errors, and errors are almost inevitable because of the imprecision of observations made from a moving vessel. Nor can you assume that the other vessel is maintaining a constant course and speed. Regular and consistent checking of observations is imperative.

Many collisions continue to happen because vessel operators base their actions on faulty assumptions. Rule 7 calls attention to the danger of basing actions on scanty information, requiring that the operator be patient and monitor other vessels in the vicinity until the risk of collision can be determined with a satisfying degree of certainty. (And remember, as long as there is doubt, you must assume that risk of collision does exist!)

INTERNATIONAL

(d) In determining if risk of collision exists the following considerations shall be among those taken into account:

(i) such risk shall be deemed to exist if the compass bearing of an approaching vessel does not appreciably change;

INLAND

(d) In determining if risk of collision exists the following considerations shall be among those taken into account:

(i) such risk shall be deemed to exist if the compass bearing of an approaching vessel does not appreciably change;

(ii) such risk may sometimes exist even when an appreciable bearing change is evident, particularly when approaching a very large vessel or a tow or when approaching a vessel at close range.

(ii) such risk may sometimes exist even when an appreciable bearing change is evident, particularly when approaching a very large vessel or a tow or when approaching a vessel at close range.

The classic test of risk of collision is given special attention in the final paragraph of Rule 7: if your vessel is holding course and speed, and you take several compass bearings on another vessel and those bearings are all about the same, then you will collide with the other vessel if it is also holding course and speed and if one does not take evasive action. Even if the compass bearings do change, there may still be the potential for a collision.

If the other vessel is maneuvering, the compass-bearing test doesn't work. Also, the test works only when the size of the vessels is small when compared with the distance between them. If you take compass bearings to the bow of an approaching ship from the bridge wing at the stern of your ship and note that the compass bearings are changing, then all you know is that a collision is probably not set up between your stern and the other vessel's bow—your bow and its stern, however, may have other ideas.

If the vessel does not have a compass suitable or convenient for taking bearings, other reference points on the vessel can be used to sight on approaching vessels. If, as the other vessel approaches, it remains lined up with the chosen reference points, then risk of collision exists. This technique, of course, is simply a tool to aid the mariner. Like all tools, it has its limitations and should not be relied upon as conclusive.

Rule 8—Action to Avoid Collision

The Rules before Rule 8 address the correct identification of potential danger. Rule 8 begins a series of Rules that prescribe what to do once the risk of collision has been determined to exist. Rule 8 tells how the avoiding action must be executed, not which vessels are required to take the avoiding action. That is left to later Rules.

The International and the Inland Rule 8 are the same. Each

applies to all vessels in all conditions of visibility. In good visibility, one vessel will usually have primary responsibility for taking avoiding action; in restricted visibility, vessels will share equally in that responsibility.

INTERNATIONAL

(a) Any action taken to avoid collision shall, if the circumstances of the case admit, be positive, made in ample time and with due regard to the observance of good seamanship.

INLAND

(a) Any action taken to avoid collision shall, if the circumstances of the case admit, be positive, made in ample time and with due regard to the observance of good seamanship.

Paragraph (a) is a general admonition to use care in avoiding collisions. Although the mandatory word "shall" appears, the paragraph also contains the escape clause "if the circumstances of the case admit." This means that in taking action you are not required to put yourself in a worse condition. You are not required to run aground (although in an extreme situation this may be the best course of action) or enter a collision situation with yet another vessel. Paragraph (a)'s admonition employs indefinite terms—actions are to be "positive," "made in ample time," and "with due regard to the observance of good seamanship."

"Positive" action is a significant change in vessel course or speed; paragraph (b) elaborates. "Ample time" and "with due regard" remind us to act early and do more than is absolutely necessary to avoid the collision, allowing a generous margin of safety both in time and in distance.

INTERNATIONAL

(b) Any alteration of course and/or speed to avoid collision shall, if the circumstances of the case admit, be large enough to be readily apparent to another vessel observing visually or by radar; a succession of small alterations of course and/or speed should be avoided.

INLAND

(b) Any alteration of course or speed to avoid collision shall, if the circumstances of the case admit, be large enough to be readily apparent to another vessel observing visually or by radar; a succession of small alterations of course or speed should be avoided.

Let the other vessel know what you are doing. Make it obvious by sight in good visibility, and obvious on the radar screen in areas of restricted visibility. The give-way vessel in a crossing situation must alter course enough that the stand-on vessel will know it will pass astern. Give the proper maneuvering signals if operating under the International Rules. Call the other vessel by radiotelephone.

INTERNATIONAL	INLAND
(c) If there is sufficient sea room, alteration of course alone may be the most effective action to avoid a close-quarters situation provided that it is made in good time, is substantial and does not result in another close-quarters situation.	(c) If there is sufficient sea room, alteration of course alone may be the most effective action to avoid a close-quarters situation provided that it is made in good time, is substantial and does not result in another close-quarters situation.

Two variables can be altered to avoid collisions: course and speed. Large commercial vessels often find it easier to change course than to change speed, especially in open water when engine room personnel may not have taken the preliminary steps for speed changes. Hence, paragraph (c) allows for a course change alone, which can be made directly and immediately from the bridge. On smaller vessels, on other vessels with direct bridge-controlled engines, or especially on vessels with a controllable-pitch propeller, a speed change may be an equal or more effective action, even when there is ample sea room for a course change.

Paragraph (c) talks about avoiding a "close-quarters" situation. Does that imply a *requirement* to avoid a "close-quarters" situation? Close-quarters situations, of course, should be avoided where possible, but in rivers, harbors, and other inland waterways close-quarters situations are unavoidable.

How does "close quarters" compare with the closest-point-of-approach distance that triggers risk of collision (see Rule 7 discussion), or with the "safe distance" of paragraph (d) of this Rule, or with the "well clear" of Rule 16? As was mentioned in the discussion of Rule 7, the projected closest point of approach between two vessels is one factor in assessing risk of collision. The distance between vessels for which "close quarters" would exist will always be less than the closest-point-of-approach distance that would trigger risk of collision; half the distance would almost certainly be "close quarters."

On the other hand, paragraph (d)'s "safe distance" and Rule 16's "well clear" mean much the same thing (the minimum passing distance permitted by the Rules), and both generally represent a smaller distance than "close-quarters." On inland waters especially, a give-way vessel passing well clear of (or at a safe distance from) another may, at the same time, be in a close-quarters/risk-of-collision situation with that vessel. Two vessels meeting in a narrow channel is an example. Extra caution makes such situations safe.

INTERNATIONAL	INLAND
(d) Action taken to avoid collision with another vessel shall be such as to result in passing at a safe distance. The effectiveness of the action shall be carefully checked until the other vessel is finally past and clear.	(d) Action taken to avoid collision with another vessel shall be such as to result in passing at a safe distance. The effectiveness of the action shall be carefully checked until the other vessel is finally past and clear.

Paragraph (d) requires that action taken result in passing at a safe distance. What distance is safe depends on the circumstances; suffice it to say that if you are obligated to take the action, the person on the other vessel should not feel compelled to act also to increase the distance still further.

Paragraph (d) also imposes the obligation to continue with the Rule 7 assessment of risk of collision until the other vessel is past and clear. You should especially consider the effects of normal maneuvers that the other vessel may begin while still in the vicinity. If in doubt, use your radiotelephone or whistle signal.

INTERNATIONAL	INLAND
(e) If necessary to avoid collision or allow more time to assess the situation, a vessel shall slacken her speed or take all way off by stop-	(e) If necessary to avoid collision or allow more time to assess the situation, a vessel shall slacken her speed or take all way off by stop-

ping or reversing her means of propulsion.

ping or reversing her means of propulsion.

Paragraph (e) should be read in conjunction with paragraph (c). It directs vessels to slow down or stop to avoid a collision or to give more time in which to determine the best course of action. This prescription is only one of several on speed—see Rule 6 (Safe Speed), and Rule 19, paragraphs (b) and (e), relating to speed in restricted visibility.

The separation within Rule 8 of the requirements for course changes (paragraph [c]) and speed changes (paragraph [e]) should not be taken to mean that one method is preferred over the other. If action is required, the mariner must take effective and readily apparent action, whether it be a course change or a speed change or a combination of the two. A course change works better for meeting situations, whereas for vessels crossing at near-right angles, a speed change (perhaps in combination with a course change) often works better.

INTERNATIONAL

(f)(i) A vessel which, by any of these Rules, is required not to impede the passage or safe passage of another vessel shall, when required by the circumstances of the case, take early action to allow sufficient sea room for the safe passage of the other vessel.

(ii) A vessel required not to impede the passage or safe passage of another vessel is not relieved of this obligation if approaching the other vessel so as to involve the risk of collision and shall, when taking action, have full regard to the action which may be required by the Rules of this part.

(iii) A vessel the passage of which is not to be impeded remains fully obliged to comply with the

INLAND

(f)(i) A vessel which, by any of these Rules, is required not to impede the passage or safe passage of another vessel shall, when required by the circumstances of the case, take early action to allow sufficient sea room for the safe passage of the other vessel.

(ii) A vessel required not to impede the passage or safe passage of another vessel is not relieved of this obligation if approaching the other vessel so as to involve the risk of collision and shall, when taking action, have full regard to the action which may be required by the Rules of this part.

(iii) A vessel the passage of which is not to be impeded remains fully obliged to comply with the

INTERNATIONAL

INLAND

Rules of this part when the two vessels are approaching one another so
as to involve risk of collision.

Rules of this part when the two vessels are approaching one another so
as to involve risk of collision.

International Rule 8(f) was added in 1989. (Parallel language was added to the Inland Rules in 1990.) This change puts to rest debates that had been ongoing for almost as long as the 72 COL-REGS have existed. The "shall not impede" language comes into play in Rule 9 (narrow channels and narrow fairways), in International Rule 10 (traffic separation schemes), and in International Rule 18 (vessels constrained by draft). In each of these cases, usually larger vessels find themselves in situations where they are at a substantial maneuvering disadvantage with respect to smaller vessels in the same area—smaller vessels that otherwise might be stand-on vessels.

The IMO Subcommittee on Safety of Navigation for a time had issued guidance on the meaning of the term "shall not impede." That guidance said that the "shall not impede" command meant to maneuver, when practicable, so far out of the way of the other vessel that risk of collision never develops, with the proviso that if risk of collision by some chance does develop, the more general Steering and Sailing Rules would take over (that is, the "shall not impede" rules would no longer be in effect).

The IMO subsequently decided that the guidance, if given at all, should be part of the Rules. During the course of the debate on the actual language, the delegates decided that the vessel that was originally directed to not impede the other should retain that burden even after risk of collision arose. That does not mean, however, that the (usually larger) vessel that was not to be impeded continues to have the right-of-way. The new Rule provides that if the not-to-be-impeded vessel would be the give-way vessel under the general rules, it has a duty to stay out of the way of the impeding vessel after risk of collision exists. Under the new Rule, which changed the earlier official guidance in this respect, the impeding vessel *also* continues to have a duty to stay out of the way after risk of collision arises, and does not gain the stand-on status that the general rules might have given it. *Both* vessels would be obligated to stay out of the way.

If, on the other hand, the not-to-be-impeded vessel would be the stand-on vessel under the general Steering and Sailing Rules, it would not lose that status. In that case, the impeding vessel would have a double duty to stay out of the way.

The "shall not impede" language in these cases creates an exception to the general rules, making them more practical. Vessels directed "not to impede" other vessels should take *early* action to keep clear by *wide* margins, thus providing sufficient sea room. The other vessel shouldn't become concerned enough to alter its course or speed, or otherwise feel obliged to act differently from the way it would if the "impeding" vessel weren't there.

Rule 9—Narrow Channels

With Rule 9, the Rules become more specific. Although Rule 9 applies in all conditions of visibility, it applies only on certain waters and to certain vessels. Rule 9 is also the first to contain significant differences between the International and Inland versions.

Two terms are used throughout the Rule that are not defined. They are "narrow channel" (namesake of the Rule) and "(narrow) fairway." We must assume that the drafters of the Rules either believed their meanings to be obvious or else were not able to formulate suitably concise definitions.

Rule 9 applies only on waters described by the two terms. What is "narrow" depends on the type of vessel and the circumstances. A "channel" is a natural or dredged lane restricted on either side by shallow water; it is often marked by buoys. A "fairway" is generally in open water, and the water on either side is not much shallower than that within the fairway. Fairways are used to route vessels away from natural hazards, oil platforms, mines, or smaller vessels. Fairways should be differentiated from the lanes in traffic separation schemes; vessels in the latter should follow Rule 10 rather than Rule 9.

INTERNATIONAL	INLAND
(a) A vessel proceeding along the course of a narrow channel or fairway shall keep as near to the outer	(a)(i)A vessel proceeding along the course of a narrow channel or fairway shall keep as near to the outer

INTERNATIONAL

limit of the channel or fairway which lies on her starboard side as is safe and practicable.

INLAND

limit of the channel or fairway which lies on her starboard side as is safe and practicable.

Just as all cars drive on the right side of the road (in the United States), paragraph (a) requires all vessels to navigate on the far right side of a narrow channel, whether or not the traffic is approaching from the other direction. If that is not "safe or practicable," however, the mariner is justified in moving closer to the center or even over the center to the left side (providing the traffic permits such action).

INLAND

(ii) Notwithstanding paragraph (a)(i) and Rule 14(a), a power-driven vessel operating in narrow channels or fairways on the Great Lakes, Western Rivers, or waters specified by the Secretary, and proceeding downbound with a following current shall have the right-of-way over an upbound vessel, shall propose the manner and place of passage, and shall initiate the maneuvering signals prescribed by Rule 34 (a)(i), as appropriate. The vessel proceeding upbound against the current shall hold as necessary to permit safe passing.

Paragraph (a) of the Inland Rules contains a provision that was added to deal with the control problems experienced by some downbound vessels on rivers. The provision concerns power-driven vessels transiting narrow channels and narrow fairways on the Great lakes and western rivers. In addition, the Coast Guard has specified other bodies of water on which the provision applies: Tennessee–Tombigbee Waterway, Tombigbee River, Black Warrior River, Alabama River, Coosa River, Mobile River above the Cochrane Bridge at St. Louis Point, Flint River, Chattachoochee

River, and the Apalachicola River above its confluence with the Jackson River (see Title 33 of the Code of Federal Regulations, Part 89, Subpart B).

The vessel proceeding downbound with a following current has the right-of-way and is given the choice of passing arrangements over an upbound vessel. The downbound vessel is *required* to contact the upbound vessel and to initiate maneuvering signals. The upbound vessel is obligated to accept the downbound vessel's proposed manner of passing unless doing so would jeopardize its safety. It is also obligated, if necessary, to hold position until the downbound vessel has passed. Normal port-to-port passing should be the rule except in the area of bends where both sides of the channel may be needed to make the turn.

INTERNATIONAL	INLAND
(b) A vessel of less than 20 meters in length or a sailing vessel shall not impede the passage of a vessel which can safely navigate only within a narrow channel or fairway.	(b) A vessel of less than 20 meters in length or a sailing vessel shall not impede the passage of a vessel which can safely navigate only within a narrow channel or fairway.

Paragraphs (b) and (c) are the same for the International and Inland Rules and direct certain vessels not to impede other vessels that can safely navigate only within the narrow channel or fairway. The 1989 Rule 8(f) "shall not impede" amendment says that vessels directed not to impede shall take early enough action that sufficient sea room exists for safe passage. If risk of collision does arise (ideally it should not), the impeding vessel retains its duty to stay out of the way, notwithstanding any stand-on rights the more general Steering and Sailing Rules may have given it. In other words, the vessel directed not to impede should stay *well* clear!

Paragraph (b) gives rights to nonsailing vessels that are over twenty meters long *and* that can safely navigate only within the narrow channel or fairway. Both conditions must be met. The Rule does not assign rights *between* power-driven vessels less than twenty meters long and sailing vessels, as these vessels fall into the same class—for Rule 9(b) purposes.

INTERNATIONAL

(c) A vessel engaged in fishing shall not impede the passage of any other vessel navigating within a narrow channel or fairway.

INLAND

(c) A vessel engaged in fishing shall not impede the passage of any other vessel navigating within a narrow channel or fairway.

Paragraph (c), unlike paragraph (b), gives rights to *any* vessel navigating within a narrow channel or fairway, not just to those that can safely operate *only* within the channel or fairway. Vessels engaged in fishing—defined in Rule 3(d)—must stay out of the way, although they are permitted to fish in the channel or fairway if it is not otherwise being used.

INTERNATIONAL

(d) A vessel shall not cross a narrow channel or fairway if such crossing impedes the passage of a vessel which can safely navigate only within such channel or fairway. The latter vessel may use the sound signal prescribed in Rule 34(d) if in doubt as to the intention of the crossing vessel.

INLAND

(d) A vessel shall not cross a narrow channel or fairway if such crossing impedes the passage of a vessel which can safely navigate only within such channel or fairway. The latter vessel may use the danger signal prescribed in Rule 34(d) if in doubt as to the intention of the crossing vessel.

Paragraph (d) of both the International and Inland Rule 9 prohibits all vessels from crossing a narrow channel or fairway in a way that would impede a vessel that could not safely operate outside of the channel or fairway. Rule 8(f) "shall not impede" language is operative here. If your vessel is directed not to impede another, try to avoid causing the other vessel to change its course or speed. If you blunder into a risk-of-collision situation, the general Steering and Sailing Rules will not apply to you—you will continue to be obliged to stay out of the way. Be mindful, however, that Rule 8(f)(iii) says that the general rules will apply to the vessel you are impeding. It may be helpful to contact the other vessel (for example, on channel 13 VHF-FM) to inform its operator of your intentions—early, of course.

The Rule also provides for the vessel constrained to the channel to sound five or more short blasts if in doubt as to the intentions of the vessel sounding the crossing signal. The International version of Rule 9 says that this sound signal "may" be used—although International Rule 34(d) *requires* its use in case of doubt—while the Inland Rule 9 says it "shall" be used.

Note that the International version refers to the "sound signal prescribed in Rule 34(d)," while the Inland Rule refers to the "danger signal prescribed in Rule 34(d)." Neither version of Rule 34(d) refers to the five or more short blasts as the "danger" signal, but rather calls for the signal's use when "either vessel fails to understand the intentions or actions of the other, or is in doubt whether sufficient action is being taken by the other to avoid collision." Thinking of the five-blast signal as a danger signal may cause a vessel operator to delay its use until a situation of *potential* danger has developed into one of *immediate* danger. Its *early* application in the circumstances of doubt described in Rule 34(d) would likely focus the attention of the parties while there is still time to act effectively in a noncrisis environment. Think of the signal as a "doubt" rather than a "danger" signal.

INTERNATIONAL

(e)(i) In a narrow channel or fairway when overtaking can take place only if the vessel to be overtaken has to take action to permit safe passing, the vessel intending to overtake shall indicate her intention by sounding the appropriate signal prescribed in Rule 34(c)(i). The vessel to be overtaken shall, if in agreement, sound the appropriate signal prescribed in Rule 34(c)(ii) and take steps to permit safe passing. If in doubt she may sound the signals prescribed in Rule 34(d).

(ii) This Rule does not relieve the overtaking vessel of her obligation under Rule 13.

INLAND

(e)(i) In a narrow channel or fairway when overtaking, the vessel intending to overtake shall indicate her intention by sounding the appropriate signal prescribed in Rule 34(c) and take steps to permit safe passing. The overtaken vessel, if in agreement, shall sound the same signal. If in doubt she shall sound the danger signal prescribed in Rule 34(d).

(ii) This Rule does not relieve the overtaking vessel of her obligation under Rule 13.

Paragraph (e) gives the procedures for overtaking in narrow channels and fairways and should be read in conjunction with Rule 13, the Rule for overtaking in general, and with Rule 34(c), which prescribes the sound signals for overtaking. The requirements for overtaking in narrow channels and fairways and the sound signals for overtaking in general vary substantially between the International Rules and the Inland Rules.

The International Rule 9 requirement for overtaking applies only when the overtaken vessel (in addition to the overtaking vessel) has to take *maneuvering action* to permit a safe passing. If the overtaken vessel agrees with the overtaking vessel's passing proposal, then the overtaken vessel is required to "take steps to permit safe passing." The Inland Rule requirements for overtaking in narrow channels and fairways are the same as the general Inland Rule requirement for overtaking and are therefore redundant.

The sound signals used for overtaking in open water are the same as for overtaking in narrow channels, although the International overtaking signals are different from those used on inland waters. The Inland Rule signals used for crossing are also used for overtaking. The International overtaking signals are longer (although perhaps less likely to cause confusion). The sound signals will be more fully discussed with Rule 34.

International Rule 9(e)(i) says that when doubt exists as to the other vessel's intentions, the overtaken vessel "may" sound the Rule 34(d) five short blast doubt signal, while the Inland version requires ("shall sound") the sounding of the signal. Both are legally superfluous and merely act as reminders of the Rule 34(d) *requirement* ("shall" in both International and Inland) for all vessels to sound the five-blast signal when doubt exists.

INTERNATIONAL	INLAND
(f) A vessel nearing a bend or an area of a narrow channel or fairway where other vessels may be obscured by an intervening obstruction shall navigate with particular alertness and caution and shall sound the appropriate signal prescribed in Rule 34(e).	(f) A vessel nearing a bend or an area of a narrow channel or fairway where other vessels may be obscured by an intervening obstruction shall navigate with particular alertness and caution and shall sound the appropriate signal prescribed in Rule 34(e).

Paragraph (f) cautions vessels nearing a blind bend or other area where an approaching vessel may be obscured and reminds them to obey the Rule 34(e) signal requirement. The requirements in this paragraph (International identical to Inland) offer nothing new—the requirements for lookout, safe speed, and so forth cover needed precautions and Rule 34(e) covers the signal requirement.

INTERNATIONAL

(g) Any vessel shall, if the circumstances of the case admit, avoid anchoring in a narrow channel.

INLAND

(g) Any vessel shall, if the circumstances of the case admit, avoid anchoring in a narrow channel.

Anchoring in a narrow channel is obviously not a good practice and is prohibited by Rule 9(g) except under pressing circumstances. A separate and older law (Section 409 of Title 33, U.S. Code) repeats the prohibition for U.S. waters: it is unlawful to tie up or anchor barges or other craft in navigable channels in such a manner as to prevent or obstruct the passage of other vessels or craft.

Anchorage regulations cover background, procedures, rules, and a list of special anchorage areas and anchorage grounds. These regulations are contained in Title 33 of the Code of Federal Regulations, Parts 109 and 110.

Rule 10—Traffic Separation Schemes/Vessel Traffic Services

Rule 10 adds an extra dose of traffic management for a number of specially designated areas having high-density traffic, converging traffic, or some exceptional hazard. In these situations, more conventional navigation rules do not provide a desirable margin of safety. Although conceptually similar, International Rule 10 and Inland Rule 10 differ completely in content and even have different names.

The International Rule's "traffic separation schemes" are coastal routing systems that guide oceangoing ships in approaching or departing busy ports and at turning points in crowded sea lanes. The Inland Rule's "vessel traffic services" are management systems tailored for particular congested ports under U.S. territorial jurisdiction. Vessel traffic services are "active" (as opposed to the "passive" traffic separation schemes) and depend on a full-time, shore-based staff and an array of electronic equipment. Because the two versions of Rule 10 are completely different, they will be considered separately.

INTERNATIONAL

Traffic Separation Schemes
(a) This Rule applies to traffic separation schemes adopted by the Organization and does not relieve any
vessel of her obligation under any
other rule.

The "Organization" is the International Maritime Organization (IMO), a body of the United Nations headquartered in London. Traffic separation schemes are adopted by the IMO after a country (or countries) submits a traffic separation scheme proposal, which must meet specific IMO guidelines. Normally a scheme will not be shown on charts until it has been formally adopted by the IMO. The IMO publishes *Ships' Routeing*, which contains design standards and a list (with diagrams and coordinates) of all adopted traffic separation schemes. Check with your local authorities for an up-to-date list.

The IMO defines "traffic separation scheme" as a plan that organizes traffic proceeding in opposite or nearly opposite directions by means of a separation zone or line, traffic line, or such. There may be obstructions within the traffic separation scheme. Efforts, however, are made to keep the lanes clear. For known obstructions, such as an oil rig or wreck, within a traffic separation scheme, notice to mariners will be given. Sometimes a traffic separation scheme will be temporarily modified to skirt a short-term obstruction. In some cases off U.S. coasts "safety fairways," in which obstructions are excluded, are superimposed over a traffic separation scheme. (In most cases safety fairways are used independently, usually in areas having concentrations of offshore petroleum production and exploration platforms.)

A vessel is said to be "using" a traffic separation scheme when the vessel is within the boundaries of the scheme and is neither

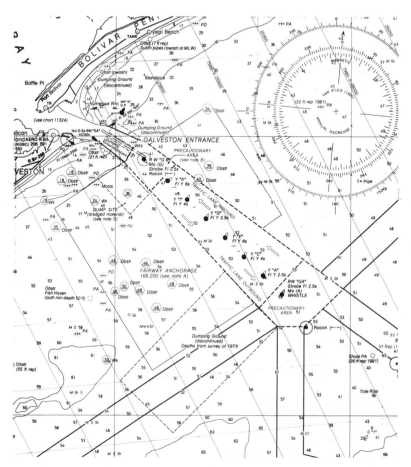

Figure 1—Example of a traffic separation scheme (*dashed lines*) and, in this case, connecting safety fairways (*solid lines*).

crossing the scheme nor fishing within the separation zone. The language on vessel obligations dispels any notion that once in a traffic lane, a vessel acquires absolute rights over vessels outside of the lane. Rule 8(f)(iii) provides an example of where a vessel in a lane would be obligated to stay out of the way of a presumably less privileged crossing vessel.

INTERNATIONAL

(b) A vessel using a traffic separation scheme shall:

(i) proceed in the appropriate traffic lane in the general direction of traffic flow for that lane;

(ii) so far as practicable keep clear of a traffic separation line or separation zone;

(iii) normally join or leave a traffic lane at the termination of the lane, but when joining or leaving from either side shall do so at as small an angle to the general direction of traffic flow as practicable.

The first rule for using a traffic separation scheme is obvious: go with the flow.

The second rule requires vessels "so far as practicable" not to get too close to a traffic separation line or zone so as not to drift accidentally into the lane of oncoming traffic or create doubt about whether or not it is using the traffic separation scheme. Unlike highways on land, traffic separation schemes do not have double yellow lines down the middle or a white line on its outside boundary.

The third rule, governing vessels entering or leaving a traffic separation lane, requires a small angle of approach or departure to differentiate that vessel from one crossing the scheme. (Crossing instructions are in Rule 10[c].)

INTERNATIONAL

(c) A vessel shall, so far as practicable, avoid crossing traffic lanes but if obliged to do so shall cross on a heading as nearly as practicable at right angles to the general direction of traffic flow.

Many schemes are short, and you can go around, not through, them. Crossing long schemes at right angles announces that vessel's intentions and minimizes the time the crossing vessel spends in the scheme. Please note that the angle of crossing is determined by the vessel's heading, not its course (which could be different, usually because of a side current). When a crossing vessel encounters a vessel using a traffic separation scheme, the vessel that is required to stay out of the way is determined by Rule 15 (Crossing Situations).

Fishing vessels, sailing vessels, and power-driven vessels less than twenty meters in length—see paragraphs (i) and (j)—that are crossing shall always stay out of the way of a vessel following a traffic lane, but be aware that the larger vessel in the traffic lane does not have absolute rights; see Rule 8(f)(iii).

INTERNATIONAL

(d)(i) A vessel shall not use an inshore traffic zone when she can safely use the appropriate traffic lane within the adjacent traffic separation scheme. However, vessels of less than 20 meters in length, sailing vessels and vessels engaged in fishing may use the inshore traffic zone.

(ii) Notwithstanding subparagraph (d)(i), a vessel may use an inshore traffic zone when en route to or from a port, offshore installation or structure, pilot station or any other place situated within the inshore traffic zone, or to avoid immediate danger.

Segregating large fast ships from smaller coastal vessels lessens the anxieties often felt when big and small vessels share a common waterway. Rule 10(d) provides this separation through "inshore traffic zones," defined as designated areas between the landward boundary of a traffic separation scheme and the adjacent coast intended for coastal traffic. The purpose of inshore traffic zones may be, for example, to keep oil tankers away from the coastline or to allow fishermen to operate away from merchant shipping.

When an inshore traffic zone has been adopted as part of a traffic separation scheme, large through vessels are in effect required to use the traffic lanes or to stay offshore beyond the traffic separation scheme. The Rule recognizes that sailing vessels and small power-driven vessels often depend on being near the coast.

INTERNATIONAL

(e) A vessel other than a crossing vessel or a vessel joining or leaving a lane shall not normally enter a separation zone or cross a separation line except:

(i) in cases of emergency to avoid immediate danger;

(ii) to engage in fishing within a separation zone.

The paragraph (e) restriction on crossing a separation line or entering a separation zone is similar to the paragraph (b)(ii) restriction, but it explicitly recognizes a right to fish within separation zones.

INTERNATIONAL

(f) A vessel navigating in areas near the terminations of traffic separation schemes shall do so with particular caution.

Most traffic separation schemes guiding traffic flow in and out of ports have "precautionary areas" at the inshore end of the scheme. Because of the concentration of meeting and crossing traffic, you should exercise particular care. Paragraph (f) makes it clear that the mariner is also required to proceed with caution near the ends of traffic separation schemes that do not have precautionary areas.

INTERNATIONAL

(g) A vessel shall so far as practicable avoid anchoring in a traffic

separation scheme or in areas near
its terminations.

Following the reasoning for prohibitions against anchoring in
narrow channels, fairways, and so forth, paragraph (g) prohibits
anchoring in a traffic separation scheme or near its ends.

INTERNATIONAL

(h) A vessel not using a traffic separation scheme shall avoid using it
by as wide a margin as is practicable.

The smooth operation of a traffic separation scheme depends
on the absence of outside disturbances. A vessel not using a traffic
separation scheme must stay far enough away that vessels within
the scheme are not obligated, via any other navigation rules—see
Rule 8(f)(iii)—to take action inconsistent with the flow of traffic.

INTERNATIONAL

(i) A vessel engaged in fishing
shall not impede the passage of any
vessel following the traffic lane.

Fishing is permitted within a traffic lane so long as the fishing
vessel proceeds along the lane with the rest of the traffic and does
not "impede" other vessels following the traffic lane. If the vessel
engaged in fishing follows a course that obliges a vessel following
the traffic lane to alter course or speed, then the fishing vessel has
impeded the other vessel and is therefore in violation of this requirement.

INTERNATIONAL

(j) A vessel of less than 20 meters
in length or a sailing vessel shall
not impede the safe passage of a
power-driven vessel following a
traffic lane.

The Rules often distinguish among size and type of vessels. Rule 10 distinguishes between large vessels (power-driven vessels twenty meters or longer) and small (power-driven vessels less than twenty meters and all sailing vessels). Just as paragraph (d) gives priority to small vessels in inshore traffic zones, paragraph (j) gives priority to large vessels in traffic lanes. Small vessels using traffic separation schemes must stay far away from ships and, whenever possible, should communicate their intentions by radiotelephone. The "shall not impede" language, discussed earlier, operates in this requirement too—see Rule 8(f).

INTERNATIONAL

(k) A vessel restricted in her ability to maneuver when engaged in an operation for the maintenance of safety of navigation in a traffic separation scheme is exempted from complying with this Rule to the extent necessary to carry out the operation.

(l) A vessel restricted in her ability to maneuver when engaged in an operation for the laying, servicing or picking up of a submarine cable, within a traffic separation scheme, is exempted from complying with this Rule to the extent necessary to carry out the operation.

Paragraphs (k) and (l) provide exemptions from Rule 10 requirements for two classes of vessels that, by the nature of their work, cannot always comply with every requirement. Vessels engaged in the maintenance of navigation safety, such as buoy tenders, are exempted *only* while they are restricted in their ability to maneuver and *only* to the extent needed to carry out their work. Vessels laying or maintaining submarine cables must go where the cable goes and while working cable are normally restricted in their ability to maneuver. Operations likely to interfere with normal separation-scheme traffic may be publicized by notices to mariners.

INLAND

Vessel Traffic Services

Each vessel required by regulation to participate in a vessel traffic service shall comply with the applicable regulations.

In the United States there are eight vessel traffic services (VTS), which the Coast Guard defines as "an integrated system encompassing the variety of technologies, equipment, and people employed to coordinate vessel movements in or approaching a port or waterway." The purpose of a VTS is to reduce the risk of collisions, rammings, and groundings and the environmental harm that often accompanies such events.

Because the success of a VTS relies on the accuracy of the information it receives about vessel traffic and marine hazards, each VTS uses a communications system known as a Vessel Movement Reporting System. In a voluntary VTS, the vessel operator is encouraged to check into the system, monitor on VHF-FM radio the VTS operating frequency, and exchange information with the VTS. In a mandatory VTS, the vessel operator must report into a VTS, provide information about the vessel (size, speed, intended movements, and so forth), and maintain a continuous monitor on the VTS operating frequency. In both voluntary and mandatory systems, VTS personnel monitor vessel movements using sensitive television cameras, radar, or both, and, in some locations, keep track of each vessel's location by computer. Should a dangerous situation develop, VTS personnel will contact the affected vessels to advise them of the danger and may, in certain instances, take specific action to manage vessel traffic. This does not reduce or remove in any way the responsibility of the operator to navigate his or her vessel safely.

The major mandatory systems are:

- Puget Sound Vessel Traffic Service (Seattle, Washington)
- Prince William Sound Vessel Traffic Service (Valdez, Alaska)
- St. Marys River Vessel Traffic Service (Sault St. Marie, Michigan)

- Berwick Bay Vessel Traffic Service (Morgan City, Louisiana)
- New York Vessel Traffic Service (New York, New York)

The voluntary systems are:

- San Francisco Vessel Traffic Service (Yerba Buena Island in San Francisco Bay, California)
- Houston/Galveston Vessel Traffic Service (Galena Park, Texas)

Vessel traffic service regulations are contained in Title 33 of the Code of Federal Regulations, Part 161 (see Appendix III of this book).

SECTION/SUBPART II—CONDUCT OF VESSELS IN SIGHT OF ONE ANOTHER

Rule 11—Application

INTERNATIONAL
Rules in this Section apply to vessels in sight of one another.

INLAND
Rules in this subpart apply to vessels in sight of one another.

Rule 11 begins Section/Subpart II and says that Rules 11 through 18 apply to vessels in sight of one another. The International and Inland versions are the same except for a difference in terms ("section" versus "subpart") that is due only to past practices between the treaty drafters and the U.S. Congress. (We will refer to either as "section.")

Rule 3(k) says that vessels shall be deemed to be in sight of one another only when *one* can visually observe the other. Rules 11–18 apply when *each* vessel can see the other. If one vessel fails to sight the other only because of an inadequate lookout (Rule 5), then that vessel is not excused from complying with the Rules in this section.

The Rules in this section in most cases assign to one vessel in a two-vessel encounter the primary responsibility for staying out of the way of the other. The vessel obliged to stay out of the way is called the "give-way" vessel; the other vessel is called the "stand-on" vessel. The theory behind these Rules is that the give-way vessel is the one better able to stay out of the way, although in practice this is not always the case. The execution of these Rules depends on the operator of each vessel being able to assess the other's relative position, course, speed, and intentions. Hence the Rules in this section depend on good visibility (day or night). In restricted visibility when vessels are not in sight of one another (when each cannot visually observe the other), Rules 11–18 *do not apply* and the vessel operators are required to follow instead Rule 19 (Conduct of Vessels in Restricted Visibility).

What Rules you should use depends on whether you can actually see that vessel, and only indirectly on the condition of visibility. If you have vessels A and B on your radar screen but can visually see only vessel A, you must follow Rules 12–18 with respect to A and Rule 19 with respect to B. In such a situation you may find that obscured vessel B moves out of its fogbank (or haze or whatever) and becomes visible. As soon as it does, and when it is clear that it also sees you, Rules 12–18 would then normally apply. If the other vessel, upon becoming visible, is too close or is coming on too fast for you to act effectively under Section II Rules (stand-on/give-way), then Section I and Section III Rules have been disobeyed (by somebody) and you must take *whatever* action is needed to avoid collision—immediately.

Rule 12—Sailing Vessels

INTERNATIONAL

(a) When two sailing vessels are approaching one another, so as to involve risk of collision, one of them shall keep out of the way of the other as follows:

INLAND

(a) When two sailing vessels are approaching one another, so as to involve risk of collision, one of them shall keep out of the way of the other as follows:

Rule 12 tells which of two sailing vessels must stay out of the way of the other and covers all situations except overtaking. Rule 13 outranks Rule 12 and says the overtaking vessel shall stay out of the way of the overtaken vessel, whether it be a sailboat overtaking another sailboat or a sailboat overtaking a power-driven vessel.

INTERNATIONAL

(i) when each has the wind on a different side, the vessel which has the wind on the port side shall keep out of the way of the other;

INLAND

(i) when each has the wind on a different side, the vessel which has the wind on the port side shall keep out of the way of the other;

Paragraph (a)(i) refers to a vessel with "the wind on the port side." In this case the "windward side," as defined in paragraph (b), would be the port side and the vessel would be said to be on the "port tack." A sailing vessel with the wind on the starboard side (that is, starboard side is windward side) carries its mainsail on the port side and stands on for vessels with the wind on the port side. Or, as more commonly expressed, the starboard-tack boat has right-of-way over the port-tack boat. This is true even if the port-tack boat is close-hauled and the starboard-tack boat is running downwind.

INTERNATIONAL

(ii) when both have the wind on the same side, the vessel which is to windward shall keep out of the way of the vessel which is to leeward;

INLAND

(ii) when both have the wind on the same side, the vessel which is to windward shall keep out of the way of the vessel which is to leeward;

When both vessels have the wind on the same side, the vessel to windward is required to stay out of the way. If you draw a line through your vessel 90 degrees to the direction of the true wind (not necessarily the "relative" wind that you feel while your boat is moving), "to windward" is everywhere on the side of the line in the direction from where the wind is blowing (upwind) and "to leeward" is everywhere on the other side of the line (downwind).

INTERNATIONAL

(iii) if a vessel with the wind on the port side sees a vessel to windward and cannot determine with certainty whether the other vessel has the wind on the port or on the

INLAND

(iii) if a vessel with the wind on the port side sees a vessel to windward and cannot determine with certainty whether the other vessel has the wind on the port or on the

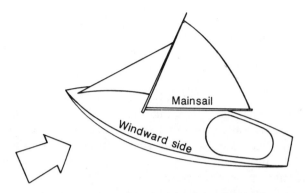

Figure 2—The windward side.

starboard side, she shall keep out of the way of the other.

starboard side, she shall keep out of the way of the other.

If you can't tell on which side the other vessel's sails are carried and you are on port tack, stay out of the way. At night it is especially difficult to determine on which tack another vessel is sailing.

INTERNATIONAL

(b) For the purposes of this Rule the windward side shall be deemed to be the side opposite to that on which the mainsail is carried or, in the case of a square-rigged vessel, the side opposite to that on which the largest fore-and-aft sail is carried.

INLAND

(b) For the purposes of this Rule the windward side shall be deemed to be the side opposite to that on which the mainsail is carried or, in the case of a square-rigged vessel, the side opposite to that on which the largest fore-and-aft sail is carried.

Rule 13—Overtaking

INTERNATIONAL

(a) Notwithstanding anything contained in the Rules of Part B, Sec-

INLAND

(a) Notwithstanding anything contained in the Rules 4 through 18,

tions I and II any vessel overtaking any other shall keep out of the way of the vessel being overtaken.

any vessel overtaking any other shall keep out of the way of the vessel being overtaken.

Overtaking on the water is much like overtaking on land: the driver of the faster car is looking forward at the car to be passed and hence is in a better position to plan and execute the maneuver. From the bridge of most larger vessels, the view to the rear is substantially more limited than the view to the front. Should there not be room to pass, the overtaking vessel always has the option of slowing down; the vessel to be overtaken will often be unable to go any faster. Rule 13 therefore requires the overtaking vessel to keep out of the way of the vessel being passed.

Rule 9(e) also has requirements for overtaking in narrow channels and fairways, and the International version of that Rule requires some action by the vessel to be overtaken. Rule 34(c) gives requirements for sounding whistle signals in overtaking situations. Rule 16 requires the give-way (overtaking) vessel to keep well clear of the vessel to be passed. Keeping well clear while overtaking is especially important because the potentially strong hydrodynamic interactive forces may cause one or both vessels to veer off course.

Paragraph (a) of this Rule requires that any vessel overtaking another keep out of the way, even if another rule required otherwise. In overtaking situations, look first to Rule 13. Despite the seemingly absolute language of paragraph (a), there are a few situations where the overtaking vessel would retain the stand-on status given by another Rule.

Rule 9(b) and (c) and Rule 10(i) and (j) say that power-driven vessels less than 20 meters in length, sailing vessels, and vessels engaged in fishing "shall not impede the passage" of larger vessels following a narrow channel, narrow fairway, or traffic lane. Smaller vessels are usually slower and larger, faster vessels commonly overtake them. Rule 13 requires overtaking vessels to put aside the other "shall not impede" requirements and to keep out of the way of the vessel being overtaken. But requiring, for example, a large and fast commercial vessel operating in a long narrow channel such that it cannot safely leave the channel to trail behind a small slow vessel might be described as an unintended result of a literal and strict following of Rule 13. Certainly the best solution to this troublesome circumstance is for both vessels to be accommodating. The smaller vessel should probably not be in the narrow channel in the first place, if it is wide enough for only one vessel, but, of course, the larger vessel would not be justified in running over the smaller vessel, no matter how tempting!

INTERNATIONAL

(b) A vessel shall be deemed to be overtaking when coming up with another vessel from a direction more than 22.5 degrees abaft her beam, that is, in such a position with reference to the vessel she is overtaking, that at night she would be able to see only the sternlight of that vessel but neither of her sidelights.

INLAND

(b) A vessel shall be deemed to be overtaking when coming up with another vessel from a direction more than 22.5 degrees abaft her beam; that is, in such a position with reference to the vessel she is overtaking, that at night she would be able to see only the sternlight of that vessel but neither of her sidelights.

Paragraph (b) says what is meant by overtaking. A vessel approaching from a direction more than 22.5 degrees aft of the beam of another vessel—or stated differently, from within a 135-degree horizontal sector centered directly astern (the same as the light from the vessel's sternlight) of that vessel—is overtaking if there is risk of collision. If the approaching vessel is within the sternlight sector of another vessel but their courses will bring them no closer together than, say, three miles, then there is no risk of collision and no overtaking situation exists.

Overtaking continues even as the overtaking vessel moves out of the sternlight sector and pulls abeam of and then ahead of the overtaken vessel. It ends only when the maneuver has been completed.

INTERNATIONAL

(c) When a vessel is in any doubt as to whether she is overtaking an-

INLAND

(c) When a vessel is in any doubt as to whether she is overtaking another, she shall assume that this is the case and act accordingly.

other, she shall assume that this is the case and act accordingly.

At night if you are approaching a white navigation light but can see no sidelights, you know you are overtaking another vessel (or perhaps approaching an anchored vessel) and so must stay clear. If you see a white light and later a colored sidelight, either you could be overtaking and have come up enough to move into the horizontal sector of the sidelight, or you could be crossing or meeting, having first seen the brighter white masthead light and then later the less visible colored sidelight. The arrangement, if discernible, should tell you which is the case. During daylight it may be difficult to estimate the angle of approach without the navigation lights as a reference. Paragraph (c) says that if you are in doubt, assume that you are overtaking and keep out of the way of the other vessel. If you are in doubt and haven't used your radar or radiotelephone, shame on you!

(d) Any subsequent alteration of the bearing between the two vessels shall not make the overtaking vessel a crossing vessel within the meaning of these Rules or relieve her of the duty of keeping clear of the overtaken vessel until she is finally past and clear.

(d) Any subsequent alteration of the bearing between the two vessels shall not make the overtaking vessel a crossing vessel within the meaning of these Rules or relieve her of the duty of keeping clear of the overtaken vessel until she is finally past and clear.

Paragraph (d) makes clear that the overtaking vessel cannot (by any action of its own) shift its give-way status to the other vessel. The overtaking vessel remains the give-way vessel until the risk of collision has passed, that is, until the overtaking vessel "is finally past and clear." This requirement is a restatement of the Rule 8 duty of all vessels required to take action to continue their vigilance "until the other vessel is finally past and clear."

Paragraph (d) was included to cover the case of one vessel overtaking on the starboard side of another and then turning left across the other's bow. In an ordinary crossing situation, the vessel on the right would have the right-of-way. If this were also the case of the overtaking vessel crossing the other, the overtaken/stand-on vessel would suddenly become the crossing/give-way vessel and might not have enough maneuvering room.

Rule 14—Head-on Situation

INTERNATIONAL

(a) When two power-driven vessels are meeting on reciprocal or nearly reciprocal courses so as to involve risk of collision each shall alter her course to starboard so that each shall pass on the port side of the other.

INLAND

(a) Unless otherwise agreed, when two power-driven vessels are meeting on reciprocal or nearly reciprocal courses so as to involve risk of collision each shall alter her course to starboard so that each shall pass on the port side of the other.

Two vessels are approaching each other rapidly head-on, and there is no way to distinguish one from the other for the purpose of assigning right-of-way. To ensure quick and predictable action, Rule 14 requires *both* vessels to do the same thing: to turn right. This procedure reduces uncertainty (and delay) and also sets Rule 14 apart from the rules around it. Rules 12, 13, 15, and 18 all assign primary responsibility for taking avoiding action to *one* vessel, the give-way vessel; Rule 14 assigns responsibility to *both*.

The Inland version of this Rule has been modified to accommodate the special needs of vessels navigating on meandering rivers, where the downbound vessel may have less ability to maneuver than the vessel it meets head-on traveling upriver. The addition of the words "Unless otherwise agreed" gives the two vessels the option of passing starboard-to-starboard that otherwise would be available only to vessels in narrow channels in certain inland waters (see Rule 9[a][ii]).

Rule 14 applies only to *power-driven vessels* meeting head-on with other *power-driven vessels*. It does not apply if one of the power-driven vessels is not an "ordinary" power-driven vessel but rather is one that is made a stand-on vessel with respect to an ordinary power-driven vessel by Rule 18(a). These other special vessels include vessels not under command, restricted in ability to maneuver, or engaged in fishing and are not required to take action (initially) when meeting an ordinary power-driven vessel head-on. Two sailing vessels meeting head-on are governed by Rule 12.

Rule 14 is easy to follow. Each power-driven vessel approaching another head-on is required to *alter her course to starboard* for a port-to-port passing—you must turn right, never left. A new Inland rule exception permits alterations of course to port for a starboard-to-starboard passing if both vessels agree in advance.

INTERNATIONAL

(b) Such a situation shall be deemed to exist when a vessel sees the other ahead or nearly ahead and by night she could see the masthead lights of the other in a line or nearly in a line and/or both sidelights and by day she observes the corresponding aspect of the other vessel.

INLAND

(b) Such a situation shall be deemed to exist when a vessel sees the other ahead or nearly ahead and by night she could see the masthead lights of the other in a line or nearly in a line or both sidelights and by day she observes the corresponding aspect of the other vessel.

Risk of collision must exist for Rule 14 to apply. In theory, two distant vessels approaching nearly head-on may by the time they near each other be so far apart (to one side or the other) that no action is required. In practice, if you are close enough to another vessel to determine that you are meeting nearly head-on, you most likely will also be in risk of collision.

Deciding whether you are in a head-on situation is also straightforward (no pun intended). Paragraph (a) describes it as a "meeting on reciprocal or nearly reciprocal courses." Paragraph (b) says what that means. The language is clear—look at the *aspect* of the other vessel. The decision should not depend on the course made good over the bottom, so do not delay your action until the path of the other vessel has been plotted. The leeway angle can be significant with a strong beam wind or current.

The navigation light technical performance requirements contained in Annex I provide for each sidelight to overlap about 2 degrees into the other light's horizontal sector. As a result, there will be approximately a 4-degree sector directly ahead of a vessel in which both sidelights may be seen. Because sidelights will not have exactly the same intensities, and because the human eye is not equally sensitive to red and green light, one sidelight may appear before the other, even if you are in a head-on situation. It is also difficult to see colors at low light intensities—a colored light will look the same as a dim white light. Use your binoculars!

INTERNATIONAL

(c) When a vessel is in any doubt as to whether such a situation exists she shall assume that it does exist and act accordingly.

INLAND

(c) When a vessel is in any doubt as to whether such a situation exists she shall assume that it does exist and act accordingly.

Paragraph (c) poses a warning. If it is not plain to you that a *crossing* situation exists, then take the action required for a *head-on* situation.

INLAND

(d) Notwithstanding paragraph (a) of this rule, a power-driven vessel operating on the Great Lakes, Western Rivers, or waters specified by the Secretary, and proceeding downbound with a following current shall have the right-of-way over an upbound vessel, shall propose the manner of passage, and shall initiate the maneuvering signals prescribed by Rule 34(a)(i), as appropriate.

Paragraph (d) extends to all channels the general right-of-way given by Inland Rule 9(a)(ii) to vessels in *narrow* channels in the Great Lakes, western rivers, and waters specified by the Secretary (see Title 33 of the Code of Federal Regulations, §89.25 for a list of those waters—contained in Appendix I of this book). Although this Rule 14(d) exception contains most of the language in the Rule 9(a)(ii) narrow-channel exception, 14(d) does not give the downbound vessel as much control as does 9(a)(i) for the trickier narrow-channel situation. The 14(d) provision does not require the downbound vessel to propose the place of passage and does not require the upbound vessel to "hold as necessary to permit safe passing." Presumably if those two added precautions were needed for a safe passing, the channel would be narrow enough to bring Rule 9 into effect.

Rule 15—Crossing Situation

INTERNATIONAL

(a) When two power-driven vessels are crossing so as to involve risk of collision, the vessel which has the other on her own starboard side shall keep out of the way and shall, if the circumstances of the case admit, avoid crossing ahead of the other vessel.

INLAND

(a) When two power-driven vessels are crossing so as to involve risk of collision, the vessel which has the other on her own starboard side shall keep out of the way and shall, if the circumstances of the case admit, avoid crossing ahead of the other vessel.

Encounters are of three types: overtaking, head-on, and crossing. Rule 15 addresses a crossing situation between two power-driven vessels. This is another simple rule, and one that is the same for International and Inland, with an exception for the rivers of the Great Lakes and western rivers.

Rule 15 does not apply to power-driven vessels restricted in ability to maneuver, engaged in fishing, or not under command. Remember, towing vessels with their tows are considered to be ordinary power-driven vessels unless they are severely restricted in their ability to deviate from their courses (see Rule 3[g]).

The crossing rule applies only to vessels in visual sight of one another. It doesn't matter whether your radar screen shows perfectly clearly the approach of another vessel in a "crossing situation"; if you can't *see* the other vessel, Rule 15 does *not* apply and Rule 19 does.

Like the other Rules in this section/subpart, Rule 15 does not apply until risk of collision exists (see Rule 7). Earlier responsibilities between vessels may exist where "shall not impede" provisions pertain. These provisions apply to small power-driven vessels, sailing vessels, and fishing vessels in narrow channels or fairways, and in traffic lanes. Once risk of collision arises, however, Rule 15 takes over and may change the obligations of the vessels. Thus, if you are operating a large vessel and are in a narrow channel, narrow fairway, or traffic lane, and you encounter a crossing smaller vessel *involving risk of collision*, you must obey Rule 15, even though the smaller vessel is also required to stay well out of your way. Because of the possible shift in responsibilities, you should resolve any doubts early by using your radiotelephone or, failing that, sounding the signal of five or more short blasts described in Rule 34(d).

Rule 15 requires the vessel that has the other on its starboard side to stay out of the way, and to pass behind. The vessel on the right becomes the stand-on vessel and must follow Rule 17 (Action by Stand-on Vessel). The vessel on the left becomes the give-way vessel and must follow Rule 16 (Action by Give-way Vessel). At night, the stand-on vessel sees the green sidelight of the give-way vessel, and the give-way vessel sees the stand-on vessel's red sidelight. A vessel approaching from the quarter so that it could not see a sidelight would be overtaking and would look to Rule 13. A vessel seeing both sidelights would be meeting head-on and would follow Rule 14.

The give-way vessel is required (if the circumstances of the case admit) to pass behind the stand-on vessel and so a turn to starboard would be in order. To keep the area to the left of the stand-on vessel clear for the give-way vessel's maneuvers, Rule 17 directs the stand-on vessel to refrain from turning to port.

There are a few situations where application of the crossing rule is not straightforward. Vessels following a winding river or channel may approach each other in what may appear to be a crossing situation. They should, however, follow Rule 9 and stay to the far right of the channel (general rule). Rule 15 does not apply in such cases, and in other cases where the apparent "stand-on" vessel cannot or does not hold a steady course.

A stopped vessel that sees another power-driven vessel approaching on its starboard side (involving risk of collision) is obligated to get out of the way unless the stopped vessel is not under command, is restricted in its ability to maneuver, or is engaged in fishing, or unless there are special circumstances. Special circumstances may consist of, for example, a stopped large

loaded tanker that is physically unable to maneuver out of the
way of a fast-approaching "stand-on" vessel or if the stopped
vessel is maneuvering and not on any course. Operators of stopped
vessels that cannot readily be maneuvered should exhibit the
lights or shapes for a hampered vessel (that is, a vessel restricted
in ability to maneuver, not under command, or constrained by
draft) and should contact approaching vessels by radiotelephone
to warn them of the situation.

INLAND

(b) Notwithstanding paragraph (a),
on the Great Lakes, Western Rivers,
or waters specified by the Secretary, a vessel crossing a river shall
keep out of the way of a power-
driven vessel ascending or de-
scending the river.

The Inland Rule 15 differs from the International Rule 15 in
that the Inland version contains an exception (paragraph [b]) to
the general rule. This exception has been extended beyond the
Great Lakes and western rivers to include the Tennessee–
Tombigbee Waterway, Tombigbee River, Black Warrior River, Alabama River, Coosa River, Mobile River above the Cochrane Bridge
at St. Louis Point, Flint River, Chattachoochee River, and the Apalachicola River above its confluence with the Jackson River.

Rule 16—Action by Give-way Vessel

INTERNATIONAL
Every vessel which is directed to
keep out of the way of another vessel shall, so far as possible, take
early and substantial action to keep
well clear.

INLAND
Every vessel which is directed to
keep out of the way of another vessel shall, so far as possible, take
early and substantial action to keep
well clear.

Rules 12, 13, 15, and 18 (all of which apply to vessels in sight
of each other) direct one of two approaching vessels to keep out
of the way of the other. Rules 16 and 17 assign respective re-

sponsibilities to each vessel. Rule 16 applies to the give-way vessel, the one directed to stay out of the way of the other. Rule 17 assigns more complicated responsibilities and privileges to the other vessel, the stand-on vessel.

Rule 16 commands the give-way vessel to take "early and substantial action to keep well clear," that is, "action to avoid collision," precisely the title of Rule 8.

Rule 8 contains some of the same tenets as Rule 16, but the language differs. Rule 16 says "take early and substantial action"; Rule 8 says take action that is "positive, made in ample time." Rule 16 says take action "to keep well clear"; Rule 8 says take action that will "result in passing at a safe distance." Rule 16 says take the prescribed action "so far as possible"; Rule 8 says take the action "if circumstances of the case admit." Although the language varies, the meaning is essentially the same.

Rule 8 also provides more specific guidance for the give-way (and other) vessels. Maneuvers should be large enough to be readily seen. The maneuver may be by course change alone but slowing or stopping may be necessary. The effectiveness of actions taken shall be observed (and further measures carried out if need be) until risk of collision has passed.

Depending on the situation, the give-way vessel may or may not be allowed to cross ahead of the stand-on vessel. Rule 15 does not permit (under normal circumstances) a power-driven give-way vessel to cross ahead of a power-driven vessel. A give-way vessel can cross ahead of a sailing vessel, hampered vessel, or vessel it is overtaking. If you cross ahead of a stand-on vessel, remember that you must pass "at a safe distance" (Rule 8) and keep "well clear" (Rule 16).

Rule 17—Action by Stand-on Vessel

INTERNATIONAL

(a)(i) Where one of two vessels is to keep out of the way the other shall keep her course and speed.

INLAND

(a)(i) Where one of two vessels is to keep out of the way the other shall keep her course and speed.

Rule 17 assigns responsibilities to the vessel with the "right-of-way"—the stand-on vessel. The text of the Rule does not use the term "stand-on vessel" but instead describes it in paragraph (a) as the "other" vessel, that is, not the give-way vessel, not the vessel required to keep out of the way. When does this Rule apply? It applies only in situations covered by Rules 12, 13, 15, and 18, which require one vessel to stay out of the way of another.

These four Rules apply *only* when the two vessels are in sight of one another and only when risk of collision exists. When three or more vessels approach with risk of collision it will likely be impossible for all of them to act according to all of the Rules; one vessel may be a stand-on vessel with respect to a second and a give-way vessel with respect to a third. Rule 17 would require one action while Rule 16 would require a conflicting action. Such a situation is one of special circumstances and is governed by Rule 2.

Give-way vessels have one obligation—to stay out of the way of stand-on vessels. Stand-on vessels, however, have more complicated responsibilities, but their basic obligation is to hold their course and speed, or to "stand on." Other actions are required or permitted depending on the circumstances.

Remember that give-way/stand-on situations do not begin until risk of collision (Rule 7) exists. You are free to maneuver before that risk arises no matter what your obligations would be later if you were to continue on your initial course.

Once risk of collision develops, however, paragraph (a)(i) requires the stand-on vessel to hold its course and speed. The purpose of this requirement is to enable the give-way vessel to predict the action of the stand-on vessel and so be able to stay out of its way. In some circumstances, the stand-on vessel's normal maneuver would be to slow down or turn (to pick up a pilot or enter a channel, for example) and such action may be expected of the stand-on vessel by those on the give-way vessel. In that case, the stand-on vessel is obligated to maneuver as expected, even though the action is something other than holding course and speed. Again, a radiotelephone confirmation of intentions is useful.

INTERNATIONAL	INLAND
(ii) The latter vessel may however take action to avoid collision by her maneuver alone, as soon as	(ii) The latter vessel may however take action to avoid collision by her maneuver alone, as soon as

it becomes apparent to her that the vessel required to keep out of the way is not taking appropriate action in compliance with these Rules.

it becomes apparent to her that the vessel required to keep out of the way is not taking appropriate action in compliance with these Rules.

The operator of a stand-on vessel that is on a collision course with another vessel expects the give-way vessel to take the *prompt* avoiding action required by the Rules. If after time has passed the give-way vessel persists in its impersonation of a stand-on vessel, it is reasonable to expect the stand-on vessel's operator to be somewhat concerned about the competence of the give-way vessel's crew.

As soon as it becomes apparent that the give-way vessel is not taking appropriate action, the stand-on vessel is free to act to avoid a collision. Rule 17(a)(ii) says that the stand-on vessel *may* maneuver at this stage, but it *does not require* the stand-on vessel to maneuver. The stand-on vessel may continue on for a while before maneuvering. As soon as the stand-on vessel feels entitled to maneuver, however, it is *required* to *immediately* sound the doubt signal of five or more short blasts prescribed by Rule 34(d). *Do not wait* until danger is imminent. *Do not wait* until you are about to crash to sound this signal.

The stand-on vessel may or may not choose to maneuver after giving the five-blast signal. If it does change direction and is operating under the International Rules, it must also then give the appropriate one-or two-blast signal to indicate that maneuver (see Rule 34[a]).

How long do you have to wait before it becomes "apparent" that the other vessel is not taking appropriate action? You may not take action until the give-way vessel has had time to assess the situation and begin to take avoiding action. Precipitous action by the stand-on vessel may result in simultaneous action by both vessels, which can greatly increase the danger. How close must you be to the other vessel before the stand-on vessel may maneuver? The same factors that determined the separation for risk of collision to exist apply here. A two-mile separation for ships crossing at sea would justify a stand-on vessel's maneuver. The particular circumstances in any given situation would, of course, determine the distance at which the stand-on vessel may maneuver to avoid the give-way vessel.

Rule 17(a)(ii) says that the stand-on vessel may act if the give-way vessel does not take "appropriate" action. Inappropriate action is no action at all or *ineffective* action.

If you are the operator of a stand-on vessel and decide to take action when the give-way vessel fails to do so, what action would be best? In a crossing situation (involving power-driven vessels), you normally would not want to slow down because that makes it more difficult for the give-way vessel to pass behind you. Remember that Rule 15 directs the give-way vessel to avoid crossing ahead of you. Rule 8 (Action to Avoid Collision) provides further guidance. For power-driven vessels, paragraph (c) of Rule 17 applies directly to this situation. It says don't turn left when the give-way vessel is on your port side. That means appropriate action is a right turn except when the give-way vessel is overtaking on your starboard side. For situations not involving two power-driven vessels, the appropriate action depends on the circumstances.

INTERNATIONAL	INLAND
(b) When, from any cause, the vessel required to keep her course and speed finds herself so close that collision cannot be avoided by the action of the give-way vessel alone, she shall take such action as will best aid to avoid collision.	(b) When, from any cause, the vessel required to keep her course and speed finds herself so close that collision cannot be avoided by the action of the give-way vessel alone, she shall take such action as will best aid to avoid collision.

You are on the stand-on vessel, and it becomes apparent that the give-way vessel on your port side is not taking appropriate action. You sound the five short blast signal, put your engines on stand-by, but continue holding your course and speed. Thirty seconds pass without any response. You again sound five short blasts. By this time you are much closer and through your binoculars observe a figure on an otherwise empty bridge jumping at what you assume to be the autopilot. The vessel's turn to the right is not fast enough to prevent a collision without your help, and you recall that Rule 17(b) now requires you to "take such action as will best aid to avoid collision." But what action? The right turn recommended for early stand-on avoiding action would at this point swing your stern into the oncoming bow of the give-way vessel. Aha! Hard left rudder. Your stern swings away just as the give-way vessel churns through your propeller wash.

Rule 17(b) describes the classic "in extremis" situation, one that every mariner wishes never to experience. Such a situation—one in which collision is imminent—is defined by the maneuverability of the give-way vessel alone. But what effect does the maneuverability of the stand-on vessel have? What will be the outcome if the stand-on vessel waits until the give-way vessel can't avoid the collision by itself?

If the two vessels are equally maneuverable, avoiding the collision will depend on the action of both vessels. If the stand-on vessel is more maneuverable, then its quick action will probably prevent a collision. If, however, the stand-on vessel is less maneuverable than the give-way vessel, then the stand-on vessel can most likely do nothing to prevent the collision.

Therefore, if you are operating a stand-on vessel approaching a more maneuverable give-way vessel, it would behoove you *not to wait* until the Rules *require* you to maneuver to avoid collision. By that time it will probably be too late. If the give-way vessel isn't doing its job, take early advantage of Rule 17(a)(ii) and maneuver before the situation becomes more distressing.

You should remember that when the stand-on vessel is required to act to avoid collision (Rule 17[b]), it must take whatever action will best prevent or minimize collision damage. At that point, other requirements saying don't cross ahead, turn right, or whatever no longer apply. Do what has to be done.

INTERNATIONAL	INLAND
(c) A power-driven vessel which takes action in a crossing situation in accordance with subparagraph (a)(ii) of this Rule to avoid collision with another power-driven vessel shall, if the circumstances of the case admit, not alter course to port for a vessel on her own port side.	(c) A power-driven vessel which takes action in a crossing situation in accordance with subparagraph (a)(ii) of this Rule to avoid collision with another power-driven vessel shall, if the circumstances of the case admit, not alter course to port for a vessel on her own port side.

Turning away from the give-way vessel decreases the rate of approach and increases the time each vessel has to take further avoiding action. Turning toward the give-way vessel may well place the stand-on vessel in a much more dangerous situation if the give-way vessel had initiated a turn to starboard just before or simultaneously with the stand-on vessel's maneuver.

INTERNATIONAL	INLAND
(d) This Rule does not relieve the give-way vessel of her obligation to keep out of the way.	(d) This Rule does not relieve the give-way vessel of her obligation to keep out of the way.

Finally, paragraph (d) of Rule 17 makes perfectly clear that the give-way vessel's responsibility to keep out of the way of the stand-on vessel is in no way diminished by the stand-on vessel's voluntary action under Rule 17(a)(ii) or by the stand-on vessel's required action under Rule 17(b). An operator of a give-way vessel is absolutely wrong in assuming he or she doesn't have to worry about staying out of the way (and passing at a safe distance) if the stand-on vessel takes avoiding action.

Rule 18—Responsibilities between Vessels

Most of the other Rules for vessels in sight of each other deal with encounters between two ordinary power-driven vessels, and Rule 12 covers encounters between sailing vessels. Rule 18 tells you what to do when you encounter a vessel that is fundamentally different from your own.

Rule 18 lists the various classes of vessels in a "pecking order" of privilege. Vessel classes perceived to be more maneuverable are directed to keep out of the way of classes thought to be less maneuverable. Naturally, there are several exceptions in the Rule because perceptions do not necessarily hold true in reality. Remember that this Rule applies only to vessels in sight of each other.

The vessel directed to keep out of the way must follow Rule 8 (Action to Avoid Collision) and Rule 16 (Action by Give-way Vessel).

INTERNATIONAL
Except where Rules 9, 10, and 13
otherwise require:

INLAND
Except where Rules 9, 10, and 13
otherwise require:

Rule 18 does not apply when a Rule 9, 10, or 13 requirement would conflict with a Rule 18 requirement. For instance, a sailing vessel *overtaking* a power-driven vessel must keep out of the way, even though Rule 18 says power-driven vessels are required to keep out of the way of sailing vessels. The Rule 13 requirement takes precedence.

As we mentioned elsewhere, the Rule 9 and 10 exceptions are trickier. Rules 9 and 10, among other things, direct sailing vessels, small power-driven vessels, and fishing vessels not to impede the passage of a larger vessel confined to a narrow channel or narrow fairway, or using a traffic lane. Under Rule 8(f) these Rule 9 and 10 proscriptions continue to be in effect after risk of collision arises, at which time the Rule 18 provisions *favoring* sailing vessels and vessels engaged in fishing would also place the duty to stay out of the way on the impeded vessel. *Both* vessels are now charged with staying out of the way!

Rule 18 discusses seven different vessel classes: power-driven, not under command, restricted in ability to maneuver, engaged in fishing, sailing, constrained by draft, and seaplane. The Inland Rule 18 does not contain the International Rule 18 provisions on vessels constrained by draft, but otherwise it is the same.

INTERNATIONAL
(a) A power-driven vessel under-way shall keep out of the way of:
    (i) a vessel not under command;
    (ii) a vessel restricted in her ability to maneuver;
    (iii) a vessel engaged in fishing;
    (iv) a sailing vessel.

INLAND
(a) A power-driven vessel under-way shall keep out of the way of:
    (i) a vessel not under command;
    (ii) a vessel restricted in her ability to maneuver;
    (iii) a vessel engaged in fishing; and
    (iv) a sailing vessel.

Ordinary power-driven vessels that are underway must stay out of the way of the other types of vessels. Power-driven vessels that are not underway—that is, that are anchored, aground, or made fast to the shore—of course do not have to keep out of the way of other vessels. Vessels that are anchored or aground must display the required lights and shapes for those situations.

INTERNATIONAL

(b) A sailing vessel underway shall keep out of the way of:

   (i) a vessel not under command;
   (ii) a vessel restricted in her ability to maneuver;
   (iii) a vessel engaged in fishing.

INLAND

(b) A sailing vessel underway shall keep out of the way of:

   (i) a vessel not under command;
   (ii) a vessel restricted in her ability to maneuver; and
   (iii) a vessel engaged in fishing.

Sailing vessels that are underway must stay out of the way of vessels not under command, restricted in ability to maneuver, or engaged in fishing. (The definitions of these vessel classes are contained in Rule 3.)

INTERNATIONAL

(c) A vessel engaged in fishing when underway shall, so far as possible, keep out of the way of:

   (i) a vessel not under command;
   (ii) a vessel restricted in her ability to maneuver.

INLAND

(c) A vessel engaged in fishing when underway shall, so far as possible, keep out of the way of:

   (i) a vessel not under command; and
   (ii) a vessel restricted in her ability to maneuver.

Vessels engaged in fishing (when underway) must keep out of the way of vessels not under command or restricted in ability to maneuver, but only "so far as possible." Some fishing operations so severely hamper a vessel's ability to maneuver that it would be physically impossible to keep out of the way of another vessel. For example, a trawler's speed is often limited to a few knots when its trawl is out, and a purse seiner may not be able to move at all while drawing in its net. Rule 18 certainly does not require that a fishing vessel cut loose its gear in order to move out of the way of another hampered vessel.

Vessels restricted in ability to maneuver and vessels not under command are given equal status. All vessels under normal circumstances are required to stay out of the way of these two classes.

What happens when a vessel not under command encounters a vessel restricted in ability to maneuver (or if both belong to the same class)? Both should take action to avoid collision.

INTERNATIONAL

(d)(i) Any vessel other than a vessel not under command or a vessel restricted in her ability to maneuver shall, if the circumstances of the case admit, avoid impeding the safe passage of a vessel constrained by her draft, exhibiting the signals in Rule 28.

Paragraph (d) of International Rule 18 concerns vessels constrained by draft to a relatively narrow natural or dredged channel. If a vessel in such a situation turned off its course, it would run aground. Predicting the action the Rule requires of a vessel constrained by draft is uncertain, so the formal concept of a vessel constrained by draft was not adopted in Inland Rule 18.

The International Rule requires that vessels (except those not under command and those restricted in ability to maneuver), if the circumstances of the case admit, avoid impeding the safe passage of a vessel constrained by draft. The general requirement attempts to resolve a situation that varies greatly with particular circumstances. As a result, there are two problems with the requirement. First, the escape clause "if the circumstances of the case admit" relies on the judgment of the operator of the vessel approaching the vessel constrained by draft. This introduces uncertainty on the part of the constrained vessel because the other operator's judgment can only be guessed.

Second, the "shall not impede the passage" requirement places responsibility on the nonconstrained vessel to stay out of the way while it is at long range. Notwithstanding that obligation, if it gets close enough for risk of collision to exist, the constrained vessel will be obligated to act according to the more general Steering and Sailing Rules, which may make it the give-way vessel. The nonconstrained vessel will in all cases continue to be charged with staying out of the way. (Confused? See Rule 8[f] for "shall not impede" guidance.)

(ii) A vessel constrained by her draft shall navigate with particular caution having full regard to her special condition.

Perhaps because of the uncertainty involved, the Rule commands vessels constrained by draft to navigate "with particular caution." This means that the constrained vessel must be ready to take collision-avoiding action at all times, which for a vessel constrained by draft means limiting speed and having engines ready for maneuver.

INTERNATIONAL	INLAND
(e) A seaplane on the water shall, in general, keep well clear of all vessels and avoid impeding their navigation. In circumstances, however, where risk of collision exists, she shall comply with the Rules of this Part.	(e) A seaplane on the water shall, in general, keep well clear of all vessels and avoid impeding their navigation. In circumstances, however, where risk of collision exists, she shall comply with the Rules of this Part.

The last paragraph in Rule 18 covers seaplanes, an encounter with which is probably a rarity for most mariners. Rule 18 directs seaplanes to stay well clear of other vessels if possible. Otherwise, a seaplane is to follow the Rules as would a comparable power-driven vessel. While landing and taking off, seaplanes cannot effectively turn, but they can maneuver when taxiing. Vessels operating in the vicinity of a seaplane taking off or landing should note, as a precaution, that during high-angle-of-attack phases of those operations, the pilot's forward visibility may become completely blocked by the aircraft's raised nose.

SECTION/SUBPART III—CONDUCT OF VESSELS IN RESTRICTED VISIBILITY

Rule 19—Conduct of Vessels in Restricted Visibility

Section/Subpart III contains but one Rule—Rule 19. Section I specified Conduct of Vessels in Any Condition of Visibility, and

Section II specified Conduct of Vessels in Sight of One Another. The title of Section III is the same as that of Rule 19—Conduct of Vessels in Restricted Visibility. International Rule 19 is identical to Inland Rule 19 except for a few minor style changes that do not affect substance.

INTERNATIONAL

(a) This Rule applies to vessels not in sight of one another when navigating in or near an area of restricted visibility.

INLAND

(a) This Rule applies to vessels not in sight of one another when navigating in or near an area of restricted visibility.

How poor must visibility be in order to be called "restricted?" The Rule 3 definition does not explain that but does give examples of natural phenomena that can impair visibility: fog, mist, falling snow, heavy rainstorms, sandstorms, and so on. Obviously, if visibility is restricted by haze to ten miles, you would not be in an area of restricted visibility. What would be called restricted visibility naturally depends on the circumstances. In open water if you cannot see five miles in all directions you are operating in or near restricted visibility. In more confined bodies of water the distance may be less.

Why is it that only one Steering and Sailing Rule is devoted exclusively to conditions of restricted visibility while there are eight Rules for much better conditions? The reason is that when a situation can be better perceived it merits more detailed and specific recommendations and requirements. In restricted visibility, on the other hand, you can't see if there are other vessels around you, where they are, how big they are, what kind they are, or what their courses and speeds are. Radar helps, but not enough. Without the benefit of good visibility, Rules 4 through 10, which apply to the conduct of vessels in any condition of visibility, become that much more important. Indeed, much of Rule 19 repeats and emphasizes the contents of Rules 4–10, and it essentially says to be extra careful.

It is important to remember that the navigation rules contain two rather distinct sets of rules: one for when you can see the other vessel, and one for when you can't. The Rules for vessels in sight of one another (11 through 18) naturally predominate and may become so second nature that they may be difficult to put aside in conditions of restricted visibility. When the visibility is so poor that you cannot see the vessels around you, you must forget about Rules 11 through 18: there will be no "stand-on vessel"; there will be no holding course and speed; the overtaken as well as the overtaking vessel are equally obligated to act to avoid collision. Restricted visibility is the great equalizer.

Paragraph (a) cites two conditions that make Rule 19 applicable. Both conditions must be present. The first is that the vessels must *not* be in sight of one another. If they are, then Rules 11 through 18 apply instead of 19. Remember that "in sight" means "observed visually." The second is that the vessel must be *in* or *near* an area of restricted visibility. Your vessel may be in an area of good visibility but may also be close to a fogbank or thundershower that is concealing one or more vessels. Even though you are in the clear, you must follow Rule 19 (and sound the signal required by Rule 35). However, with respect to another vessel in your area of good visibility or a vessel that emerges from the fogbank, you must follow Rules 11 through 18 (and sound any signals required by Rule 34). It is therefore possible for you to be following at the same time the rules for good visibility and the rules for restricted visibility.

INTERNATIONAL	INLAND
(b) Every vessel shall proceed at a safe speed adapted to the prevailing circumstances and conditions of restricted visibility. A power-driven vessel shall have her engines ready for immediate maneuver.	(b) Every vessel shall proceed at a safe speed adapted to the prevailing circumstances and conditions of restricted visibility. A power-driven vessel shall have her engines ready for immediate maneuver.

Paragraph (b) repeats the mandate of Rule 6 to proceed at a safe speed, making explicit the requirement to have engines ready for immediate maneuvering when in restricted visibility. This applies to open waters as well as more confined waters.

Safe speed does not necessarily mean slow speed. Sometimes it is better to proceed fast enough for effective rudder action.

INTERNATIONAL

(c) Every vessel shall have due regard to the prevailing circumstances and conditions of restricted visibility when complying with the Rules of Section I of this Part.

INLAND

(c) Every vessel shall have due regard to the prevailing circumstances and conditions of restricted visibility when complying with Rules 4 through 10.

Paragraph (c) adds no new requirement but does push mariners into closer scrutiny of Rules 4 through 10. Rules 5, 6, and 7 are particularly important for vessels navigating in restricted visibility.

INTERNATIONAL

(d) A vessel which detects by radar alone the presence of another vessel shall determine if a close-quarters situation is developing and/or risk of collision exists. If so, she shall take avoiding action in ample time, provided that when such action consists of an alteration of course, so far as possible the following shall be avoided:

(i) an alteration of course to port for a vessel forward of the beam, other than for a vessel being overtaken;

(ii) an alteration of course towards a vessel abeam or abaft the beam.

INLAND

(d) A vessel which detects by radar alone the presence of another vessel shall determine if a close-quarters situation is developing or risk of collision exists. If so, she shall take avoiding action in ample time, provided that when such action consists of an alteration of course, so far as possible the following shall be avoided:

(i) an alteration of course to port for a vessel forward of the beam, other than for a vessel being overtaken; and

(ii) an alteration of course toward a vessel abeam or abaft the beam.

Paragraph (d) summarizes the more detailed provisions in Rules 7 and 8 and adds specific guidance on evasive maneuvering. The recommended course changes are intended to prevent ships from turning into each other. Not surprisingly, this provision works only if both vessels follow it. What is surprising is the number of collisions that result because one operator thought turning the other way would work better. In any case, nothing in this paragraph suggests that course changes could be made in lieu of a speed reduction in areas of restricted visibility.

INTERNATIONAL

(e) Except where it has been determined that a risk of collision does not exist, every vessel which hears apparently forward of her beam the fog signal of another vessel, or which cannot avoid a close-quarters situation with another vessel forward of her beam, shall reduce her speed to the minimum at which she can be kept on her course. She shall if necessary take all her way off and in any event navigate with extreme caution until danger of collision is over.

INLAND

(e) Except where it has been determined that a risk of collision does not exist, every vessel which hears apparently forward of her beam the fog signal of another vessel, or which cannot avoid a close-quarters situation with another vessel forward of her beam, shall reduce her speed to the minimum at which she can be kept on course. She shall if necessary take all her way off and, in any event, navigate with extreme caution until danger of collision is over.

Paragraph (e) directs *every* vessel to slow down or stop when it hears the fog signal of another vessel forward of the beam or knows another vessel lies ahead. This requirement no longer applies once the vessel *knows for sure* that risk of collision does not exist and will not develop. Paragraph (e) adds to Rule 6 (Safe Speed) and relies on the proper execution of Rule 7 (Risk of Collision). This provision applies to *every* vessel, not just the *other* vessel.

After detecting another vessel forward of the beam, a vessel must reduce its speed to the point of bare steerageway. Stopping engines will both slow the vessel and make it easier to hear the other vessel's signals. Do not change course until you know the other vessel's position, course, and speed. The other vessel's signals should indicate whether it is making way, stopped, or anchored, but do not rely on signals alone. Use all other means available for collecting information, including radar and radiotelephone. If you cannot quickly clarify the situation, do not continue blindly into the great unknown. Stop your vessel until you establish the location and intentions of the vessel(s) ahead.

PART C

Lights and Shapes

Navigation lights are a critical part of obeying the Steering and Sailing Rules at night. If you have ever passed close by a vessel operating without lights, you have no doubt gained some appreciation for them. Part C of the Rules defines several types of navigation lights, specifies the minimum ranges, and gives the combination of lights that identifies each vessel by size, type, function, and activity. Annex I to the Rules provides technical details of performance and positioning that are essential for the manufacturers of navigation lights but less useful for the mariner.

Shapes convey information about a vessel, its situation, or its activity that would not be obvious even by day. The technical details on shape, size, color, and spacing are contained in Annex I.

Part C contains Rules 20 through 31. Rule 20 tells when lights and shapes must be displayed. Rule 21 contains the definitions or descriptions of navigation lights. Rule 22 marks the minimum distances at which the lights can be seen. The rest of the Rules in Part C specify what vessels must display what array of navigation lights and shapes.

Rule 20—Application

The International and Inland versions of the Rule are the same.

INTERNATIONAL
(a) Rules in this Part shall be complied with in all weathers.

INLAND
(a) Rules in this Part shall be complied with in all weathers.

Paragraph (a) assures us that bad weather is not an excuse for not displaying the required navigation lights. In the era of electric navigation lights, this perhaps is directed at those vessels still using oil and wicks to show their presence, but it also applies to those operators who would prefer to wait for a nice day to change a burned-out electric lamp.

INTERNATIONAL
(b) The Rules concerning lights shall be complied with from sunset to sunrise, and during such times no other lights shall be exhibited, except such lights as cannot be mistaken for the lights specified in these Rules or do not impair their visibility or distinctive character, or interfere with the keeping of a proper look-out.

INLAND
(b) The Rules concerning lights shall be complied with from sunset to sunrise, and during such times no other lights shall be exhibited, except such lights as cannot be mistaken for the lights specified in these Rules or do not impair their visibility or distinctive character, or interfere with the keeping of a proper look-out.

Paragraph (b) begins by saying that navigation lights are to be displayed between sunset and sunrise. This part of the paragraph is generally adhered to, but the rest is often ignored. When your navigation lights are on, the display of other colored or bright white lights may be mistaken for navigation lights, may impair the visibility or character of the navigation lights, or may interfere with the lookout. Such displays would put you in violation of the navigation rules and could lead to an accident.

INTERNATIONAL
(c) The lights prescribed by these Rules shall, if carried, also be exhibited from sunrise to sunset in restricted visibility and may be exhibited in all other circumstances when it is deemed necessary.

INLAND
(c) The lights prescribed by these Rules shall, if carried, also be exhibited from sunrise to sunset in restricted visibility and may be exhibited in all other circumstances when it is deemed necessary.

Navigation lights must be turned on when you are operating in restricted visibility unless your vessel is used only during the day and does not have navigation lights. Navigation lights *may* be displayed at other times at the option of the operator.

INTERNATIONAL

(d) The Rules concerning shapes shall be complied with by day.

INLAND

(d) The Rules concerning shapes shall be complied with by day.

Shapes are displayed during the day, that is, from sunrise to sunset. Because the transition from light to dark and back again is gradual, it is a good idea to display both lights and shapes at dawn and dusk.

INTERNATIONAL

(e) The lights and shapes specified in these Rules shall comply with the provisions of Annex I to these Regulations.

INLAND

(e) The lights and shapes specified in these Rules shall comply with the provisions of Annex I of these Rules.

Paragraph (e) contains the formal reference in the Rules to the Annex I technical requirements for lights and shapes. All mariners should read the annex at least once, to garner an idea of the requirements all designers and manufacturers should meet.

Rule 21—Definitions

Rule 21 lists the types of navigation lights making up the various arrays specified in Rules 23 to 31. There are no other types of navigation lights and each one has only one name. Other navigation light terms, such as "steaming light" or "bow light," are from popular slang or from old rules no longer in effect.

INTERNATIONAL

(a) "Masthead light" means a white light placed over the fore and aft centerline of the vessel showing an unbroken light over an arc of the horizon of 225 degrees and so fixed

INLAND

(a) "Masthead light" means a white light placed over the fore and aft centerline of the vessel showing an unbroken light over an arc of the horizon of 225 degrees and so fixed

INTERNATIONAL

INLAND

as to show the light from right ahead to 22.5 degrees abaft the beam on either side of the vessel.

as to show the light from right ahead to 22.5 degrees abaft the beam on either side of the vessel, except that on a vessel of less than 12 meters in length the masthead light shall be placed as nearly as practicable to the fore and aft centerline of the vessel.

The masthead light is used in a number of ways but always has the same characteristics and orientation. It points forward and is normally the highest navigation light on a vessel. There may be only one masthead light (on smaller vessels), or two may be carried—one on a forward mast and another further aft and higher on another mast. Two or three may be carried in a vertical line on a single mast (for towing) with perhaps another single masthead light carried on another mast. On sailing vessels, on rowboats, and with some optional lighting configurations on smaller power-driven vessels, there may be no masthead light at all.

The Inland Rule definition of masthead light permits it to be mounted to one side on small vessels, while a similar provision in Rule 23 of the International Rules permits the same offset for power-driven vessels only. Otherwise, the light must be placed on the centerline.

INTERNATIONAL

INLAND

(b) "Sidelights" means a green light on the starboard side and a red light on the port side each showing an unbroken light over an arc of the horizon of 112.5 degrees and so fixed as to show the light from right ahead to 22.5 degrees abaft the beam on its respective side. In a vessel of less than 20 meters in length the sidelights may be combined in one lantern carried on the fore and aft centerline of the vessel.

(b) "Sidelights" means a green light on the starboard side and a red light on the port side each showing an unbroken light over an arc of the horizon of 112.5 degrees and so fixed as to show the light from right ahead to 22.5 degrees abaft the beam on its respective side. On a vessel of less than 20 meters in length the sidelights may be combined in one lantern carried on the fore and aft centerline of the vessel, except that on a vessel of less than

12 meters in length the sidelights when combined in one lantern shall be placed as nearly as practicable to the fore and aft centerline of the vessel.

Sidelights are the green and red lights mounted on either side of a vessel. If you are in a power-driven vessel and see another power-driven vessel (recognized by its "picture" of navigation lights) with its green light showing, then your vessel is the stand-on vessel and you should hold your course and speed. If you see the red light, you should keep out of the way.

Under the Inland Rules combined sidelights on small vessels may be mounted off the centerline. (A comparable International Rule provision for power-driven vessels only is in Rule 23.) Otherwise the International and Inland sidelights are the same.

INTERNATIONAL

(c) "Sternlight" means a white light placed as nearly as practicable at the stern showing an unbroken light over an arc of the horizon of 135 degrees and so fixed as to show the light 67.5 degrees from right aft on each side of the vessel.

INLAND

(c) "Sternlight" means a white light placed as nearly as practicable at the stern showing an unbroken light over an arc of the horizon of 135 degrees and so fixed as to show the light 67.5 degrees from right aft on each side of the vessel.

The sternlight is pointed directly aft and is normally mounted right on the very stern, often on the centerline. It does not *have* to be on the centerline and it does not *have* to be at the stern, but "as nearly as practicable" at the stern. It is not unusual for it to be quite some distance from the stern on vessels where the stern is perhaps low and exposed to rough use, as on a stern trawler or an offshore oil-platform supply vessel.

INTERNATIONAL

(d) "Towing light" means a yellow light having the same characteristics as the "sternlight" defined in paragraph (c) of this Rule.

INLAND

(d) "Towing light" means a yellow light having the same characteristics as the "sternlight" defined in paragraph (c) of this Rule.

Towing lights may be used either with or without stern lights, depending on whether you are using the International or the Inland Rules.

INTERNATIONAL
(e) "All-round light" means a light showing an unbroken light over an arc of the horizon of 360 degrees.

INLAND
(e) "All-round light" means a light showing an unbroken light over an arc of the horizon of 360 degrees.

All-round lights have many applications and come in red, green, yellow, and white.

INTERNATIONAL
(f) "Flashing light" means a light flashing at regular intervals at a frequency of 120 flashes or more per minute.

INLAND
(f) "Flashing light" means a light flashing at regular intervals at a frequency of 120 flashes or more per minute.

A flashing light is used only on air-cushion vehicles and is yellow. The flash characteristic was chosen to distinguish the light from the slower flashing of many lighted aids to navigation (buoys and markers).

INLAND
(g) "Special flashing light" means a yellow light flashing at regular intervals at a frequency of 50 to 70 flashes per minute, placed as far forward and as nearly as practicable on the fore and aft centerline of the tow and showing an unbroken light over an arc of the horizon of not less than 180 degrees nor more than 225 degrees and so fixed as to show the light from right ahead to abeam and no more than 22.5 degrees abaft the beam on either side of the vessel.

The special flashing light is also yellow but exists only in the Inland Rules. It is used at the head of barges being pushed ahead.

The light can have the 225-degree horizontal arc characteristic of a masthead light or anything down to 180 degrees. If a 225-degree light is mounted on top of the front of a barge, it could be seen through the full 225-degree arc, but if mounted on the front face of the barge, it would only be seen through a 180-degree horizontal arc. The flexibility in the requirement permits different light construction and mounting techniques.

Rule 22—Visibility of Lights

INTERNATIONAL

The lights prescribed in these Rules shall have an intensity as specified in Section 8 of Annex I to these Regulations so as to be visible at the following minimum ranges:

(a) In vessels of 50 meters or more in length:

—a masthead light, 6 miles;

—a sidelight, 3 miles;

—a sternlight, 3 miles;

—a towing light, 3 miles;

—a white, red, green or yellow all-round light, 3 miles.

(b) In vessels of 12 meters or more in length but less than 50 meters in length:

—a masthead light, 5 miles; except that where the length of the vessel is less than 20 meters, 3 miles;

—a sidelight, 2 miles;

—a sternlight, 2 miles;

—a towing light, 2 miles;

—a white, red, green or yellow all-round light, 2 miles.

INLAND

The lights prescribed in these Rules shall have an intensity as specified in Annex I to these Rules, so as to be visible at the following minimum ranges:

(a) In a vessel of 50 meters or more in length:

—a masthead light, 6 miles;

—a sidelight, 3 miles;

—a sternlight, 3 miles;

—a towing light, 3 miles;

—a white, red, green or yellow all-round light, 3 miles; and

—a special flashing light, 2 miles.

(b) In a vessel of 12 meters or more in length but less than 50 meters in length:

—a masthead light, 5 miles; except that where the length of the vessel is less than 20 meters, 3 miles;

—a sidelight, 2 miles;

—a sternlight, 2 miles;

—a towing light, 2 miles;

—a white, red, green or yellow all-round light, 2 miles; and

—a special flashing light, 2 miles.

(c) In vessels of less than 12 meters in length:
—a masthead light, 2 miles;
—a sidelight, 1 mile;
—a sternlight, 2 miles;
—a towing light, 2 miles;
—a white, red, green or yellow all-round light, 2 miles.

(d) In inconspicuous, partly submerged vessels or objects being towed:
—a white all-round light, 3 miles.

(c) In a vessel of less than 12 meters in length:
—a masthead light, 2 miles;
—a sidelight, 1 mile;
—a sternlight, 2 miles;
—a towing light, 2 miles;
—a white, red, green or yellow all-round light, 2 miles; and
—a special flashing light, 2 miles.

(d) In an inconspicuous, partly submerged vessel or object being towed:
—a white all-round light, 3 miles.

Almost all of Rule 22 informs, but does not require. Only the first sentence requires anything, which is that navigation lights be as bright as the technical specifications of Annex I say they must be. Rule 22 does *not* say that navigation lights shall be visible at the distances given. If a navigation light meets the minimum Annex I intensity requirement, but is no brighter than required, and if the visibility is good, then that navigation light could first be seen at the distance given in Rule 22. Keeping those conditions in mind, the list of minimum ranges gives you a good idea of the relative performances of navigation lights. You will know, for example, that the masthead light can be seen long before the sidelights appear.

How far away a navigation light will project varies greatly. A light may be twice as bright as required, and therefore could be seen farther away. A light is more visible on a clear dark night in midocean than on a muggy night near a big city. The distances given by Rule 22 were based on a somewhat arbitrarily chosen value for atmospheric light transmissivity—one that represents "good" visibility. The mathematical formula used to determine visibility (in nautical miles) from the laboratory-measured light intensity is given in Annex I.

Rule 23—Power-driven Vessels Underway

This Rule is the first of those Rules that describe the navigation light "picture" displayed by each vessel. Rule 23 covers power-driven vessels and gives the basic array of navigation lights—masthead lights, sidelights, and sternlight—from which the arrays for other vessel types are derived.

You will note that significant differences exist between the International Rules and the Inland Rules with regard to navigation lights. The Inland Rules allow more optional displays and are less stringent in the positioning requirements. (These more relaxed provisions were often concessions to special-interest groups who wished to retain their traditional light configurations.)

Rule 23 applies to ordinary power-driven vessels of all sizes—from the recreational boat to the supertanker. It applies to power-driven fishing vessels when they are not engaged in fishing. It applies to tugboats assisting in ship maneuvering either not connected to the ship or connected with a short line or cable. It does not apply to power-driven vessels that are anchored, aground, or tied to a dock.

INTERNATIONAL	INLAND
(a) A power-driven vessel underway shall exhibit:	(a) A power-driven vessel underway shall exhibit:
(i) a masthead light forward;	(i) a masthead light forward; except that a vessel of less than 20 meters in length need not exhibit this light forward of amidships but shall exhibit it as far forward as is practicable;
(ii) a second masthead light abaft of and higher than the forward one; except that a vessel of less than 50 meters in length shall not be obliged to exhibit such light but may do so;	(ii) a second masthead light abaft of and higher than the forward one; except that a vessel of less than 50 meters in length shall not be obliged to exhibit such light but may do so;
(iii) sidelights;	(iii) sidelights; and
(iv) a sternlight.	(iv) a sternlight.

Paragraph (a) lists the navigation lights for ordinary power-driven vessels. Two masthead lights are required—one forward and one aft—except that small vessels only need one forward. The forward masthead light is placed in the forward half of the vessel, except that under the Inland Rules this light does not have to be forward of amidships on small vessels. Sidelights and a sternlight are also required. Details on the orientation and positioning of these navigation lights are in Rule 21 and in Annex I. Alternative navigation light configurations for vessels less than twelve meters in length are contained in paragraph (c).

INTERNATIONAL

(b) An air-cushion vessel when operating in the nondisplacement mode shall, in addition to the lights prescribed in paragraph (a) of this Rule, exhibit an all-round flashing yellow light.

INLAND

(b) An air-cushion vessel when operating in the nondisplacement mode shall, in addition to the lights prescribed in paragraph (a) of this Rule, exhibit an all-round flashing yellow light where it can best be seen.

Air-cushion vessels are given a distinctive yellow flashing light in paragraph (b). The flashing (120 regular flashes per minute) all-round light is displayed only when the vessel is operating on its cushion of air. Air-cushion vessels may operate at high speeds, may tend to travel a little sideways in a crosswind, and may not be able to turn quickly, depending upon the design of the vessel. A U.S. Navy regulation (Title 32 of the Code of Federal Regulations, §707.7) permits the use of a flashing yellow light on submarines, but the flash characteristic is not the same.

INTERNATIONAL

(c)(i) A power-driven vessel of less than 12 meters in length may in lieu of the lights prescribed in paragraph (a) of this Rule exhibit an all-round white light and sidelights;

INLAND

(c) A power-driven vessel of less than 12 meters in length may, in lieu of the lights prescribed in paragraph (a) of this Rule, exhibit an all-round white light and sidelights.

Some owners, operators, or builders of power-driven vessels under twelve meters in length feel that the conventional masthead light, sidelights, and sternlight array is too complicated, consumes too much power, or just costs too much. For them, paragraph (c) provides one or two alternatives.

Vessels less than twelve meters long may display an all-round white light and sidelights. The all-round white light is commonly mounted at the stern on the starboard side, but that location is a carry-over from superseded navigation rules. Under the current Rules, the all-round white light can be placed anywhere, so long as it is on a level one meter higher than the sidelights. Putting the all-round light above the operator lessens interference with his or her night vision. In addition, carrying the all-round light in the forward part of the boat closer to the sidelights minimizes the decrease in vertical separation (all-round light/sidelights) when the boat assumes a bow-high trim (planing boat).

INTERNATIONAL

(ii) a power-driven vessel of less than 7 meters in length whose maximum speed does not exceed 7 knots may in lieu of the lights prescribed in paragraph (a) of this Rule exhibit an all-round white light and shall, if practicable, also exhibit sidelights;

Under the International Rules, but not the Inland Rules, a power-driven vessel less than seven meters long may dispense with the sidelights, displaying only an all-round white light, *providing* that its "maximum speed does not exceed 7 knots." This means that its maximum speed during the time it is operating at night does not exceed seven knots. One school of thought interprets "maximum speed does not exceed 7 knots" to mean "maximum speed could not exceed 7 knots" or "which is not capable of more than 7 knots," but that is not what the Rule says. The Rule says "does not," present tense. If a single white light is safe for a five-knot boat going five knots, then it should also be safe for a twenty-five-knot boat going five knots.

INTERNATIONAL

(iii) the masthead light or all-round white light on a power-driven vessel of less than 12 meters in length may be displaced from the fore and aft centerline of the vessel if centerline fitting is not practicable, provided that the sidelights are combined in one lantern which shall be carried on the fore and aft centerline of the vessel or located as nearly as practicable in the same fore and aft line as the masthead light or the all-round white light.

Both the International and Inland Rules allow for the off-centerline positioning of masthead or substitute all-round white light. The International Rule provision in Rule 23(c)(iii) is more restrictive than the Inland Rule provisions contained in Rule 21.

INLAND

(d) A power-driven vessel when operating on the Great Lakes may carry an all-round white light in lieu of the second masthead light and sternlight prescribed in paragraph (a) of this Rule. The light shall be carried in the position of the second masthead light and be visible at the same minimum range.

Paragraph (d) of Inland Rule 23 contains an alternative light configuration for Great Lakes vessels, in which an all-round white light replaces the after masthead light and sternlight. This provision is in the Rules not because the conditions or vessels on the Great Lakes are unique, but rather because when the Rules were rewritten, some Great Lakes mariners did not wish to give up their traditional navigation light arrangement.

Rule 24—Towing and Pushing

Rule 24 tells us which navigation lights towing vessels must display as well as those the towed vessel (or object) must display. Some of the Inland provisions are the same as the International in this Rule, but others, particularly for pushing ahead or towing alongside, are different. The first four paragraphs, (a) through (d), apply to *towing* vessels, while paragraphs (e) through (h) apply to *towed* vessels. Paragraph (i), found only in the Inland Rules, exempts western rivers towboats from the general requirements.

INTERNATIONAL

(a) A power-driven vessel when towing shall exhibit:

(i) instead of the light prescribed in Rule 23(a)(i) or (a)(ii), two masthead lights in a vertical line. When the length of the tow, measuring from the stern of the towing vessel to the after end of the tow exceeds 200 meters, three such lights in a vertical line;

(ii) sidelights;

(iii) a sternlight;

(iv) a towing light in a vertical line above the sternlight;

(v) when the length of the tow exceeds 200 meters, a diamond shape where it can best be seen.

INLAND

(a) A power-driven vessel when towing astern shall exhibit:

(i) instead of the light prescribed either in Rule 23(a)(i) or 23(a)(ii), two masthead lights in a vertical line. When the length of the tow, measuring from the stern of the towing vessel to the after end of the tow exceeds 200 meters, three such lights in a vertical line;

(ii) sidelights;

(iii) a sternlight;

(iv) a towing light in a vertical line above the sternlight; and

(v) when the length of the tow exceeds 200 meters, a diamond shape where it can best be seen.

Paragraph (a) presents the lighting requirements for vessels towing astern. Although the International version says "when towing" and does not employ the explicit Inland language, "when towing astern," the International requirement nevertheless applies only to vessels towing astern.

Subparagraph (i) needs special comment. Here the length of the vessel and tow determines the arrangement of masthead lights. Vessels less than fifty meters in length (those that have to display only one masthead light when underway without a tow) are required to display two masthead lights in a vertical line, or, if the tow length is over two hundred meters, three in a vertical line.

Vessels over fifty meters when underway without a tow must display both a forward and, mounted higher, an after masthead light. The masthead lights, forward and aft, thus act as a range, giving others an idea of the vessel's orientation or relative course. When underway *with* a tow, these larger vessels are required to replace either (not both) the forward or the after masthead light with a vertical array of either two or three masthead lights, depending on the length of the tow. A vessel over fifty meters long with a tow less than two hundred meters long must display two masthead lights on its forward mast and one on its after mast. Alternatively, it could display two lights on its after mast and one on its forward mast. Such a vessel would also, of course, display the requisite sidelights, sternlight, and yellow towing light.

INTERNATIONAL	INLAND
(b) When a pushing vessel and a vessel being pushed ahead are rigidly connected in a composite unit they shall be regarded as a power-driven vessel and exhibit the lights prescribed in Rule 23.	(b) When a pushing vessel and a vessel being pushed ahead are rigidly connected in a composite unit they shall be regarded as a power-driven vessel and exhibit the lights prescribed in Rule 23.

Paragraph (b) of Rule 24 is less of a requirement than a statement that certain specialized tug–barge combinations do not fall under Rule 24 but rather under the rules governing lighting of ordinary power-driven vessels. This provision applies only to *pushing ahead.* Described as being "rigidly connected in a composite unit," these vessels are usually designed so that the pushing vessel's bow fits into a matching notch in the stern of the "barge." A locking device holds them so rigidly together that little or no independent motion is permitted. These rigid tug–barge combinations do not need to be certified or classified in order to display the navigation lights of a power-driven vessel. (See also the interpretative rules in Title 33, Code of Federal Regulations, §82.3/International, and §90.3/Inland.)

INTERNATIONAL

(c) A power-driven vessel when pushing ahead or towing alongside, except in the case of a composite unit, shall exhibit:

(i) instead of the light prescribed in Rule 23(a)(i) or (a)(ii), two masthead lights in a vertical line;

(ii) sidelights;

(iii) a sternlight.

INLAND

(c) A power-driven vessel when pushing ahead or towing alongside, except as required by paragraphs (b) and (i) of this Rule, shall exhibit:

(i) instead of the light prescribed either in Rule 23(a)(i) or 23(a)(ii), two masthead lights in a vertical line;

(ii) sidelights; and

(iii) two towing lights in a vertical line.

Paragraph (c) specifies the lights for vessels pushing ahead or towing alongside. Significant differences exist between the International and Inland versions. Both require sidelights. Both require two masthead lights carried in a vertical line. But the Inland Rule exempts (in paragraph [i]) towboats on western rivers from having to display masthead lights. In lieu of the sternlight required by the International version, two yellow towing lights are required by the Inland Rules.

INTERNATIONAL

(d) A power-driven vessel to which paragraphs (a) or (c) of this Rule apply shall also comply with Rule 23(a)(ii).

INLAND

(d) A power-driven vessel to which paragraphs (a) or (c) of this Rule apply shall also comply with Rule 23(a)(i) and 23(a)(ii).

The wording in paragraphs (a) and (c) did not make clear the requirement for larger towing vessels to display both forward and after masthead lights, so paragraph (d) was added. Yet its inclusion seems only to have made the requirement more confusing. Paragraph (d) is aimed at vessels over fifty meters in length and says if you elect to display your two or three masthead lights (in a vertical line) for towing on the forward mast, then you must also display another masthead light on the after mast. If the two or three masthead light towing array is mounted on the after mast, a single masthead light must be displayed on the forward mast.

Whether to display the vertical array masthead lights on the forward mast or on the after mast is the decision of the builder/operator.

Because towing vessels under fifty meters need carry masthead lights on only one mast, they can ignore paragraph (d), although they may voluntarily carry both forward and after masthead lights.

INTERNATIONAL

(e) A vessel or object being towed, other than those mentioned in paragraph (g) of this Rule, shall exhibit:
    (i) sidelights;
    (ii) a sternlight;
    (iii) when the length of the tow exceeds 200 meters, a diamond shape where it can best be seen.

INLAND

(e) A vessel or object other than those referred to in paragraph (g) of this Rule being towed shall exhibit:
    (i) sidelights;
    (ii) a sternlight; and
    (iii) when the length of the tow exceeds 200 meters, a diamond shape where it can best be seen.

Paragraph (e) of both the International and Inland Rules begins the lighting requirements for vessels *being towed*, stipulating that vessels being towed astern have sidelights and a sternlight. The intensity of the lights is based on the length of the towed vessel, excluding towline and towing vessel. Annex I to the Inland Rules contains a special provision affecting the intensity of battery-powered navigation lights on unmanned barges. A diamond shape is displayed by day when the length of the tow, including towed vessel and towing line, exceeds two hundred meters.

INTERNATIONAL

(f) Provided that any number of vessels being towed alongside or pushed in a group shall be lighted as one vessel,
    (i) a vessel being pushed ahead, not being part of a composite unit, shall exhibit at the forward end, sidelights;

    (ii) a vessel being towed alongside shall exhibit a sternlight and at the forward end, sidelights.

INLAND

(f) Provided that any number of vessels being towed alongside or pushed in a group shall be lighted as one vessel:
    (i) a vessel being pushed ahead, not being part of a composite unit, shall exhibit at the forward end sidelights, and a special flashing light; and
    (ii) a vessel being towed alongside shall exhibit a sternlight and at the forward end sidelights.

Paragraph (f) specifies the navigation lights for vessels being pushed ahead or towed alongside. If several barges are tied together and towed as a unit, then they must be lighted as though a single vessel. The light must be intense enough to meet the requirement for the length of the group, not the length of a single barge within the group (see Rule 22).

Vessels being *towed alongside* have the same requirement under both International and Inland Rules: sidelights and a sternlight.

Vessels being *pushed ahead* carry sidelights, as required by both sets of Rules, but the Inland Rules also demand a special flashing light at the front of the tow. Inland Rule 21(g) describes this flashing yellow light, whose display is not allowed on vessels being towed alongside.

INTERNATIONAL	INLAND
(g) An inconspicuous, partly submerged vessel or object, or combination of such vessels or objects being towed, shall exhibit:	(g) An inconspicuous, partly submerged vessel or object being towed shall exhibit:
(i) if it is less than 25 meters in breadth, one all-round white light at or near the forward end and one at or near the after end except that dracones need not exhibit a light at or near the forward end;	(i) if it is less than 25 meters in breadth, one all-round white light at or near each end;
(ii) if it is 25 meters or more in breadth, two additional all-round white lights at or near the extremities of its breadth;	(ii) if it is 25 meters or more in breadth, four all-round white lights to mark its length and breadth;
(iii) if it exceeds 100 meters in length, additional all-round white lights between the lights prescribed in subparagraphs (i) and (ii) so that the distance between the lights shall not exceed 100 meters;	(iii) if it exceeds 100 meters in length, additional all-round white lights between the lights prescribed in subparagraphs (i) and (ii) so that the distance between the lights shall not exceed 100 meters: *Provided,* That any vessels or objects being towed alongside each other shall be lighted as one vessel or object;
(iv) a diamond shape at or near	(iv) a diamond shape at or near

the aftermost extremity of the last vessel or object being towed and if the length of the tow exceeds 200 meters an additional diamond shape where it can best be seen and located as far forward as is practicable.

the aftermost extremity of the last vessel or object being towed; and

(v) the towing vessel may direct a searchlight in the direction of the tow to indicate its presence to an approaching vessel.

Paragraph (g) provides for lighting "inconspicuous, partly submerged" vessels or objects that, by their very nature, cannot be provided with conventional side- and sternlights. This "vessel" class includes dracones, which are large flexible bags used for transporting liquids.

The International and Inland versions differ slightly in language and detail. Both require an all-round white light at each end of the towed vessel, although the International version exempts dracones from the forward light stipulation. Both require two additional white lights to mark the beam on wide (twenty-five meters or more) tows. For long tows, subparagraph (g)(iii) provides for extra lights so that there will not be an unlighted span of more than one hundred meters. These intermediate lights on long tows should be mounted singly if the tow is less than twenty-five meters wide or in pairs for wider tows.

The Inland subparagraph (g)(iii) says that when several vessels are being towed alongside one another, the extra intermediate lights for very long tows shall be displayed—that is, as though the several vessels were one. The International version does not contain a similar caveat because all of the International paragraph (g) requirements are applied to combinations of inconspicuous, partly submerged vessels or objects as if they were one. In the Inland version, however, only the (g)(iii) requirement applies to combinations.

By day both the International and Inland Rules demand a diamond shape at the "aftermost extremity" of the tow. For tows exceeding two hundred meters in length (including towline) the International Rules (but not the Inland) require an additional diamond shape displayed on the towed vessel or object "where it can best be seen and located as far forward as is practicable."

The Inland paragraph (g) includes a statement permitting but not mandating the use of a searchlight aimed toward the tow for the benefit of an approaching vessel. Although the International version of paragraph (g) does not explicitly state that such a searchlight is permitted, its use for the purpose of illuminating a tow would be allowed under International Rules 2 and 36.

INTERNATIONAL

(h) Where from any sufficient cause it is impracticable for a vessel or object being towed to exhibit the lights or shapes prescribed in paragraph (e) or (g) of this Rule, all possible measures shall be taken to light the vessel or object towed or at least to indicate the presence of such vessel or object.

INLAND

(h) Where from any sufficient cause it is impracticable for a vessel or object being towed to exhibit the lights prescribed in paragraph (e) or (g) of this Rule, all possible measures shall be taken to light the vessel or object towed or at least to indicate the presence of the unlighted vessel or object.

In some situations a vessel being towed astern cannot be fitted with proper navigation lights. For example, a vessel disabled by storm or accident may be without power and the urgency of rescue efforts may prevent the fitting of emergency lighting. In such a case, paragraph (h) excuses compliance with conventional lighting requirements but says every effort must be made to indicate to other vessels in the area that a vessel (or object) is being towed. Searchlights, the towed vessel's deck lighting, illumination flares, radar, radiotelephone, or whatever else is available should be used.

INLAND

(i) Notwithstanding paragraph (c), on the Western Rivers (except below the Huey P. Long Bridge on the Mississippi River) and on waters specified by the Secretary, a power-driven vessel when pushing ahead or towing alongside, except as paragraph (b) applies, shall exhibit:

(i) sidelights; and

(ii) two towing lights in a vertical line.

Towing vessels pushing barges ahead need not display mast-head lights when on certain inland waters, including the western rivers above the Huey P. Long Bridge, the Tennessee–Tombigbee Waterway, Tombigbee River, Black Warrior River, Alabama River, Coosa River, Mobile River above the Cochrane Bridge at St. Louis Point, Flint River, Chattachoochee River, and the Apalachicola River above its confluence with the Jackson River (see Title 33, Code of Federal Regulations, Part 89, Subpart B).

This Inland Rule provision was added not because the absence of masthead lights contributed to safety but rather because their height made passing under low bridges more difficult. If towing vessels operating on these waters wish to have the higher visibility that masthead lights afford, they may display masthead lights according to the paragraph (c) general requirements for inland waters. The display of masthead lights on western rivers while pushing ahead should not cause confusion because such display is permitted (and required) in the case of towboats complying with the International Rules and operating on western rivers, and their display is required for all towing vessels on western rivers below the Huey P. Long Bridge.

INTERNATIONAL

(i) Where from any sufficient cause it is impracticable for a vessel not normally engaged in towing operations to display the lights prescribed in paragraph (a) or (c) of this Rule, such vessel shall not be required to exhibit those lights when engaged in towing another vessel in distress or otherwise in need of assistance. All possible measures shall be taken to indicate the nature of the relationship between the towing vessel and the vessel being towed as authorized by Rule 36, in particular by illuminating the towline.

INLAND

(j) Where from any sufficient cause it is impracticable for a vessel not normally engaged in towing operations to display the lights prescribed by paragraph (a), (c) or (i) of this Rule, such vessel shall not be required to exhibit those lights when engaged in towing another vessel in distress or otherwise in need of assistance. All possible measures shall be taken to indicate the nature of the relationship between the towing vessel and the vessel being assisted. The searchlight authorized by Rule 36 may be used to illuminate the tow.

The final provision in Rule 24 concerns so-called good Samaritan towing. International paragraph (i) and Inland paragraph (j), which are essentially the same, permit a vessel to tow another without displaying the navigation lights of a towing vessel. The towing vessel must not have expected to become involved in towing, having only fortuitously encountered another vessel "in distress or otherwise in need of assistance." Good Samaritans must indicate to others, by whatever means available, that they are engaged in towing.

Obviously, commercial towing operations do not qualify under this provision. Nor do vessels whose normal activities include the towing (or expectation of towing) of disabled vessels, regardless of whether a fee is collected.

Rule 25—Sailing Vessels Underway and Vessels Under Oars

The International and Inland versions of this Rule are identical but for one Inland provision exempting small vessels from having to carry a day shape. The navigation light rules for sailing vessels have one basic lighting configuration (sidelights and sternlight) and several optional configurations.

INTERNATIONAL	INLAND
(a) A sailing vessel underway shall exhibit:	(a) A sailing vessel underway shall exhibit:
(i) sidelights;	(i) sidelights; and
(ii) a sternlight.	(ii) a sternlight.

Paragraph (a) presents the fundamental requirement for sidelights and sternlight. Remember that the definition of sidelights for vessels less than twenty meters in length allows them to be either separate or combined in a single fixture. The combined sidelights reduce power consumption, as they use one lamp instead of two.

INTERNATIONAL	INLAND
(b) In a sailing vessel of less than 20 meters in length the lights prescribed in paragraph (a) of this Rule	(b) In a sailing vessel of less than 20 meters in length the lights prescribed in paragraph (a) of this Rule

may be combined in one lantern carried at or near the top of the mast where it can best be seen.

may be combined in one lantern carried at or near the top of the mast where it can best be seen.

Paragraph (b) carries this power savings even further for sailing vessels under twenty meters by allowing sidelights *and* sternlight to be combined into a single fixture and carried at the masthead. This combined navigation light is often called a "tricolor" light. It cannot be used, however, while an auxiliary engine propels the boat, so a sailing vessel equipped with an engine must be fitted with regular sidelights and sternlight even if a "tricolor" light is used when under sail alone. The "tricolor" light may not be used when the regular sidelights are on. Display one or the other but not both.

INTERNATIONAL

(c) A sailing vessel underway may, in addition to the lights prescribed in paragraph (a) of this Rule, exhibit at or near the top of the mast, where they can best be seen, two all-round lights in a vertical line, the upper being red and the lower green, but these lights shall not be exhibited in conjunction with the combined lantern permitted by paragraph (b) of this Rule.

INLAND

(c) A sailing vessel underway may, in addition to the lights prescribed in paragraph (a) of this Rule, exhibit at or near the top of the mast, where they can best be seen, two all-round lights in a vertical line, the upper being red and the lower green, but these lights shall not be exhibited in conjunction with the combined lantern permitted by paragraph (b) of this Rule.

Paragraph (c) presents an optional display that is much less popular than the "tricolor" light but that can be employed on sailing vessels over (as well as under) twenty meters. The all-round red over the all-round green light are to be used with the regular sidelights and sternlight. Annex I requires that the red and green lights be mounted vertically two meters apart for vessels over twenty meters in length and one meter apart for smaller vessels. This arrangement makes it difficult not to obstruct the arc of visibility of the lower (green) all-round light, so this option will probably rarely be seen.

INTERNATIONAL

(d)(i)A sailing vessel of less than 7 meters in length shall, if practicable, exhibit the lights prescribed in paragraph (a) or (b) of this Rule, but if she does not, she shall have ready at hand an electric torch or lighted lantern showing a white light which shall be exhibited in sufficient time to prevent collision.

(ii)A vessel under oars may exhibit the lights prescribed in this Rule for sailing vessels, but if she does not, she shall have ready at hand an electric torch or lighted lantern showing a white light which shall be exhibited in sufficient time to prevent collision.

INLAND

(d)(i)A sailing vessel of less than 7 meters in length shall, if practicable, exhibit the lights prescribed in paragraph (a) or (b) of this Rule, but if she does not, she shall have ready at hand an electric torch or lighted lantern showing a white light which shall be exhibited in sufficient time to prevent collision.

(ii) A vessel under oars may exhibit the lights prescribed in this Rule for sailing vessels, but if she does not, she shall have ready at hand an electric torch or lighted lantern showing a white light which shall be exhibited in sufficient time to prevent collision.

Paragraph (d) deals with small sailboats and rowboats. You can expect to see either sidelights and sternlight or a flashlight when approaching these vessels at night. Sailboats under seven meters are to display sidelights and sternlight "if practicable." If the boat has a motor equipped with a battery, then it is probably practicable, not to mention wise, to display sidelights and sternlight.

INTERNATIONAL

(e) A vessel proceeding under sail when also being propelled by machinery shall exhibit forward where it can best be seen a conical shape, apex downwards.

INLAND

(e) A vessel proceeding under sail when also being propelled by machinery shall exhibit forward where it can best be seen a conical shape, apex downward. A vessel of less than 12 meters in length is not required to exhibit this shape, but may do so.

The final paragraph requires that a conical shape (point down) be displayed on a sailing vessel propelled by both sail and machinery. The conical shape indicates to other vessels that the "sailing" vessel is a power-driven vessel for purposes of the navigation rules. The Inland Rule version says that sailing vessels less than twelve meters long do not have to display this shape when motorsailing. Annex I to both sets of Rules permits vessels less than twenty meters long to display shapes smaller than full size.

Rule 26—Navigation Lights for Fishing Vessels

INTERNATIONAL

(a) A vessel engaged in fishing, whether underway or at anchor, shall exhibit only the lights and shapes prescribed in this Rule.

INLAND

(a) A vessel engaged in fishing, whether underway or at anchor, shall exhibit only the lights and shapes prescribed in this Rule.

The rules for navigation lights on fishing vessels are relatively straightforward. There are no exceptions for particular geographic areas, and the International and Inland versions are the same. The navigation lights in this Rule are *only* for those vessels "engaged in fishing" as defined in Rule 3 whose maneuverability is restricted by their fishing apparatus.

INTERNATIONAL

(b) A vessel when engaged in trawling, by which is meant the dragging through the water of a dredge net or other apparatus used as a fishing appliance, shall exhibit:

(i) two all-round lights in a vertical line, the upper being green and the lower white, or a shape consisting of two cones with their apexes together in a vertical line one above the other; a vessel of less than 20 meters in length may instead of this shape exhibit a basket;

(ii) a masthead light abaft of and higher than the all-round green light; a vessel of less than 50 meters in length shall not be obliged to exhibit such a light but may do so;

INLAND

(b) A vessel when engaged in trawling, by which is meant the dragging through the water of a dredge net or other apparatus used as a fishing appliance, shall exhibit:

(i) two all-round lights in a vertical line, the upper being green and the lower white, or a shape consisting of two cones with their apexes together in a vertical line one above the other; a vessel of less than 20 meters in length may instead of this shape exhibit a basket;

(ii) a masthead light abaft of and higher than the all-round green light; a vessel of less than 50 meters in length shall not be obliged to exhibit such a light but may do so; and

(iii) when making way through the water, in addition to the lights prescribed in this paragraph, sidelights and a sternlight.

(c) A vessel engaged in fishing, other than trawling, shall exhibit:

(i) two all-round lights in a vertical line, the upper being red and the lower white, or a shape consisting of two cones with apexes together in a vertical line one above the other; a vessel of less than 20 meters in length may instead of this shape exhibit a basket;

(ii) when there is outlying gear extending more than 150 meters horizontally from the vessel, an all-round white light or a cone apex upwards in the direction of the gear;

(iii) when making way through the water, in addition to the lights prescribed in this paragraph, sidelights and a sternlight.

(iii) when making way through the water, in addition to the lights prescribed in this paragraph, sidelights and a sternlight.

(c) A vessel engaged in fishing, other than trawling, shall exhibit:

(i) two all-round lights in a vertical line, the upper being red and the lower white, or a shape consisting of two cones with apexes together in a vertical line one above the other; a vessel of less than 20 meters in length may instead of this shape exhibit a basket;

(ii) when there is outlying gear extending more than 150 meters horizontally from the vessel, an all-round white light or a cone apex upward in the direction of the gear; and

(iii) when making way through the water, in addition to the lights prescribed in this paragraph, sidelights and a sternlight.

Rule 26 separates vessels engaged in fishing into two classes: vessels trawling, and all others. The basic lighting rules are the same for the two classes except that trawlers use a green all-round light while others use a red one.

The lighting requirements for vessels engaged in fishing distinguish between vessels making way through the water and those that are stopped, that is, drifting or anchored. Also related to that is the provision that anchored vessels engaged in fishing be lighted as would a drifting fishing vessel. Hence, those vessels should ignore the Rule 30 lighting requirements. (See paragraph [a], Rule 26.)

INTERNATIONAL

(d) A vessel engaged in fishing in close proximity to other vessels en-

INLAND

(d) A vessel engaged in fishing in close proximity to other vessels en-

INTERNATIONAL

gaged in fishing may exhibit the additional signals described in Annex II to these Regulations.

INLAND

gaged in fishing may exhibit the additional signals described in Annex II to these Rules.

Paragraph (d) refers the reader to the Annex II optional lights for vessels fishing in a "fleet." These Annex II lights, which provide close-by fishing vessels with information, can only be displayed in the company of other vessels engaged in fishing.

One of the Annex II displays, a white light over a red light for a trawler hauling its nets, could be mistaken for the lights of a pilot vessel. While Rule 29 requires a pilot vessel to display a white over a red light, with either sidelights and sternlight if underway or anchor light if anchored, Rule 26 requires a trawler to display green over white lights. Note that the optional white-over-red Annex II lights will be displayed at a lower level than the green-over-white and that they will not be as bright.

INTERNATIONAL

(e) A vessel when not engaged in fishing shall not exhibit the lights or shapes prescribed in this Rule, but only those prescribed for a vessel of her length.

INLAND

(e) A vessel when not engaged in fishing shall not exhibit the lights or shapes prescribed in this Rule, but only those prescribed for a vessel of her length.

Fishing vessels not "engaged in fishing" must display not Rule 26 lights but instead the lights for an ordinary power-driven or sailing vessel, whichever is appropriate.

Rule 27—Vessels Not Under Command or Restricted in Their Ability to Maneuver

Vessels not under command and vessels restricted in their ability to maneuver are treated similarly under the Rules, as their combined status under Rule 27 reflects. The Rule 3 definition of a "vessel not under command" is that of a vessel "unable to maneuver as required" of ordinary vessels because of "exceptional circumstance." Rule 3 defines a "vessel restricted in her ability to maneuver" as one unable to keep out of the way because of "the nature of her work." In both cases, the vessels cannot physically comply with the Rules for ordinary vessels, and so they are granted special privileges. Rule 18 requires all other vessels to keep out of the way of these two classes of vessels.

INTERNATIONAL

(a) A vessel not under command shall exhibit:

(i) two all-round red lights in a vertical line where they can best be seen;

(ii) two balls or similar shapes in a vertical line where they can best be seen;

(iii) when making way through the water, in addition to the lights prescribed in this paragraph, sidelights and a sternlight.

INLAND

(a) A vessel not under command shall exhibit:

(i) two all-round red lights in a vertical line where they can best be seen;

(ii) two balls or similar shapes in a vertical line where they can best be seen; and

(iii) when making way through the water, in addition to the lights prescribed in this paragraph, sidelights and a sternlight.

A vessel not under command has usually suffered a disability, which is not easy to predict or classify. An example would be a vessel with a disabled rudder. The navigation light requirement is, therefore, brief and general.

INTERNATIONAL

(b) A vessel restricted in her ability to maneuver, except a vessel engaged in mineclearance operations, shall exhibit:

(i) three all-round lights in a vertical line where they can best be seen. The highest and lowest of these lights shall be red and the middle light shall be white;

(ii) three shapes in a vertical line where they can best be seen. The highest and lowest of these shapes shall be balls and the middle one a diamond;

INLAND

(b) A vessel restricted in her ability to maneuver, except a vessel engaged in mineclearance operations, shall exhibit:

(i) three all-round lights in a vertical line where they can best be seen. The highest and lowest of these lights shall be red and the middle light shall be white;

(ii) three shapes in a vertical line where they can best be seen. The highest and lowest of these shapes shall be balls and the middle one a diamond;

INTERNATIONAL

(iii) when making way through the water, a masthead light or lights, sidelights and a sternlight, in addition to the lights prescribed in subparagraph (i);

(iv) when at anchor, in addition to the lights or shapes prescribed in subparagraphs (i) and (ii), the light, lights or shape prescribed in Rule 30.

INLAND

(iii) when making way through the water, masthead lights, sidelights and a sternlight, in addition to the lights prescribed in subparagraph (b)(i); and

(iv) when at anchor, in addition to the lights or shapes prescribed in subparagraphs (b)(i) and (ii), the light, lights or shape prescribed in Rule 30.

Unlike the not-under-command category, vessel classifications within the restricted-in-ability-to-maneuver category are predictable and are listed in the Rule 3 definition. Rule 27, starting with paragraph (b), gives general navigation light requirements and then more specific requirements for several vessel activities that restrict maneuverability.

The lights described in paragraph (b) are not to be displayed by a vessel engaged in mineclearance, even though the mineclearing vessel is regarded as being restricted in its ability to maneuver. Separate lighting requirements for mineclearance are given in paragraph (f).

As is also the case with vessels engaged in fishing, vessels restricted in ability to maneuver are required to display additional lights when making way through the water. Anchor lights, as described in Rule 30, are to be displayed while at anchor in addition to the lights indicating restricted ability to maneuver, *except that vessels restricted in ability to maneuver because of dredging or underwater operations, and when an obstruction exists, do not* display Rule 30 anchor lights when anchored (see paragraph [d]).

INTERNATIONAL

(c) A power-driven vessel engaged in a towing operation such as severely restricts the towing vessel and her tow in their ability to deviate from their course shall, in addition to the lights or shapes pre-

INLAND

(c) A vessel engaged in a towing operation which severely restricts the towing vessel and her tow in their ability to deviate from their course shall, in addition to the lights or shapes prescribed in subscribed in Rule 24(a), exhibit the lights or shapes prescribed in subparagraphs (b)(i) and (ii) of this Rule.

paragraphs (b)(i) and (ii) of this Rule, exhibit the lights or shape prescribed in Rule 24.

Under most circumstances, vessels engaged in towing do not have any privileges over ordinary power-driven vessels. In cases where a towing operation "severely restricts the towing vessel and her tow in their ability to deviate from their course," the towing vessel is considered to be restricted in its ability to maneuver and is accorded special status. In such situations Rule 27(c) requires the display of *both* Rule 24 towing lights and Rule 27(b) restricted-in-ability-to-maneuver lights. The latter lights are to be displayed where they can best be seen. They should be at a lower level than the masthead lights if practicable, but they may be higher; see Annex I 2(f)(ii)/§84.03(f)(2). The red-white-red all-round lights do not have to be in a vertical line with the masthead lights and may be off the centerline. Only the towing vessel displays the lights for a vessel restricted in ability to maneuver, not the vessel being towed.

INTERNATIONAL

(d) A vessel engaged in dredging or underwater operations, when restricted in her ability to maneuver, shall exhibit the lights and shapes prescribed in subparagraphs (b)(i), (ii) and (iii) of this Rule and shall in addition, when an obstruction exists, exhibit:

(i) Two all-round red lights or two balls in a vertical line to indicate the side on which the obstruction exists;

(ii) Two all-round green lights or two diamonds in a vertical line to indicate the side on which another vessel may pass;

INLAND

(d) A vessel engaged in dredging or underwater operations, when restricted in her ability to maneuver, shall exhibit the lights and shapes prescribed in subparagraphs (b)(i), (ii), and (iii) of this Rule and shall in addition, when an obstruction exists, exhibit:

(i) two all-round red lights or two balls in a vertical line to indicate the side on which the obstruction exists;

(ii) two all-round green lights or two diamonds in a vertical line to indicate the side on which another vessel may pass; and

INTERNATIONAL

(iii) When at anchor, the lights or shapes prescribed in this paragraph instead of the lights or shape prescribed in Rule 30.

INLAND

(iii) when at anchor, the lights or shape prescribed by this paragraph, instead of the lights or shapes prescribed in Rule 30 for anchored vessels.

Paragraphs (d) and (e) give further details for vessels restricted in ability to maneuver because they are engaged in dredging or underwater operations, including diving. Paragraph (d) gives new requirements only for hampered vessels having an obstruction projecting out from one side of the vessel. The obstruction could be a dredging arm or a float or other equipment used to support underwater operations. (Separate requirements for special lighting of dredge pipelines are contained in Annex V to the Inland Rules.) Vessels displaying the obstruction lights required by this paragraph do not also display Rule 30 anchor lights, when anchored, but vessels engaged in dredging and underwater operations when no obstruction exists are required to comply with Rule 30 when anchored.

INTERNATIONAL

(e) Whenever the size of a vessel engaged in diving operations makes it impracticable to exhibit all lights and shapes prescribed in paragraph (d) of this Rule, the following shall be exhibited:

(i) Three all-round lights in a vertical line where they can best be seen. The highest and lowest of these lights shall be red and the middle light shall be white;

(ii) A rigid replica of the International Code flag "A" not less than 1 meter in height. Measures shall be taken to ensure its all-round visibility.

INLAND

(e) Whenever the size of a vessel engaged in diving operations makes it impracticable to exhibit all lights and shapes prescribed in paragraph (d) of this Rule, the following shall instead be exhibited:

(i) Three all-round lights in a vertical line where they can best be seen. The highest and lowest of these lights shall be red and the middle light shall be white.

(ii) A rigid replica of the International Code flag "A" not less than 1 meter in height. Measures shall be taken to ensure its all-round visibility.

Paragraph (e) provides for vessels too small to comply with the requirements of paragraph (d) for vessels engaged in diving operations. Paragraph (e) is clearly aimed at the small vessel conducting diving operations, regardless of whether an obstruction on one side of the vessel exists. The paragraph (b) requirements for sidelights and sternlight when making way cannot be disregarded for small vessels engaged in diving operations, nor can the Rule 30 requirement to display an anchor light when anchored. Paragraph (g) of Rule 27 makes clear the intent. Paragraph (e) excuses the display of obstruction lights and shapes and excuses the display of the ball-diamond-ball day shape array if the proper-size International Code flag "A" is displayed instead. Flags smaller than one meter are not permitted for small vessels, even though shapes of reduced size are permitted on vessels less than twenty meters long. Although a flag that big will seem large to people on a relatively small dive boat, a smaller flag would probably go undetected by a larger vessel approaching the area.

INTERNATIONAL

(f) A vessel engaged in mineclearance operations shall in addition to the lights prescribed for a power-driven vessel in Rule 23 or to the lights or shape prescribed for a vessel at anchor in Rule 30 as appropriate, exhibit three all-round green lights or three balls. One of these lights or shapes shall be exhibited near the foremast head and one at each end of the fore yard. These lights or shapes indicate that it is dangerous for another vessel to approach within 1000 meters of the mineclearance vessel.

INLAND

(f) A vessel engaged in mineclearance operations shall, in addition to the lights prescribed for a power-driven vessel in Rule 23 or to the lights or shape prescribed for a vessel at anchor in Rule 30 as appropriate, exhibit three all-round green lights or three balls. One of these lights or shapes shall be exhibited near the foremast head and one at each end of the fore yard. These lights or shapes indicate that it is dangerous for another vessel to approach within 1000 meters of the mineclearance vessel.

Vessels engaged in clearing mines (or the old term "minesweeping") display a unique combination of navigation lights to warn others of their dangerous operations. These lights are carried in addition to the lights carried by an ordinary vessel.

INTERNATIONAL

(g) Vessels of less than 12 meters in length, except those engaged in

INLAND

(g) A vessel of less than 12 meters in length, except when engaged in

INTERNATIONAL
diving operations, shall not be required to exhibit the lights and
shapes prescribed in this Rule.

INLAND
diving operations, is not required
to exhibit the lights or shapes prescribed in this Rule.

Paragraph (g) exempts small vessels from the light and shape requirements for vessels not under command and restricted in ability to maneuver. Such small vessels presumably could not then claim the status of vessels in such situations and would not be given the privileges accompanying such status unless the small vessel's predicament were recognized by other means. Small vessels engaged in diving operations do not have this blanket exemption but may comply with the alternative requirements of paragraph (e).

INTERNATIONAL
(h) The signals prescribed in this
Rule are not signals of vessels in
distress and requiring assistance.
Such signals are contained in
Annex IV to these Regulations.

INLAND
(h) The signals prescribed in this
Rule are not signals of vessels in
distress and requiring assistance.
Such signals are contained in
Annex IV to these Rules.

The final paragraph in Rule 27 makes clear that even though a vessel not under command (or less likely, a vessel restricted in ability to maneuver) may actually be in distress, the lights and shapes required by this Rule do *not* indicate distress and need of assistance. If you do in fact need assistance, use one or more of the signals listed in Annex IV. A vessel may be not under command for any number of reasons, and many of those would not require outside assistance.

Rule 28—Vessels Constrained by Their Draft

INTERNATIONAL
A vessel constrained by her draft
may, in addition to the lights prescribed for power-driven vessels
in Rule 23, exhibit where they
can best be seen three all-round
red lights in a vertical line, or a
cylinder.

International Rule 18(d) provides for vessels constrained by their draft and attempts to favor them with regard to other vessels because of the restrictions on their movement. This Rule gives the special navigation lights and shape that mark a vessel constrained by draft. The Inland Rules did not adopt the concept of "vessel constrained by draft," and there is, therefore, no Inland Rule 28.

Rule 29—Pilot Vessels

INTERNATIONAL

(a) A vessel engaged on pilotage duty shall exhibit:

(i) at or near the masthead, two all-round lights in a vertical line, the upper being white and the lower red;

(ii) when underway, in addition, sidelights and a sternlight;

(iii) when at anchor, in addition to the lights prescribed in subparagraph (i), the light, lights or shape prescribed in Rule 30 for vessels at anchor.

(b) A pilot vessel when not engaged on pilotage duty shall exhibit the lights or shapes prescribed for a similar vessel of her length.

INLAND

(a) A vessel engaged on pilotage duty shall exhibit:

(i) at or near the masthead, two all-round lights in a vertical line, the upper being white and the lower red;

(ii) when underway, in addition, sidelights and a sternlight; and

(iii) when at anchor, in addition to the lights prescribed in subparagraph (i), the anchor light, lights, or shape prescribed in Rule 30 for anchored vessels.

(b) A pilot vessel when not engaged on pilotage duty shall exhibit the lights or shapes prescribed for a vessel of her length.

The International and Inland Rule 29 requirements are the same. Rule 29 is simple and straightforward. The white-over-red all-round lights are also used as an optional display on trawlers hauling in their nets, but the white-over-red lights in that application are used in combination with a green-over-white all-round light display and then only when close to other fishing vessels. There is very little chance, then, that a pilot vessel would be confused with a vessel engaged in fishing.

Rule 30—Anchored Vessels and Vessels Aground

INTERNATIONAL

(a) A vessel at anchor shall exhibit where it can best be seen:

INLAND

(a) A vessel at anchor shall exhibit where it can best be seen:

(i) in the fore part, an all-round white light or one ball;

(ii) at or near the stern and at a lower level than the light prescribed in subparagraph (i), an all-round white light.

(b) A vessel of less than 50 meters in length may exhibit an all-round white light where it can best be seen instead of the lights prescribed in paragraph (a) of this Rule.

(c) A vessel at anchor may, and a vessel of 100 meters and more in length shall, also use the available working or equivalent lights to illuminate her decks.

(i) in the fore part, an all-round white light or one ball; and

(ii) at or near the stern and at a lower level than the light prescribed in subparagraph (i), an all-round white light.

(b) A vessel of less than 50 meters in length may exhibit an all-round white light where it can best be seen instead of the lights prescribed in paragraph (a) of this Rule.

(c) A vessel at anchor may, and a vessel of 100 meters or more in length shall, also use the available working or equivalent lights to illuminate her decks.

The basic lighting requirements for anchoring are given in the first three paragraphs: two white lights for vessels fifty meters or more in length; one white light for vessels less than fifty meters in length; and deck lights for vessels one hundred meters or more in length. Smaller vessels may at their option show the extra lights required for big vessels. These requirements are the same for the International and Inland Rules.

A vessel is anchored when its anchor touches bottom; a vessel is no longer anchored when the anchor is lifted off the bottom. A vessel dragging its anchor is underway and therefore not "anchored." A vessel fastened to a mooring is "at anchor."

(d) A vessel aground shall exhibit the lights prescribed in paragraph (a) or (b) of this Rule and in addition, where they can best be seen:

(i) two all-round red lights in a vertical line;

(ii) three balls in a vertical line.

(d) A vessel aground shall exhibit the lights prescribed in paragraph (a) or (b) of this Rule and in addition, if practicable, where they can best be seen:

(i) two all-round red lights in a vertical line; and

(ii) three balls in a vertical line.

Paragraph (d) tells you what lights to display when you run aground. You are not considered to be "aground" for purposes of the navigation rules if you have intentionally moved your vessel against the bottom or bank of a river or other body of water to hold your position. If you have to keep your engines engaged to maintain your position, or if you are free to move away from your holding position at any time, then you are not considered to be "aground." You would be underway but not making way through the water.

The Inland and International versions of paragraph (d) vary slightly. Both require that vessels aground display the navigation lights and shapes for a vessel at anchor. The International version also requires the display of two all-round red lights (or three balls), whereas the Inland version requires the display of these extra lights and shapes only "if practicable."

INTERNATIONAL	INLAND
(e) A vessel of less than 7 meters in length, when at anchor, not in or near a narrow channel, fairway or anchorage, or where other vessels normally navigate, shall not be required to exhibit the lights or shape prescribed in paragraphs (a) and (b) of this Rule.	(e) A vessel of less than 7 meters in length, when at anchor, not in or near a narrow channel, fairway or anchorage, or where other vessels normally navigate, shall not be required to exhibit the lights or shape prescribed in paragraphs (a) and (b) of this Rule.
(f) A vessel of less than 12 meters in length, when aground, shall not be required to exhibit the lights or shapes prescribed in subparagraphs (d)(i) and (ii) of this Rule.	(f) A vessel of less than 12 meters in length when aground shall not be required to exhibit the lights or shapes prescribed in subparagraphs (d)(i) and (ii) of this Rule.

Paragraphs (e) and (f) excuse small vessels from the display of anchor lights and shapes under certain circumstances and from the display of aground lights and shapes.

INLAND

(g) A vessel of less than 20 meters in length, when at anchor in a special anchorage area designated by

INLAND

the Secretary, shall not be required to exhibit the anchor lights and shapes required by this Rule.

Inland Rule 30 alone contains a paragraph (g). This provision allows small vessels to anchor without displaying lights if they are in a "special anchorage area." These special areas are listed in Title 33 of the Code of Federal Regulations, Part 110, and can also be found in the *Coast Pilot*.

Rule 31—Seaplanes

INTERNATIONAL

Where it is impracticable for a seaplane to exhibit lights and shapes of the characteristics or in the positions prescribed in the Rules of this Part she shall exhibit lights and shapes as closely similar in characteristics and position as is possible.

INLAND

Where it is impracticable for a seaplane to exhibit lights and shapes of the characteristics or in the positions prescribed in the Rules of this Part she shall exhibit lights and shapes as closely similar in characteristics and position as is possible.

The International and Inland versions of this short Rule are the same. For obvious reasons, airplanes may have difficulty complying with navigation light requirements that were written for ships.

Airplanes of all sorts (not just seaplanes) display a green "sidelight" on the right wingtip, a red "sidelight" on the left, and a white "sternlight" aft. Most aircraft also have provisions to make these lights blink when they are on the ground. This blinking mode, if available on a seaplane, should not be used on the water.

Seaplane manufacturers often provide an all-round white light on a portable mast primarily intended for use when the seaplane is anchored. The mast usually has provisions for displaying a shape. This mast is often difficult to mount and dismount, and requires the seaplane to be stopped before mounting. In short, seaplanes in sea—air transition should not be expected to conform to the lights and shapes as closely as when they are anchored.

PART D

Sound and Light Signals

Part D contains the Rules for mandatory and voluntary signals, particularly sound signals—maneuvering signals and "fog" signals—and other signaling means as well.

Rules 32 through 37 make up Part D. Rule 32 defines the most common terms; Rule 33 tells you what sound-signaling equipment you must carry; Rule 34 describes the signals given to other vessels you can see while Rule 35 is for signals to vessels you can't see; Rule 36 tells you what you can do if you want to reach out to people on another vessel; and, finally, Rule 37 is for vessels in distress.

Rule 32—Definitions

INTERNATIONAL

(a) The word "whistle" means any sound signalling appliance capable of producing the prescribed blasts and which complies with the specifications in Annex III to these Regulations.

INLAND

(a) The word "whistle" means any sound signaling appliance capable of producing the prescribed blasts and which complies with specifications in Annex III to these Rules.

The term "whistle" is used for devices that sound like whistles or horns, no matter what the frequency or tonal quality. There are no references to "foghorns" in the navigation rules.

INTERNATIONAL

(b) The term "short blast" means a blast of about one second's duration.

(c) The term "prolonged blast" means a blast of from four to six seconds' duration.

INLAND

(b) The term "short blast" means a blast of about 1 second's duration.

(c) The term "prolonged blast" means a blast of from 4 to 6 seconds' duration.

Whistles give coded signals that are made up of one or more "blasts," each of which will last either about one second (short blast) or from four to six seconds (prolonged blast). There are no "long" blasts in the navigation rules.

Rule 33—Equipment for Sound Signals

INTERNATIONAL

(a) A vessel of 12 meters or more in length shall be provided with a whistle and a bell and a vessel of 100 meters or more in length shall, in addition, be provided with a gong, the tone and sound of which cannot be confused with that of the bell. The whistle, bell and gong shall comply with the specifications in Annex III to these Regulations. The bell or gong or both may be replaced by other equipment having the same respective sound characteristics, provided that manual sounding of the prescribed signals shall always be possible.

INLAND

(a) A vessel of 12 meters or more in length shall be provided with a whistle and a bell and a vessel of 100 meters or more in length shall, in addition, be provided with a gong, the tone and sound of which cannot be confused with that of the bell. The whistle, bell and gong shall comply with the specifications in Annex III to these Rules. The bell or gong or both may be replaced by other equipment having the same respective sound characteristics, provided that manual sounding of the prescribed signals shall always be possible.

From the mariner's perspective, the sound-signal equipment requirement is simple for vessels twelve meters or more in length. For the vessel's builder or marine supplier, the requirements become more technical and more complex. Annex III to the Rules contains the technical requirements, and although the International and Inland versions of Rule 33 are substantively identical, the respective versions of Annex III are not. The Inland Annex III was developed from the International Annex III and corrected many of its shortcomings. The mariner should be familiar enough with the basic principles of Annex III to be able to distinguish between different sizes of vessels.

Today's electronics can reproduce almost any sound to any level of amplification, and this, of course, includes the sounds of bells and gongs. These synthesized sounds, often more convenient than the real thing, are preferred by many vessel operators. Rule 33 permits the use of these electronic bells and gongs, but also imposes the requirement of manual sounding. If you hit a transistor with a hammer, you don't produce a very satisfying sound. Therefore, real bells and gongs must also be installed for emergency use.

INTERNATIONAL	INLAND
(b) A vessel of less than 12 meters in length shall not be obliged to carry the sound signalling appliances prescribed in paragraph (a) of this Rule but if she does not, she shall be provided with some other means of making an efficient sound signal.	(b) A vessel of less than 12 meters in length shall not be obliged to carry the sound signaling appliances prescribed in paragraph (a) of this Rule but if she does not, she shall be provided with some other means of making an efficient sound signal.

Boats less than twelve meters in length do not have to carry a specific sound-signal appliance. The old Inland Rules (in force through 1981) contained a specific requirement for small boats, and some authorities may erroneously continue to press those repealed requirements. The current requirement is contained in paragraph (b) of Rule 33 and is for some "means of making an efficient sound signal." An efficient signal is one that can be heard and understood by other vessels in ample time for proper operation of the Steering and Sailing Rules. Clearly, the signal appliance needed for a twelve-meter boat in New York Harbor would not be needed on a three-meter outboard dinghy operated on a small inland lake or in a yacht club's moorings. Depending on the circumstances the requirement could be met by a lung-powered horn, a portable compressed-gas "air horn," a police whistle, or the enthusiastic use of one's own vocal cords.

Rule 34—Maneuvering and Warning Signals

Rule 34 provides the mariner with coded signals for communicating essential navigation information with other vessels in sight. To adhere to this Rule, therefore, you must maintain a proper lookout. If you did not give a required signal because you did not see another vessel, be sure the reason you did not see it was not that you did not look.

One provision in the Inland (only) Rule 34 applies all the time, whether in sight of another vessel or not. That provision requires power-driven vessels to signal when leaving a berth or dock.

Rule 34 is one of the few areas in the navigation rules where the requirements of the International Rules and Inland Rules are so different that each version must be discussed separately. Maneuvering signals are one of the major areas of difference between the two sets of Rules and may well be the most significant difference. Although the basic International and Inland maneuvering signals bear no resemblance to each other, several Rule 34 provisions are the same. Paragraphs (d)/doubt signal, (e)/bend signal, and (f)/whistle separation, are identical.

What is the basic difference between the two? The International Rule maneuvering signals are often said to be signals of *action:* I *am turning* right. The Inland Rule signals, on the other hand, communicate not what you are doing now but what you intend to do; they are signals of *intent:* I *plan* to leave you to port. Your Inland maneuvering signal is not a statement, but rather a question, or perhaps more exactly a proposition. You propose your intention to the other vessel—"I intend such-and-such a maneuver, unless you have any objection." You wait for a definite response before acting, for the other vessel has veto power. More on that later.

INTERNATIONAL

(a) When vessels are in sight of one another, a power-driven vessel underway, when maneuvering as authorized or required by these Rules, shall indicate that maneuver by the following signals on her whistle:

—one short blast to mean "I am altering my course to starboard";

—two short blasts to mean "I am altering my course to port";

—three short blasts to mean "I am operating astern propulsion".

Paragraphs (a) and (b) present the basic maneuvering signals: paragraph (a) the whistle signals, and paragraph (b) the corresponding light signals.

The International Rule requirements apply to power-driven vessels in sight of another vessel (power-driven or not) when maneuvering as authorized or required by the Rules. In good visibility you may be able to see another vessel ten to twenty miles away, but you need not give signals for such long ranges because the other vessel wouldn't hear you anyhow. On even the largest vessels, the required range of whistles is only two miles. On smaller vessels, the required range is much less (see Annex III).

Second, a maneuver made at very long range will not likely be one "authorized or required" by the Rules. A maneuver made to get you to your destination or to avoid a buoy or other hazard, for example, is not one that need be signaled to others in sight. When vessels get close enough together to be thinking of risk of collision, then signals must be given. When a "shall not impede" situation exists, whistle signals should be given even earlier because the vessel required not to impede the passage of a large power-driven vessel needs to know the large vessel's course changes in order to keep well clear before risk of collision arises.

If you are relatively close to another vessel and find that you must execute a maneuver not explicitly "authorized or required" by the Rules (say, to avoid running aground or into a buoy), then you would go ahead and signal that maneuver so as not to catch the other vessel by surprise.

International paragraph (a) requires signals for three maneuvers: right turn, left turn, and astern propulsion. The right or left turns may be the maneuvers used by a give-way vessel to keep out of the way or by a stand-on vessel when it becomes apparent that the give-way vessel is not taking appropriate action or when collision cannot be avoided by the action of the give-way vessel alone. The turns may be made by two vessels, both of which are directed to keep out of the way, for example, in head-on situations. Remember that Rule 8 normally requires course changes to be large enough to be readily apparent.

The third maneuver is "operating astern propulsion." This is not the same as "proceeding astern." You may be moving forward or astern or be stopped when your astern propulsion is engaged. The state of the machinery, not motion through the water, constitutes the distinction here.

INTERNATIONAL

(b) Any vessel may supplement the whistle signals prescribed in paragraph (a) of this Rule by light signals, repeated as appropriate, whilst the maneuver is being carried out:

(i) these light signals shall have the following significance:

—one flash to mean "I am altering my course to starboard";

—two flashes to mean "I am altering my course to port";

—three flashes to mean "I am operating astern propulsion";

(ii) the duration of each flash shall be about one second, the interval between flashes shall be about one second, and the interval between successive signals shall be not less than ten seconds;

(iii) the light used for this signal shall, if fitted, be an all-round white light, visible at a minimum range of 5 miles, and shall comply with the provisions of Annex I to these Regulations.

The International version of paragraph (b) adds supplemental light signals to the paragraph (a) sound signals. They are the same as the sound signals, except they are given with light, and although the sound signals *must* be made, the light signals are optional. The sound signals are given only once per maneuver, but the light signals may be repeated. The light and whistle need not be synchronized. Light signals may also be used to supplement the paragraph (d) doubt signal but not the paragraph (c) overtaking signals.

INTERNATIONAL

(c) When in sight of one another in a narrow channel or fairway:

(i) a vessel intending to overtake another shall in compliance with Rule 9(e)(i) indicate her intention by the following signals on her whistle:

—two prolonged blasts followed by one short blast to mean "I intend to overtake you on your starboard side";

—two prolonged blasts followed by two short blasts to mean "I intend to overtake you on your port side."

(ii) the vessel about to be overtaken when acting in accordance with Rule 9(e)(i) shall indicate her agreement by the following signal on her whistle:

—one prolonged, one short, one prolonged and one short blast, in that order.

Whistle signals are sounded in overtaking maneuvers, by both the overtaking vessel and the overtaken. The International paragraph (c) requirements for these signals, however, apply *only* in those situations where one vessel is overtaking another in a narrow channel *and* the overtaken vessel must maneuver to allow the other to pass. All of the requirements for this overtaking action are in Rule 9(e), but the description of the signals is in Rule 34. Both must be read together. The signal of agreement for the over-taken vessel is provided in Rule 34(c), which gives no signal for disagreement. Rule 9(e), however, says such disagreement (or doubt) may be signaled by the Rule 34(d) doubt signal, five or more short blasts.

INLAND

(a) When power-driven vessels are in sight of one another and meeting or crossing at a distance within half a mile of each other, each vessel underway, when maneuvering as authorized or required by these Rules:

(i) shall indicate that maneuver by the following signals on her whistle: one short blast to mean "I intend to leave you on my port side"; two short blasts to mean "I intend to leave you on my starboard side"; and three short blasts to mean "I am operating astern pro-pulsion."

(ii) upon hearing the one or two blast signal of the other shall, if in agreement, sound the same whistle signal and take the steps necessary to effect a safe passing. If, however, from any cause, the vessel doubts the safety of the proposed maneu-ver, she shall sound the danger sig-nal specified in paragraph (d) of this Rule and each vessel shall take appropriate precautionary action until a safe passing agreement is made.

We have been talking about the first three paragraphs of the International Rule 34. The Inland versions are quite different. The

Inland signals of "intent and reply" represent a "discussion" between two vessels that must result in agreement on a course of action before the maneuver can begin.

The maneuver agreed upon will normally conform with action required by the Rules. You should avoid any agreement that involves a departure from the Rules because chances for misunderstanding are great, especially if only whistle signals are used. Nor does local custom justify a departure from the Rules. What is "custom" for one person may be foolishness to another and news to yet another.

The first two paragraphs of Inland Rule 34 apply only to power-driven vessels meeting or crossing *another* power-driven vessel. Power-driven vessels do not give signals if they are in meeting or crossing situations with vessels not power-driven.

Inland signals are given only for vessels in sight, but not for all vessels with whom risk of collision exists. Signals are given only if the two vessels will meet or cross so that their closest distance of approach is less than one-half mile. For larger vessels, the signals are given well before the half mile distance is reached, when the vessels are close enough to hear one another, in ample time for agreement to be reached before the meeting or crossing maneuver begins. The Inland Annex III audibility requirements are the same as the International: two miles for the largest vessels down to one-half mile for vessels twelve to twenty meters long.

The size and speed of vessel, the type of waterway, and the amount of traffic will affect the distance at which maneuvering signals should be started. Smaller and slower vessels will signal at closer distances than larger and faster ones. Vessels approaching each other on open waters or from opposite directions in a river should signal earlier than vessels maneuvering in confined waters.

Vessels maneuvering in areas of heavy congestion have to take special care in signaling. If more than one vessel is close by, there may be confusion as to which is the intended recipient, especially as the signals for meeting and crossing are also those for overtaking. Other vessels, not knowing for whom the signal was intended, may signal an erroneous reply or not reply when they should.

To avoid such confusion in congested waters many mariners simply do not give whistle signals. This is illegal, unless such departure from the Rules is justified by the Rule 2 caveat allowing a departure when "necessary to avoid immediate danger." Paragraph (h) of Inland Rule 34 excuses whistle signals when agreement has been reached over the radiotelephone.

The Inland whistle signals themselves indicate an intention to leave the other vessel on one side or the other, or agreement with the proposed maneuver, or that astern propulsion is being used.

What does the phrase "I intend to leave you on my port [or starboard] side" mean? To leave another vessel means to go away from the other vessel. Leaving a vessel on your port side means that the other vessel is on your port side as you go away.

In meeting situations the other vessel will be on one side before, during, and after the "meeting" and the proper signal will be obvious. When crossing at close to right angles the side on which you leave the other vessel will also be obvious even though the vessel starts out on the opposite side. When two vessels proceeding in the same direction cross at a small angle, however, the side on which each "leaves" the other may not seem to be too clear.

Figure 3 may make some sense of the wording of Inland Rule 34(a)(i) as applied to vessels converging on near-parallel courses. First, the term "leave" can be understood to mean when one vessel starts to draw away from the path of the other vessel. This happens when the vessel crosses the projected track of the other vessel. Before it reaches this point, it is converging on the track of the other vessel, and hence it is not yet "leaving" it. After it reaches this point, it leaves the other vessel on whatever side (port or starboard) the other vessel happens to be on at that time. The reference point is the intersection of the two vessels' track lines; the time for the determination is the respective time that each vessel reaches that reference point. Each vessel leaves the other on the same side—that is, the passing is a port-to-port or starboard-to-starboard, never a port-to-starboard. Each vessel gives the same signal, either one blast or two.

As mentioned, the Inland Rule passing signal is a proposition for a maneuver. The other vessel must answer agreement before the maneuver can proceed. If in agreement, the other vessel responds with the same signal. If not in agreement, the other vessel sounds a signal of five or more short blasts and each vessel then takes "appropriate precautionary action." This would normally

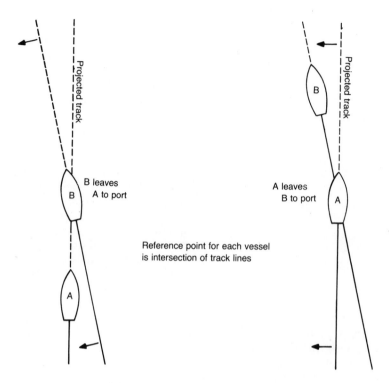

Figure 3—Port-to-port "leaving."

mean to slow or stop and communicate with the other vessel to identify the problem and work out a solution. You may not simply ignore a negative response to your maneuvering signal. Neither may you charge ahead if you get no response at all. You should not assume that the other vessel will always be in agreement. The lack of a reply does not indicate agreement. When you are in doubt, slow down and use your radiotelephone.

INLAND

(b) A vessel may supplement the whistle signals prescribed in paragraph (a) of this Rule by light signals:

INLAND

(i) These signals shall have the following significance: one flash to mean "I intend to leave you on my port side"; two flashes to mean "I intend to leave you on my starboard side"; three flashes to mean "I am operating astern propulsion";

(ii) The duration of each flash shall be about 1 second; and

(iii) The light used for this signal shall, if fitted, be one all-round white or yellow light, visible at a minimum range of 2 miles, synchronized with the whistle, and shall comply with the provisions of Annex I to these Rules.

As with the International Rules, the Inland Rule maneuvering signals may be supplemented by light signals. The Inland light signals, which may be either white or yellow, must be synchronized with the sound signals.

INLAND

(c) When in sight of one another:

(i) a power-driven vessel intending to overtake another power-driven vessel shall indicate her intention by the following signals on her whistle: one short blast to mean "I intend to overtake you on your starboard side"; two short blasts to mean "I intend to overtake you on your port side"; and

(ii) the power-driven vessel about to be overtaken shall, if in agreement, sound a similar sound signal. If in doubt she shall sound the danger signal prescribed in paragraph (d).

Paragraph (c) gives the Inland Rule for overtaking signals. These signals must be given in all overtaking situations involving two power-driven vessels, whether in open waters or confined. The signals are given whether or not the overtaken vessel must act to permit a safe overtaking. The signals for overtaking are the same as for passing—one or two short blasts. Although simpler than the International signals, they are more ambiguous when more than two vessels are in the area.

The overtaken vessel signals its disagreement to the overtaking by giving five or more short blasts. The overtaken vessel may *not* answer a two-blast signal with one blast (or vice versa) to indicate that the overtaking vessel should pass on the other side. If the overtaking vessel hears a doubt signal response, it should propose passing on the other side, wait until later to overtake, or contact the vessel to be overtaken on the radiotelephone.

INTERNATIONAL

(d) When vessels in sight of one another are approaching each other and from any cause either vessel fails to understand the intentions or actions of the other, or is in doubt whether sufficient action is being taken by the other to avoid collision, the vessel in doubt shall immediately indicate such doubt by giving at least five short and rapid blasts on the whistle. Such signal may be supplemented by a light signal of at least five short and rapid flashes.

INLAND

(d) When vessels in sight of one another are approaching each other and from any cause either vessel fails to understand the intentions or actions of the other, or is in doubt whether sufficient action is being taken by the other to avoid collision, the vessel in doubt shall immediately indicate such doubt by giving at least five short and rapid blasts on the whistle. This signal may be supplemented by a light signal of at least five short and rapid flashes.

Paragraphs (d), (e), and (f) of the International and Inland Rule 34 are the same. Paragraph (d) describes the "doubt" signal, also referred to in the Inland Rules as the "danger" signal. The signal is five or more short and rapid blasts, which may be supplemented by a light signal. Give the signal as soon as you are in doubt about the action of another approaching vessel—when you don't know what the other vessel is doing or when you think it is doing the wrong thing.

The signal is designed to give the operators a chance to resolve any confusion or disagreement *early*. Do not wait until you think you are about to crash. It is not intended as a signal to alert crew members to don their life jackets.

INTERNATIONAL

(e) A vessel nearing a bend or an area of a channel or fairway where other vessels may be obscured by an intervening obstruction shall sound one prolonged blast. Such signal shall be answered with a prolonged blast by any approaching vessel that may be within hearing around the bend or behind the intervening obstruction.

INLAND

(e) A vessel nearing a bend or an area of a channel or fairway where other vessels may be obscured by an intervening obstruction shall sound one prolonged blast. This signal shall be answered with a prolonged blast by any approaching vessel that may be within hearing around the bend or behind the intervening obstruction.

Paragraph (e) in both versions of the Rule gives a "blind bend" signal, which you sound when you are about to come around a corner to alert other vessels to watch out for you. Listen for a reply from another vessel that may indeed be approaching from just around the bend.

INTERNATIONAL

(f) If whistles are fitted on a vessel at a distance apart of more than 100 meters, one whistle only shall be used for giving maneuvering and warning signals.

INLAND

(f) If whistles are fitted on a vessel at a distance apart of more than 100 meters, one whistle only shall be used for giving maneuvering and warning signals.

Paragraph (f) of both sets of Rules seeks to avoid double signals. Because sound travels relatively slowly, a single blast sounded simultaneously on two widely separated whistles could sound like two blasts to someone ahead or astern of the signaling vessel.

INLAND

(g) When a power-driven vessel is leaving a dock or berth, she shall sound one prolonged blast.

The International Rule 34 ends here; the Inland version has two more paragraphs. Paragraph (g) provides a signal (the same as paragraph [e]'s blind-bend signal) for vessels getting underway from a dock or berth.

INLAND

(h) A vessel that reaches agreement with another vessel in a meeting, crossing, or overtaking situation by using the radiotelephone as prescribed by the Bridge-to-Bridge Radiotelephone Act (85 Stat. 165; 33 U.S.C. 1207), is not obliged to sound the whistle signals prescribed by this Rule, but may do so. If agreement is not reached, then whistle signals shall be exchanged in a timely manner and shall prevail.

Paragraph (h) says that if you reach a passing agreement on channel 13 of your radiotelephone, you don't have to give whistle signals. It is very important that you speak over the radio with the right vessel, the one you intend to move in relation to. If you're not sure you have reached the right vessel, then you still have to sound whistle signals before executing the maneuver.

Rule 35—Sound Signals in Restricted Visibility

Rule 35 tells us about what are colloquially called "fog" signals. The Rules themselves do not use the term. Restricted visibility, however, can be caused by conditions other than fog. Rule 3 attributed restricted visibility to "fog, mist, falling snow, heavy rainstorms, sandstorms or any other similar causes." In the following pages, we will refer to the signals as "restricted-visibility signals," but when people mention "fog" signals, this is what they are talking about. There are only small differences between the International and Inland versions of this Rule.

INTERNATIONAL
In or near an area of restricted visibility, whether by day or night, the signals prescribed in this Rule shall be used as follows:

INLAND
In or near an area of restricted visibility, whether by day or night, the signals prescribed in this Rule shall be used as follows:

The signals in Rule 35 are used in conjunction with Rule 19 (Conduct of Vessels in Restricted Visibility) and, as in that Rule, apply both in or near an area of restricted visibility, and by day or night. How bad must the visibility become before you have to give the signals? Giving the signals when nobody is close enough to hear them will only dull your hearing and deprive the off-watch of their sleep. Use the signals when you can't see as far as your whistle can be heard. Minimum audibility range is two miles for large ships, but they may be heard three or four miles away depending on the particular whistle and the atmospheric conditions.

INTERNATIONAL
(a) A power-driven vessel making way through the water shall sound at intervals of not more than 2 minutes one prolonged blast.
(b) A power-driven vessel underway but stopped and making no way through the water shall sound at intervals of not more than 2 minutes two prolonged blasts in succession with an interval of about 2 seconds between them.

INLAND
(a) A power-driven vessel making way through the water shall sound at intervals of not more than 2 minutes one prolonged blast.
(b) A power-driven vessel underway but stopped and making no way through the water shall sound at intervals of not more than 2 minutes two prolonged blasts in succession with an interval of about 2 seconds between them.

Paragraphs (a) and (b) give the most common signals, those for ordinary power-driven vessels underway. The signal is one prolonged blast or two, depending on whether the vessel is making way or stopped. If you hear a two-blast signal, don't assume that the vessel making it will stay stopped.

Rule 32 defines a prolonged blast as one lasting from four to six seconds. The required interval between signals is two minutes or less. Don't let a signal repeated every thirty seconds or every minute confuse you. Shorter intervals are desirable when other vessels are near.

INTERNATIONAL

(c) A vessel not under command, a vessel restricted in her ability to maneuver, a vessel constrained by her draft, a sailing vessel, a vessel engaged in fishing and a vessel engaged in towing or pushing another vessel shall, instead of the signals prescribed in paragraphs (a) or (b) of this Rule, sound at intervals of not more than 2 minutes three blasts in succession, namely one prolonged followed by two short blasts.

INLAND

(c) A vessel not under command; a vessel restricted in her ability to maneuver, whether underway or at anchor; a sailing vessel; a vessel engaged in fishing, whether underway or at anchor; and a vessel engaged in towing or pushing another vessel shall, instead of the signals prescribed in paragraphs (a) or (b) of this Rule, sound at intervals of not more than 2 minutes, three blasts in succession; namely, one prolonged followed by two short blasts.

Paragraph (c) gives a third signal for vessels that are likely to be less maneuverable than ordinary power-driven vessels, although Rule 19 does not treat them any differently from ordinary power-driven vessels. Nevertheless, the special signal—one prolonged blast followed by two short—does give other vessels more information. If and when the impaired vessels finally do loom into view, however, the Rules in force change and they may become stand-on vessels.

The impaired vessels covered by paragraph (c) include those not under command, restricted in ability to maneuver, sailing, and engaged in towing or pushing another vessel. The International version also includes vessels constrained by draft (a concept rejected in the Inland Rules).

INTERNATIONAL

(d) A vessel engaged in fishing, when at anchor, and a vessel restricted in her ability to maneuver when carrying out her work at anchor, shall instead of the signals prescribed in paragraph (g) of this Rule sound the signal prescribed in paragraph (c) of this Rule.

Vessels engaged in fishing while anchored and vessels restricted in ability to maneuver while anchored must also sound one prolonged plus two short blasts. This requirement, treated differently in the two versions, is more successful in the International version. The issue is whether the hampered and anchored vessels give both the signal for hampered vessels *and* the paragraph (g)/International or (f)/Inland signal for anchored vessels.

International paragraph (d) tells us to give the paragraph (c) signal instead of the signal for anchored vessels. The Inland version attempts to treat the special case of vessels fishing or restricted in ability to maneuver while also anchored within paragraph (c) rather than adding a separate paragraph. Inland paragraph (c) (like the International version) says to use the one-long, two-short signal, instead of the paragraph (a) and (b) signals, *and also* paragraph (f) signals for anchored vessels. The Inland Rule would seem, then, to require anchored vessels engaged in fishing or restricted in ability to maneuver to give both the paragraph (c) and paragraph (f) signals. To be on the safe side, you had better follow the wording, even though the drafters of the Inland Rules probably intended much the same message as the International version. Few vessels will be affected by this particular provision.

INTERNATIONAL	INLAND
(e) A vessel towed or if more than one vessel is towed the last vessel of the tow, if manned, shall at intervals of not more than 2 minutes sound four blasts in succession, namely one prolonged followed by three short blasts. When practicable, this signal shall be made immediately after the signal made by the towing vessel.	(d) A vessel towed or if more than one vessel is towed the last vessel of the tow, if manned, shall at intervals of not more than 2 minutes sound four blasts in succession; namely, one prolonged followed by three short blasts. When practicable, this signal shall be made immediately after the signal made by the towing vessel.

These identical paragraphs address the signals to be given by barges and other vessels towed *astern*. Unmanned towed vessels do not have to give signals nor would a manned barge if it was not the last vessel in the tow. Nevertheless, the prudent mariner would arrange, if possible, for automatic signals to be given on the last barge of any long tow.

INTERNATIONAL

(f) When a pushing vessel and a vessel being pushed ahead are rigidly connected in a composite unit they shall be regarded as a power-driven vessel and shall give the signals prescribed in paragraphs (a) or (b) of this Rule.

INLAND

(e) When a pushing vessel and a vessel being pushed ahead are rigidly connected in a composite unit they shall be regarded as a power-driven vessel and shall give the signals prescribed in paragraphs (a) or (b) of this Rule.

Paragraph (f/e) is the sound-signal counterpart of Rule 24(b), which requires rigidly connected tug–barge composites to be lighted as a single power-driven vessel. The corresponding Rule 35 provision similarly treats these composite units as ordinary power-driven vessels. Towing vessels that push ahead but are not rigidly connected use the sound signals in paragraph (c), and the barges being pushed ahead do not sound any signals.

INTERNATIONAL

(g) A vessel at anchor shall at intervals of not more than one minute ring the bell rapidly for about 5 seconds. In a vessel of 100 meters or more in length the bell shall be sounded in the forepart of the vessel and immediately after the ringing of the bell the gong shall be sounded rapidly for about 5 seconds in the after part of the vessel. A vessel at anchor may in addition sound three blasts in succession, namely one short, one prolonged and one short blast, to give warning of her position and of the possibility of collision to an approaching vessel.

INLAND

(f) A vessel at anchor shall at intervals of not more than one minute ring the bell rapidly for about 5 seconds. In a vessel of 100 meters or more in length the bell shall be sounded in the forepart of the vessel and immediately after the ringing of the bell the gong shall be sounded rapidly for about 5 seconds in the after part of the vessel. A vessel at anchor may in addition sound three blasts in succession; namely, one short, one prolonged and one short blast, to give warning of her position and of the possibility of collision to an approaching vessel.

The sound signals for anchored vessels in or near areas of restricted visibility are relatively straightforward. All vessels sound their bells, after which larger vessels also sound their gongs. Any vessel may also use a whistle signal. The whistle signal can be heard farther away than the bell and should be used when background noise is high or when another vessel is approaching too rapidly. The whistle signal also gives a better indication of your position.

INTERNATIONAL

(h) A vessel aground shall give the bell signal and if required the gong signal prescribed in paragraph (g) of this Rule and shall, in addition, give three separate and distinct strokes on the bell immediately before and after the rapid ringing of the bell. A vessel aground may in addition sound an appropriate whistle signal.

INLAND

(g) A vessel aground shall give the bell signal and if required the gong signal prescribed in paragraph (f) of this Rule and shall, in addition, give three separate and distinct strokes on the bell immediately before and after the rapid ringing of the bell. A vessel aground may in addition sound an appropriate whistle signal.

The bell and gong signals required for anchored vessels are also required for vessels aground (another form of anchoring), except that the bell signal is modified by the distinctive three rings before and after the usual five seconds of rapid ringing. You are also permitted to give an "appropriate whistle signal." The Defense Mapping Agency's *H.O. 102 International Code of Signals* is full of signals. For example, if you were on a coral reef and knew other vessels were headed your way, you might want to send the Morse code for "U"—two short plus one prolonged blast—to signal, "You are running into danger."

INTERNATIONAL

(i) A vessel of less than 12 meters in length shall not be obliged to give the above-mentioned signals but, if she does not, shall make some other efficient sound signal at intervals of not more than 2 minutes.

INLAND

(h) A vessel of less than 12 meters in length shall not be obliged to give the above-mentioned signals but, if she does not, shall make some other efficient sound signal at intervals of not more than 2 minutes.

International paragraph (i) and Inland paragraph (h) exempt small vessels from making the Rule 35 sound signals, but only on the condition that they give some other signal that can be understood (as coming from a small vessel) and heard early enough to prevent a collision. Any alternative signal must be repeated every two minutes or less, the same as for the prescribed signals. Note that this exemption dovetails with the Rule 33(b) provision saying that vessels less than twelve meters need not carry sound-signal appliances meeting the technical specifications of Annex III.

INTERNATIONAL

(j) A pilot vessel when engaged on pilotage duty may in addition to the signals prescribed in paragraphs (a), (b) or (g) of this Rule sound an identity signal consisting of four short blasts.

INLAND

(i) A pilot vessel when engaged on pilotage duty may in addition to the signals prescribed in paragraphs (a), (b) or (f) of this Rule sound an identity signal consisting of four short blasts.

Pilot vessels have their own whistle signal for restricted visibility. It is *four* short blasts. Count them. The doubt signal described in Rule 34(d) is *five* or more short blasts and is only for use between vessels in sight of each other. It is possible, however, for both signals to be heard in the same area; Rule 35 requirements apply in or near an area of restricted visibility, and, unless the visibility is zero, vessels will come into sight of each other as they get close. Remember, *four* short blasts signal a pilot vessel.

INLAND

(j) The following vessels shall not be required to sound signals as prescribed in paragraph (f) of this Rule when anchored in a special anchorage area designated by the Secretary:

(i) a vessel of less than 20 meters in length; and

(ii) a barge, canal boat, scow, or other nondescript craft.

The Inland version of Rule 35 contains this additional paragraph covering signals in designated "special anchorage areas." A list of these areas is contained in Title 33 of the Code of Federal Regulations, Part 110. About a hundred of these areas are scattered around the country. Small vessels and unpowered vessels normally towed need not give sound signals if they are anchored in one of these places.

Rule 36—Signals to Attract Attention

INTERNATIONAL

If necessary to attract the attention of another vessel, any vessel may make light or sound signals that cannot be mistaken for any signal authorized elsewhere in these Rules, or may direct the beam of her searchlight in the direction of the danger, in such a way as not to embarrass any vessel. Any light to attract the attention of another vessel shall be such that it cannot be mistaken for any aid to navigation. For the purpose of this Rule the use of high intensity intermittent or revolving lights, such as strobe lights, shall be avoided.

INLAND

If necessary to attract the attention of another vessel, any vessel may make light or sound signals that cannot be mistaken for any signal authorized elsewhere in these Rules, or may direct the beam of her searchlight in the direction of the danger, in such a way as not to embarrass any vessel.

What do you do when your radio is broken or the other vessel doesn't have a radio? Rule 36 makes one suggestion, but mostly it tells you what you can't do to attract attention.

If you want to warn another vessel about danger, if you have a searchlight, and if it is dark, then you just direct your beam toward the dangerous area, being careful not to shine your light in others' faces (or you will embarrass them, not to mention making it difficult for them to see anything but spots).

The International version adds that you must not use a signal that could be mistaken for an aid to navigation. This prohibition aims to stop the use of flash tubes or "strobe lights" to attract attention. These lights have often been used by commercial fishing vessels and some recreational vessels to warn other vessels away. Such use is not legal on International Rules waters except under Rule 2 when a need to avoid *immediate* danger would justify a departure from Rule 36.

Even under Inland Rule 36, which does not distinctly prohibit strobe lights, you may not use to attract attention a strobe light that has the flash characteristic described for distress in Rule 37, that is, fifty to seventy flashes per minute.

Rule 37—Distress Signals

INTERNATIONAL

When a vessel is in distress and requires assistance she shall use or exhibit the signals described in Annex IV to these Regulations.

INLAND

When a vessel is in distress and requires assistance she shall use or exhibit the signals described in Annex IV to these Rules.

If your vessel is in distress and in need of assistance, you must use one or more of the signals listed in Annex IV. The distress signals themselves are not contained in Rule 37 because they do not prevent collisions.

All of the distress signals in the International Annex IV are in the Inland Annex IV. The Inland version adds one more distress signal—a high-intensity (about one flash per second) white flashing light or "strobe light."

Annex IV contains more rules relating to distress signals, and these will be discussed under that annex.

PART E

Exemptions

Rule 38—Exemptions

INTERNATIONAL

Any vessel (or class of vessels) provided that she complies with the requirements of the International Regulations for Preventing Collisions at Sea, 1960, the keel of which is laid or which is at a corresponding stage of construction before the entry into force of these Regulations may be exempted from compliance therewith as follows:

INLAND

Any vessel or class of vessels, the keel of which is laid or which is at a corresponding stage of construction before the date of enactment of this Act, provided that she complies with the requirements of—

(a) The Act of June 7, 1897 (30 Stat. 96), as amended (33 U.S.C. 154–232) for vessels navigating the waters subject to that statute;

(b) Section 4233 of the Revised Statutes (33 U.S.C. 301–356) for vessels navigating the waters subject to that statute;

(c) The Act of February 8, 1895 (28 Stat. 645), as amended (33 U.S.C. 241–295) for vessels navigating the waters subject to that statute; or

(d) Sections 3, 4, and 5 of the Act of April 25, 1940 (54 Stat. 163), as amended (46 U.S.C. 526 b, c, and

d) for motorboats navigating the waters subject to that statute; shall be exempted from compliance with the technical Annexes to these Rules as follows:

(a) The installation of lights with ranges prescribed in Rule 22, until four years after the date of entry into force of these Regulations.

(i) the installation of lights with ranges prescribed in Rule 22, until 4 years after the effective date of these Rules, except that vessels of less than 20 meters in length are permanently exempt;

(b) The installation of lights with color specifications as prescribed in Section 7 of Annex I to these Regulations, until four years after the date of entry into force of these Regulations.

(ii) the installation of lights with color specifications as prescribed in Annex I to these Rules, until 4 years after the effective date of these Rules, except that vessels of less than 20 meters in length are permanently exempt;

(c) The repositioning of lights as a result of conversion from Imperial to metric units and rounding off measurement figures, permanent exemption.

(iii) the repositioning of lights as a result of conversion to metric units and rounding off measurement figures, are permanently exempt; and

(d)(i) The repositioning of masthead lights on vessels of less than 150 meters in length, resulting from the prescriptions of Section 3(a) of Annex I to these Regulations, permanent exemption.

(iv) the horizontal repositioning of masthead lights prescribed by Annex I to these Rules:

(ii) The repositioning of masthead lights on vessels of 150 meters or more in length, resulting from the prescriptions of Section 3(a) of Annex I to these Regulations, until nine years after the date of entry into force of these Regulations.

(1) on vessels of less than 150 meters in length, permanent exemption.

(2) on vessels of 150 meters or more in length, until 9 years after the effective date of these Rules.

(e) The repositioning of masthead lights resulting from the prescriptions of Section 2(b) of Annex I to

(v) the restructuring or repositioning of all lights to meet the prescriptions of Annex I to these

these Regulations, until nine years after the date of entry into force of these Regulations.

(f) The repositioning of sidelights resulting from the prescriptions of Sections 2(g) and 3(b) of Annex I to these Regulations, until nine years after the date of entry into force of these Regulations.

(g) The requirements for sound signal appliances prescribed in Annex III to these Regulations, until nine years after the date of entry into force of these Regulations.

(h) The repositioning of all-round lights resulting from the prescription of Section 9(b) of Annex I to these Regulations, permanent exemption.

Rules, until 9 years after the effective date of these Rules;

(vi) power-driven vessels of 12 meters or more but less than 20 meters in length are permanently exempt from the provisions of Rule 23(a)(i) and 23(a)(iv) provided that, in place of these lights, the vessel exhibits a white light aft visible all round the horizon; and

(vii) the requirements for sound signal appliances prescribed in Annex III to these Rules, until 9 years after the effective date of these Rules.

The International and Inland navigation rules now in effect are relatively new. The International Rules (International Regulations for Preventing Collisions at Sea, 1972) became effective on 15 July 1977, and the Inland Rules went into effect (except on the Great Lakes) on 24 December 1981. Each set contains specifications for the performance and positioning of navigation lights and sound-signal appliances, technical details that were not in the previous rules. Because it would have been unreasonable to require vessels to replace navigation lights, sound-signal appliances, and perhaps even supporting structure as soon as the new rules came into effect, Rule 38 allows mariners to make changes over time and excuses them from some changes entirely.

Rule 38 begins by explaining which vessels are eligible for exemptions. For a vessel to be exempt, its construction must have been started before 15 July 1977 (International) or 24 December 1980 (the date of *enactment* of the Inland Rules was one year before the *effective* date). In addition, the vessel must have been in compliance with the 1960 International Regulations or with the old inland, western rivers, or Great Lakes rules or the Motorboat Act of 1940. Vessels built since 15 July 1977 (International) and 24 December 1980 (Inland) are *not* eligible for any exemptions.

The numbering of paragraphs in Inland Rule 38 is somewhat confusing. The paragraphs labeled (i), (ii), (iii), and so forth are not subsections of the paragraph labeled (d), but rather follow from and are on equal footing with the unnumbered introductory paragraph that contains (a), (b), (c), and (d). The final sentence of the introductory paragraph (that is, the last sentence in [d]), which ends with "shall be exempted from compliance with the technical Annexes to these Rules as follows," is misleading because it mentions only exemptions from the "technical Annexes." Paragraph (i) of Rule 38 gives exemptions to provisions of Rule 22, and paragraph (vi) gives exemptions to provisions of Rule 23.

The permanent exemption for conversion to metric units refers to old requirements that were retained but were converted to the metric system of measurement. For example, an old requirement might have called for six feet of spacing between lights. The new requirement would round off the measurement to two meters, a little more than six feet. If your lights were separated by six feet, you would be exempt from having to adjust them to meet the exact metric requirement.

There are other differences between the International and Inland versions of Rule 38 besides the date from which the clock begins to run. The Inland exemptions are broader in scope, for example, and small vessels with Inland Rule lighting are permanently exempt from virtually all changes.

Note that the Inland Rule date is the date of "enactment" (when the Inland Rules were signed into law) rather than the date the Rules became effective. This is probably the result of another quirk in the drafting of those Rules rather than the intent. Relaxed enforcement may be used to ease the burden on affected vessels (built between the two dates), since the technical annexes were not published before the effective date.

Rule 38 is addressed more to the vessel owner than to the crew, as it is the owner who exercises control over vessel modifications and equipment. Rule 38 also implies a warning for the mariner, though. Not everything on the water will conform exactly to the new requirements, and the mariner should be alert for the unusual and unexpected.

ANNEX I

Positioning and Technical Details of Lights and Shapes

Annex I tells us how navigation lights have to perform and where they must be located. It doesn't say what lights to display—the Rules do that. Annex I also describes the size, color, and spacing for day shapes.

The International Annex I came first. The Inland Annex I is very similar but many specifications differ to suit the particular conditions of inland waterways.

The Inland Annex I is a regulation. It is marked with "section" symbols (§) and numbers beginning with "84," because it is Part 84, Title 33 of the Code of Federal Regulations. The other four Inland annexes are Parts 85, 86, 87, and 88.

1. Definition
The term "height above the hull" means height above the uppermost continuous deck. This height shall be measured from the position vertically beneath the location of the light.

§ 84.01 Definitions
(a) The term "height above the hull" means height above the uppermost continuous deck. This height shall be measured from the position vertically beneath the location of the light.

Annex I normally expresses the vertical position of lights as "height above the hull." This is measured from the highest deck (directly below the light, in the center of the vessel if the light is in the center) that extends over the length of the ship or nearly so.

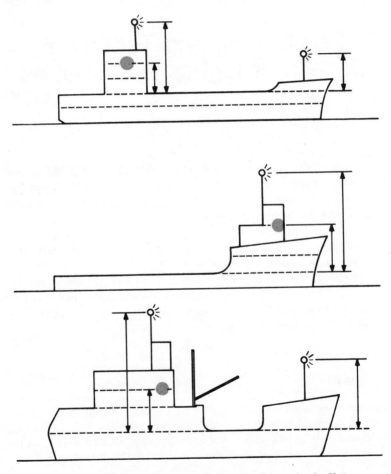

Figure 4—Measurement of "height above the hull."

INLAND
(b) The term "practical cut-off" means, for vessels 20 meters or more in length, 12.5 percent of the minimum luminous intensity (Table 84.15(b)) corresponding to the greatest range of visibility for which the requirements of Annex I are met.

Many navigation lights give you a rough idea of the orientation of a vessel, depending on whether you see a green sidelight, a red sidelight, masthead lights, or whatever. In other words, you know that, in relation to the observed vessel, you are within a certain horizontal sector. The term "horizontal sector" refers to the arc around the horizon through which each navigation light is supposed to shine. When you move from inside to outside the sector, the light "cuts off."

In theory, a light should have full intensity everywhere inside the sector and be absolutely dark outside the sector. In practice this level of performance hasn't yet been achieved using common technology and at a reasonable cost. Cut-off isn't instant and complete. Some light, undesirably because it affects perceptions of orientation, leaks outside of the sector. Annex I requires that "practical cut-off" be a reduction of the light intensity down to below 12.5 percent of what must be shown inside the sector. This is for lights designed for vessels twenty meters or longer.

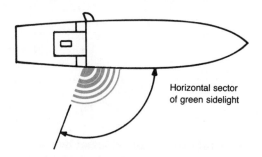

Figure 5—Example of a "horizontal sector."

The term "practical cut-off" is defined only in Inland Annex I, but the U.S. Coast Guard is using the same definition in its International Rules navigation light approval program for inspected vessels. The United States does not define practical cut-off for lights designed for vessels less than twenty meters, although a number of European countries do. These countries also certify or approve their own small-vessel navigation lights as meeting the International Annex I specifications.

The Inland Rule definition for practical cut-off is worded so that a navigation light may be used on a vessel smaller than the size class for which it was designed. The language "corresponding to the greatest range of visibility for which the requirements of Annex I are met" results in a single practical cut-off for any particular light rather than a different practical cut-off for each class of vessel.

For example, a masthead light designed for vessels twenty to fifty meters long has a minimum required range of five miles (see Rule 22). Annex I requires an intensity of at least fifty-two candelas for a five-mile light (see §84.15). A six-mile light needs ninety-four candelas, almost twice as bright; a three-mile light, twelve candelas. We'll say in our example that the actual "five-mile" light has an intensity of sixty-three candelas in the sector and is being used on a boat eighteen meters long. The practical cut-off in this case would be 12.5 percent of *fifty-two* candelas or 6.5. We don't base practical cut-off on the sixty-three candela actual intensity or on the twelve-candela minimum required intensity for the size vessel (eighteen meters) on which the light is installed.

INLAND

(c) The term "Rule" or "Rules" means the Inland Navigation Rules contained in Sec. 2 of the Inland Navigational Rules Act of 1980 (Pub. L. 96–591, 94 Stat. 3415, 33 U.S.C. 2001, December 24, 1980) as amended.

The Inland navigation rules were enacted by Congress through legislation, whereas the annexes were enacted by the Coast Guard as regulations.

INTERNATIONAL

2. Vertical positioning and spacing of lights

(a) On a power-driven vessel of 20 meters or more in length the masthead lights shall be placed as follows:

(i) the forward masthead light, or if only one masthead light is carried, then that light, at a height above the hull of not less than 6 meters, and, if the breadth of the vessel exceeds 6 meters, then at a height above the hull not less than such breadth, so however that the light need not be placed at a greater height above the hull than 12 meters;

(ii) when two masthead lights are carried the after one shall be at least 4.5 meters vertically higher than the forward one.

(b) The vertical separation of masthead lights of power-driven vessels shall be such that in all normal conditions of trim the after light will be seen over and separate from the forward light at a distance of 1000 meters from the stem when viewed from sea level.

INLAND

§ 84.03 Vertical positioning and spacing of lights

(a) On a power-driven vessel of 20 meters or more in length the masthead lights shall be placed as follows:

(1) The forward masthead light, or if only one masthead light is carried, then that light, at a height above the hull of not less than 5 meters, and, if the breadth of the vessel exceeds 5 meters, then at a height above the hull not less than such breadth, so however that the light need not be placed at a greater height above the hull than 8 meters;

(2) When two masthead lights are carried the after one shall be at least 2 meters vertically higher than the forward one.

(b) The vertical separation of masthead lights of power-driven vessels shall be such that in all normal conditions of trim the after light will be seen over and separate from the forward light at a distance of 1000 meters from the stem when viewed from sea level.

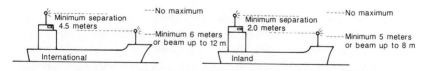

Figure 6—Vertical placement of masthead lights: vessels 20 meters or more in length.

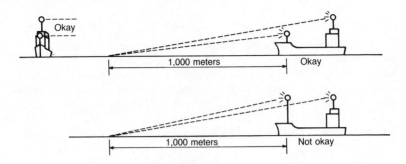

Figure 7—Vertical placement of masthead lights: sight picture.

INTERNATIONAL

(c) The masthead light of a power-driven vessel of 12 meters but less than 20 meters in length shall be placed at a height above the gunwale of not less than 2.5 meters.

(d) A power-driven vessel of less than 12 meters in length may carry the uppermost light at a height of less than 2.5 meters above the gunwale. When however, a masthead light is carried in addition to sidelights and a sternlight or the all-round light prescribed in rule 23(c)(i) is carried in addition to sidelights, then such masthead light or all-round light shall be carried at least 1 meter higher than the sidelights.

INLAND

(c) The masthead light of a power-driven vessel of 12 meters but less than 20 meters in length shall be placed at a height above the gunwale of not less than 2.5 meters.

(d) The masthead light, or the all-round light described in Rule 23(c), of a power-driven vessel of less than 12 meters in length shall be carried at least 1 meter higher than the sidelights.

Under International Rule 23, power-driven vessels less than twelve meters long may display the following: (1) sidelights, masthead light, and sternlight; (2) sidelights and all-round light; or (3) an all-round light, depending on boat size, speed, and preference of builder or owner. The Inland Rules permit only the first two options.

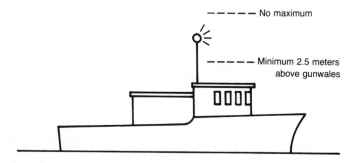

Figure 8—Vertical placement of masthead lights: power-driven vessels 12–20 meters in length.

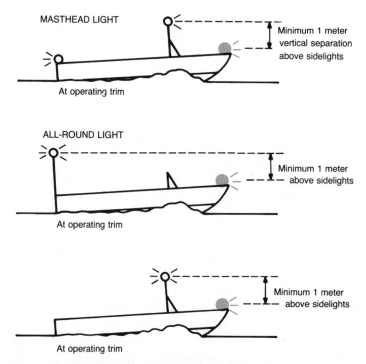

Figure 9—Vertical placement of masthead lights: power-driven vessels less than 12 meters in length.

If sidelights are displayed, the masthead light or all-round light must be at least one meter above the sidelights. The vertical separation is measured at operating trim, which is often different from static trim. Because boat trim may change significantly with speed changes, vertical separation may be decreased substantially (from what deckline-to-light measurement would indicate) if the masthead/all-round light is mounted very far aft of the sidelights. This is especially a problem if the all-round light is mounted all the way aft, as was required by the now-repealed Motorboat Act of 1940, and the sidelights are mounted all the way forward. The all-round light (or masthead light) may now be mounted anywhere from stem to stern. Mounting it horizontally close to the sidelights will minimize the adverse effect of trim changes on vertical separation.

INTERNATIONAL	INLAND
(e) One of the two or three masthead lights prescribed for a power-driven vessel when engaged in towing or pushing another vessel shall be placed in the same position as either the forward masthead light or the after masthead light; provided that if carried on the after-mast, the lowest after masthead light shall be at least 4.5 meters vertically higher than the highest forward masthead light.	(e) One of the two or three masthead lights prescribed for a power-driven vessel when engaged in towing or pushing another vessel shall be placed in the same position as either the forward masthead light or the after masthead light, provided that the lowest after masthead light shall be at least 2 meters vertically higher than the highest forward masthead light.

In most cases, vessels engaged in towing display either one or two masthead lights in addition to the normal one(s) prescribed for ordinary power-driven vessels (see Rules 23 and 24). Although the language in the Rules says two (or three) masthead lights "instead of" an ordinary masthead light, Annex I 2(e)/§84.03(e) makes clear that the Rule 23 masthead light is to be one of the two or three in a vertical row, and paragraph (f)(i) says that of the two or three masthead lights carried in a vertical line for towing, the Rule 23 masthead light must be the highest one.

Vessels fifty meters or longer must carry both forward and after

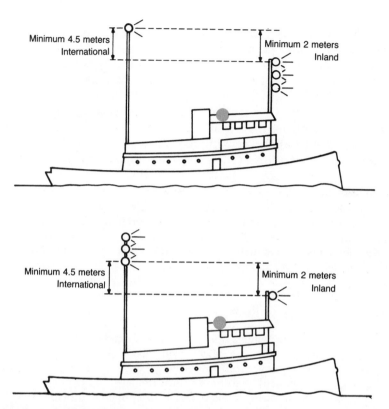

Figure 10—Vertical placement of masthead lights: towing vessels 50 meters or more in length and smaller vessels voluntarily carrying both forward and after masthead lights.

masthead lights (smaller vessels may do so). Vessels carrying both forward and after masthead lights (Rule 23[a]) also carry forward and after masthead lights when towing (Rule 24 [d]). For towing, the additional masthead lights (one, or two if the tow length exceeds two hundred meters) can be carried under either the forward masthead light or the after masthead light. If carried under the forward masthead light, the vertical separation between forward and after masthead lights will be unchanged from the nontowing display. If the additional lights are carried under the after masthead light, the vertical separation between masthead lights on forward and after masts will be reduced. Annex I 2(e)/§84.03(e) requires that at least the minimum vertical separation be maintained between the lowest after masthead light and the forward masthead light. Thus, if you carry your additional masthead lights on the after mast, your ordinary Rule 23 after masthead light must be mounted higher than would otherwise be required by Annex I 2(a)(ii)/§84.03(a)(2). The minimum vertical separation differs between the International (4.5 meters) and Inland (2 meters) Rules.

INTERNATIONAL

(f)(i) The masthead light or lights prescribed in Rule 23(a) shall be so placed as to be above and clear of all other lights and obstructions except as described in subparagraph (ii).

(ii) When it is impracticable to carry the all-round lights prescribed by Rule 27(b)(i) or Rule 28 below the masthead lights, they may be carried above the after masthead light(s) or vertically in between the forward masthead light(s) and after masthead light(s), provided that in the latter case the requirement of Section 3(c) of this Annex shall be complied with.

INLAND

(f)(1) The masthead light or lights prescribed in Rule 23(a) shall be so placed as to be above and clear of all other lights and obstructions except as described in paragraph (f)(2) of this section.

(2) When it is impracticable to carry the all-round lights prescribed in Rule 27(b)(i) below the masthead lights, they may be carried above the after masthead light(s) or vertically in between the forward masthead light(s) and after masthead light(s), provided that in the latter case the requirement of § 84.05(d) shall be complied with.

The Rule 23 masthead lights are considered to be of great importance. As the brightest lights, they function as the reference by which other navigation lights are evaluated. Annex I 2(f)/§84.03(f) therefore requires that they be mounted high and be unobstructed. The exception was added after problems were experienced with all-round lights, which are difficult to see "all-round" if they are mounted below a structure holding up the masthead light. All-round lights may now be placed above masthead lights, but only in the fashion described, which is designed to minimize interference from the masthead lights.

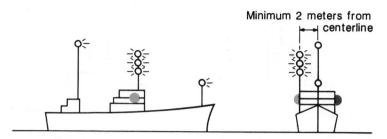

Figure 11—Vertical placement of masthead lights with respect to all-round lights.

The exempted all-round lights are those for vessels restricted in ability to maneuver (Rule 17[b][i]) and for vessels constrained by draft (Rule 28, International only).

When all-round lights are above the after masthead light, they are usually directly above, not because it is required but because it is practical.

The all-round lights can be mounted on a mast or hung from a yardarm.

The exception permitting the display of all-round lights above masthead lights applies only when it is not practicable to mount the all-round lights below the masthead light(s). If practicable, it must be done.

INTERNATIONAL

(g) The sidelights of a power-driven vessel shall be placed at a height above the hull not greater than three quarters of that of the forward masthead light. They shall not be so low as to be interfered with by deck lights.

INLAND

(g) The sidelights of a power-driven vessel shall be placed at least one meter lower than the forward masthead light. They shall not be so low as to be interfered with by deck lights.

The requirement in the International version of this paragraph is modified or supplemented by paragraphs 2(d) and 2(h) of Annex I for vessels less than twelve and twenty meters, respectively.

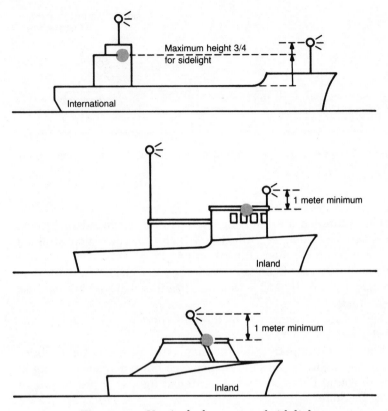

Figure 12—Vertical placement of sidelights.

INTERNATIONAL

(h) The sidelights, if in a combined lantern and carried on a power-driven vessel of less than 20 meters in length, shall be placed not less than 1 meter below the masthead light.

INLAND

(h) [Reserved]

Only the International version has a paragraph (h). A similar Inland requirement would have duplicated the Inland paragraph §84.03(g) requirement. Inland paragraph (h) was reserved so that

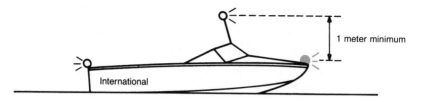

1 meter minimum

International

Figure 13—Vertical placement of sidelights on boats.

corresponding International/Inland paragraphs would be numbered (or lettered) the same.

INTERNATIONAL

(i) When the Rules prescribe two or three lights to be carried in a vertical line, they shall be spaced as follows:

(i) on a vessel of 20 meters in length or more such lights shall be spaced not less than 2 meters apart, and the lowest of these lights shall, except where a towing light is required, be placed at a height of not less than 4 meters above the hull;

(ii) on a vessel of less than 20 meters in length such lights shall be spaced not less than 1 meter apart and the lowest of these lights shall, except where a towing light is required, be placed at a height of not less than 2 meters above the gunwale;

(iii) when three lights are carried they shall be equally spaced.

INLAND

(i) When the Rules prescribe two or three lights to be carried in a vertical line, they shall be spaced as follows:

(1) On a vessel of 20 meters in length or more such lights shall be spaced not less than 1 meter apart, and the lowest of these lights shall, except where a towing light is required, be placed at a height of not less than 4 meters above the hull;

(2) On a vessel of less than 20 meters in length such lights shall be spaced not less than 1 meter apart and the lowest of these lights shall, except where a towing light is required, be placed at a height of not less than 2 meters above the gunwale;

(3) When three lights are carried they shall be equally spaced.

The navigation rules frequently require the display of two or three lights in a vertical line—all-round lights, masthead lights, or lights aimed aft for towing. Annex I prescribes the spacing between the lights and the height above the hull (above the gun-

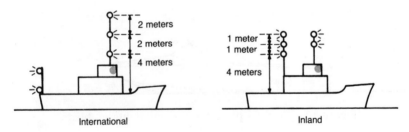

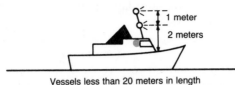

Figure 14—Minimum spacing of lights carried in a vertical line.

wale for smaller vessels) for the lowest light. Vertical height above the "hull" is above the uppermost continuous deck.

When a yellow towing light is displayed above the sternlight or above another towing light, the height-above-the-hull requirements do not apply. The sternlight, of course, is the same one used when not towing and may be placed right on the uppermost continuous deck or even below it. The same principle operates when two towing lights (no sternlight) are displayed in a vertical line (Inland Rules only).

INTERNATIONAL

(j) The lower of the two all-round lights prescribed for a vessel when engaged in fishing shall be at a height above the sidelights not less than twice the distance between the two vertical lights.

(k) The forward anchor light prescribed in Rule 30(a)(i), when two are carried, shall not be less than 4.5 meters above the after one. On

INLAND

(j) The lower of the two all-round lights prescribed for a vessel when engaged in fishing shall be at a height above the sidelights not less than twice the distance between the two vertical lights.

(k) The forward anchor light prescribed in Rule 30(a)(i), when two are carried, shall not be less than 4.5 meters above the after one. On a vessel 50 meters or more in length this forward anchor light shall be placed at a height of not less than 6 meters above the hull.

a vessel 50 meters or more in length this forward anchor light shall be placed at a height of not less than 6 meters above the hull.

Rule 30 requires two anchor lights for vessels fifty meters or longer. Smaller vessels may display two anchor lights but are required to display only one (where it can best be seen).

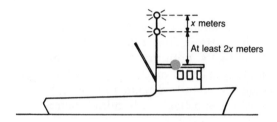

x equals distance between upper and lower all-round lights. For example, if the vertical distance between the two all-round lights is 2 meters, then the lower all-round light must be at least 4 meters above the sidelights.

Figure 15—Vertical spacing of lights on fishing vessels.

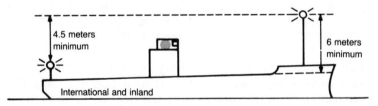

Figure 16—Vertical placement of anchor lights: vessels 50 meters or more in length.

INTERNATIONAL

3. Horizontal positioning and spacing of lights

(a) When two masthead lights are prescribed for a power-driven ves-

INLAND

§ 84.05 Horizontal positioning and spacing of lights

(a) Except as specified in paragraph (b) of this section, when two

sel, the horizontal distance between them shall not be less than one half of the length of the vessel but need not be more than 100 meters. The forward light shall be placed not more than one quarter of the length of the vessel from the stem.

masthead lights are prescribed for a power-driven vessel, the horizontal distance between them shall not be less than one quarter of the length of the vessel but need not be more than 50 meters. The forward light shall be placed not more than one half of the length of the vessel from the stem.

This provision affects primarily vessels fifty meters or longer because smaller vessels do not have to display both forward and after masthead lights. Both the International and the Inland minimum separation is based on the length of the vessel. For power-driven vessels two hundred meters or more, the minimum horizontal separation is a flat one hundred meters for International and fifty meters for Inland.

(b) On power-driven vessels 50 meters but less than 60 meters in length operated on the Western Rivers, the horizontal distance between masthead lights shall not be less than 10 meters.

Western rivers towboats fifty to sixty meters long have a slightly relaxed requirement because their typical house arrangement makes meeting the full one-quarter-length separation more costly.

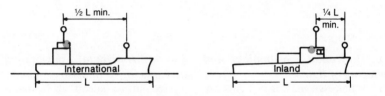

Figure 17—Horizontal spacing of masthead lights.

INTERNATIONAL

(b) On a power-driven vessel of 20 meters or more in length the sidelights shall not be placed in front of the forward masthead lights. They shall be placed at or near the side of the vessel.

(c) When the lights prescribed in Rule 27(b)(i) or Rule 28 are placed vertically between the forward masthead light(s) and the after masthead light(s) these all-round lights shall be placed at a horizontal distance of not less than 2 meters from the fore and aft centerline of the vessel in the athwartship direction.

INLAND

(c) On a power-driven vessel of 20 meters or more in length the sidelights shall not be placed in front of the forward masthead lights. They shall be placed at or near the side of the vessel.

(d) When the lights prescribed in Rule 27(b)(i) are placed vertically between the forward masthead light(s) and the after masthead light(s) these all-round lights shall be placed at a horizontal distance of not less than 2 meters from the fore and aft centerline of the vessel in the athwartship direction.

This provision is linked with the Annex I 2(f)/§ 84.03(f) requirement and is illustrated with the discussion of that vertical-positioning requirement.

INTERNATIONAL

4. Details of location of direction-indicating lights for fishing vessels, dredgers and vessels engaged in underwater operations
(a) The light indicating the direction of the outlying gear from a vessel engaged in fishing as prescribed in Rule 26(c)(ii) shall be placed at a horizontal distance of not less than 2 meters and not more than 6 meters away from the two all-round red and white lights. This light shall be placed not higher than the all-round white light prescribed in Rule 26(c)(i) and not lower than the sidelights.

INLAND

§ 84.07 Details of location of direction-indicating lights for fishing vessels, dredgers and vessels engaged in underwater operations
(a) The light indicating the direction of the outlying gear from a vessel engaged in fishing as prescribed in Rule 26(c)(ii) shall be placed at a horizontal distance of not less than 2 meters and not more than 6 meters away from the two all-round red and white lights. This light shall be placed not higher than the all-round white light prescribed in Rule 26(c)(i) and not lower than the sidelights.

Rule 26(c) applies to vessels engaged in fishing by means other than trawling. The identifying lights are an all-round red in a vertical line over an all-round white. When outlying fishing gear extends more than 150 meters from the vessel, an all-round white

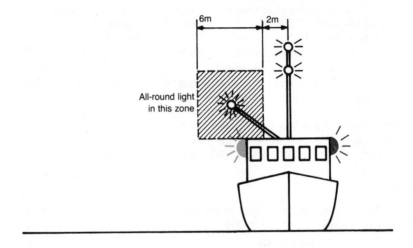

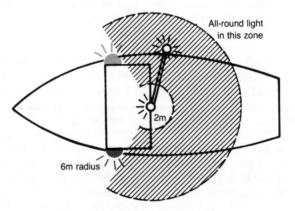

Figure 18—Placement of direction-indicating lights.

light must be displayed in the direction of the gear. This all-round light must be outside a circle with a two-meter radius and inside a circle with a six-meter radius, as viewed from above the vessel and with the center of both circles at the vertical line running through the red and white all-round identifying lights.

INTERNATIONAL

(b) The lights and shapes on a vessel engaged in dredging or underwater operations to indicate the obstructed side and/or the side on which it is safe to pass, as prescribed in Rule 27(d)(i) and (ii), shall be placed at the maximum practical horizontal distance, but in no case less than 2 meters, from the lights or shapes prescribed in Rule 27(b)(i) and (ii). In no case shall the upper of these lights or shapes be at a greater height than the lower of the three lights or shapes prescribed in Rule 27(b)(i) and (ii).

INLAND

(b) The lights and shapes on a vessel engaged in dredging or underwater operations to indicate the obstructed side and/or the side on which it is safe to pass, as prescribed in Rule 27(d)(i) and (ii), shall be placed at the maximum practical horizontal distance, but in no case less than 2 meters, from the lights or shapes prescribed in Rule 27(b)(i) and (ii). In no case shall the upper of these lights or shapes be at a greater height than the lower of the three lights or shapes prescribed in Rule 27(b)(i) and (ii).

Rule 27(d) applies to vessels engaged in dredging or underwater operations when their work involves placing an obstruction to one side of the vessel. The vessel displays the 27(b) red-white-red vertical light array to indicate restricted ability to maneuver, the 27(d) red-over-red all-round lights to indicate the side having the obstruction, and green-over-green all-round lights to indicate on which side it is safe to pass.

These Annex I provisions also apply to the corresponding shapes during the day.

INTERNATIONAL

5. Screens for sidelights

The sidelights of vessels of 20 meters or more in length shall be fitted with inboard screens painted matt

INLAND

§ 84.09 Screens

(a) The sidelights of vessels of 20 meters or more in length shall be fitted with mat black inboard

INTERNATIONAL

black, and meeting the require-ments of Section 9 of this Annex. On vessels of less than 20 meters in length the sidelights, if neces-sary to meet the requirements of Section 9 of this Annex, shall be fitted with inboard matt black screens. With a combined lantern, using a single vertical filament and a very narrow division between the green and red sections, external screens need not be fitted.

INLAND

screens and meet the requirements of § 84.17. On vessels of less than 20 meters in length, the sidelights, if necessary to meet the require-ments of § 84.17, shall be fitted with mat black inboard screens. With a combined lantern, using a single vertical filament and a very narrow division between the green and red sections, external screens need not be fitted.

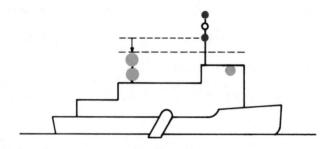

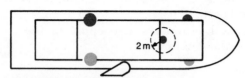

Red and green pairs must be displayed outside 2-meter-radius circle surrounding red-white-red all-round lights, as far away as "practical."

Figure 19—Lights for vessels engaged in dredging or underwater op-erations.

The sidelights on vessels twenty meters or more must be fitted with screens, which are used to keep the light from being seen across the bow (or, in other words, to help the sidelights meet the horizontal sector cut-off requirements of Annex I). In practice, some sidelights meet the cut-off requirements (see Section 9/ §84.17) without screens, but screens must still be fitted. The length of the screens is not specified, so they may be very short if not needed to meet other requirements.

Rule 21 permits vessels less than twenty meters long to combine their sidelights into one lantern using a single filament as the light source (to conserve electricity). Many of these lights are constructed with the green lens and the red lens butted together (often glued together to keep out moisture and to prevent light leaks). Since a vertical filament will be parallel with the lens joint, the transition from green to red will be almost instant rather than gradual, and therefore a screen is not needed.

INLAND

(b) On power-driven vessels less than 12 meters in length constructed after July 31, 1983, the masthead light, or the all-round light described in Rule 23(c) shall be screened to prevent direct illumination of the vessel forward of the operator's position.

The Inland version of the section on screens also contains a provision for screening navigation lights to prevent them from shining down on the boat where the glare would impair the operator's night vision.

INTERNATIONAL	INLAND
6. Shapes	**§ 84.11 Shapes**
(a) Shapes shall be black and of the following sizes:	(a) Shapes shall be black and of the following sizes:
(i) a ball shall have a diameter of not less than 0.6 meter;	(1) A ball shall have a diameter of not less than 0.6 meter;

If a masthead light is fitted, placement far forward is best—little or no screening will be necessary.

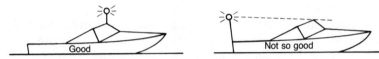

If an all-round light is fitted, the best placement (on an open boat) is over the operator—only moderate screening would be required. Placement of the all-round light farther forward may result in the light shining back in the operator's eyes; placement of the all-round light near the stern may make it impossible to screen in a way that both prevents glare and satisfies the requirement (Annex I, 10/§84.19) that the light shine down to 7.5 degrees below the horizontal.

Figure 20—Screening of masthead/all-round lights on boats.

INTERNATIONAL

(ii) a cone shall have a base diameter of not less than 0.6 meter and a height equal to its diameter;

(iii) a cylinder shall have a diameter of at least 0.6 meter and a height of twice its diameter;

(iv) a diamond shape shall consist of two cones as defined in (ii) above having a common base.

(b) The vertical distance between shapes shall be at least 1.5 meter.

(c) In a vessel of less than 20 meters in length shapes of lesser dimensions but commensurate with the size of the vessel may be used and the distance apart may be correspondingly reduced.

INLAND

(2) A cone shall have a base diameter of not less than 0.6 meter and a height equal to its diameter;

(3) A diamond shape shall consist of two cones (as defined in Paragraph (a)(2) of this section) having a common base.

(b) The vertical distance between shapes shall be at least 1.5 meter.

(c) In a vessel of less than 20 meters in length shapes of lesser dimensions but commensurate with the size of the vessel may be used and the distance apart may be correspondingly reduced.

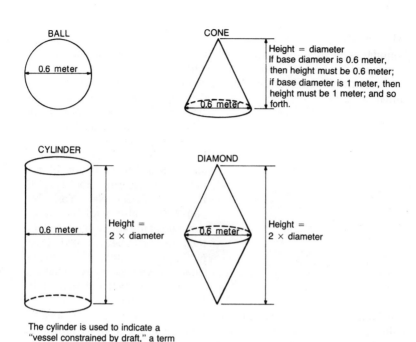

BALL

0.6 meter

CONE

0.6 meter

Height = diameter
If base diameter is 0.6 meter,
then height must be 0.6 meter;
if base diameter is 1 meter, then
height must be 1 meter; and so
forth.

CYLINDER

0.6 meter

Height =
2 × diameter

DIAMOND

0.6 meter

Height =
2 × diameter

The cylinder is used to indicate a
"vessel constrained by draft," a term
used only in the International Rules.

Figure 21—Shapes.

The minimum distance between shapes displayed in a vertical line is one and a half meters. This is measured from the top of one shape to the bottom of the one above it.

The size and spacing of shapes for small vessels may be less than specified in Annex I but not too much less. A vessel nineteen meters long would certainly not be justified in displaying shapes one-half normal size, although an eight-meter vessel would.

INTERNATIONAL

7. Color specification of lights

The chromaticity of all navigation lights shall conform to the following standards, which lie within the

INLAND

§ 84.13 Color specification of lights

(a) The chromaticity of all navigation lights shall conform to the boundaries of the area of the diagram specified for each color by the International Commission on Illumination (CIE).

The boundaries of the area for each color are given by indicating the corner coordinates, which are as follows:

   (i) *White:*
     x 0.525 0.525 0.452 0.310
       0.310 0.443
     y 0.382 0.440 0.440 0.348
       0.283 0.382
   (ii) *Green:*
     x 0.028 0.009 0.300 0.203
     y 0.385 0.723 0.511 0.356
   (iii) *Red:*
     x 0.680 0.660 0.735 0.721
     y 0.320 0.320 0.265 0.259
   (iv) *Yellow:*
     x 0.612 0.618 0.575 0.575
     y 0.382 0.382 0.425 0.406

following standards, which lie within the boundaries of the area of the diagram specified for each color by the International Commission on Illumination (CIE), in the "Colors of Light Signals," which is incorporated by reference. It is Publication CIE No. 2.2. (TC–16), 1975, and is available from the Illumination Engineering Society, 345 East 47th Street, New York, NY 10017. It is also available for inspection at the Office of the Federal Register, Room 8401, 1100 L Street N.W., Washington, D.C. 20408. This incorporation by reference was approved by the Director of the Federal Register.

(b) The boundaries of the area for each color are given by indicating the corner coordinates, which are as follows:

   (1) *White:*
     x 0.525 0.525 0.452 0.310
       0.310 0.443
     y 0.382 0.440 0.440 0.348
       0.283 0.382
   (2) *Green:*
     x 0.028 0.009 0.300 0.203
     y 0.385 0.723 0.511 0.356
   (3) *Red:*
     x 0.680 0.660 0.735 0.721
     y 0.320 0.320 0.265 0.259
   (4) *Yellow:*
     x 0.612 0.618 0.575 0.575
     y 0.382 0.382 0.425 0.406

This section of Annex I is for the manufacturer of navigation lights and their lenses. The numbers given describe the exact shade and hue of green, yellow, red, and white light required. The color measurements are made using the lamp and voltage for which the navigation light is designed.

INTERNATIONAL

8. Intensity of lights

(a) The minimum luminous intensity of lights shall be calculated by using the formula:

$$I = 3.43 \times 10^6 \times T \times D^2 \times K^{-D}$$

where I is luminous intensity in candelas under service conditions,

T is threshold factor 2×10^7 lux,

D is range of visibility (luminous range) of the light in nautical miles,

K is atmospheric transmissivity. For prescribed lights the value of K shall be 0.8, corresponding to a meteorological visibility of approximately 13 nautical miles.

(b) A selection of figures derived from the formula is given in the following table:

Range of visibility (luminous range) of light in nautical miles D	Luminous intensity of light in candelas for K = 0.8 I
1	0.9
2	4.3
3	12
4	27
5	52
6	94

Note: The maximum luminous intensity of navigation lights should be limited to avoid undue glare. This shall not be achieved by a variable control of the luminous intensity.

INLAND

§ 84.15 Intensity of lights

(a) The minimum luminous intensity of lights shall be calculated by using the formula:

$$I = 3.43 \times 10^6 \times T \times D^2 \times K^{-D}$$

where I is luminous intensity in candelas under service conditions,

T is threshold factor 2×10^7 lux,

D is range of visibility (luminous range) of the light in nautical miles,

K is atmospheric transmissivity. For prescribed lights the value of K shall be 0.8, corresponding to a meteorological visibility of approximately 13 nautical miles.

(b) A selection of figures derived from the formula is given in Table 84.15(b):

Table 84.15 (b)

Range of visibility (luminous range) of light in nautical miles D	Minimum luminous intensitiy of light in candelas for K = 0.8 I
1	0.9
2	4.3
3	12
4	27
5	52
6	94

This section gives the minimum required light intensities (measured in candelas) corresponding to ranges of visibility at a standard atmospheric clearness. The required range of visibility for any particular navigation light is given in Rule 22. This section is another used by the manufacturer of navigation lights.

A note at the end of the International version of this section cautions against lights that are so bright that they impair the night vision of the vessel's operator or lookout. Because this is a suggestion ("should") and not a requirement, it is not contained in the regulatory Inland Annex I. The International Rule proscription against a variable voltage control to vary light intensity is not contained in the Inland version because of a different philosophy: a device that would permit an increase in intensity in open water or when the air is not so clear, but which could not be manipulated to reduce the intensity below the minimum required, would be an advantage.

INTERNATIONAL

9. Horizontal sectors

(a)(i) In the forward direction, sidelights as fitted on the vessel shall show the minimum required intensities. The intensities shall decrease to reach practical cut-off between 1 degree and 3 degrees outside the prescribed sectors.

(ii) For sternlights and masthead lights and at 22.5 degrees abaft the beam for sidelights, the minimum required intensities shall be maintained over the arc of the horizon up to 5 degrees within the limits of the sectors prescribed in Rule 21. From 5 degrees within the prescribed sectors the intensity may decrease by 50 percent up to the prescribed limits; it shall decrease steadily to reach practical cut-off at not more than 5 degrees outside the prescribed sectors.

INLAND

§ 84.17 Horizontal sectors

(a)(1) In the forward direction, sidelights as fitted on the vessel shall show the minimum required intensities. The intensities shall decrease to reach practical cut-off between 1 and 3 degrees outside the prescribed sectors.

(2) For sternlights and masthead lights and at 22.5 degrees abaft the beam for sidelights, the minimum required intensities shall be maintained over the arc of the horizon up to 5 degrees within the limits of the sectors prescribed in Rule 21. From 5 degrees within the prescribed sectors the intensity may decrease by 50 percent up to the prescribed limits; it shall decrease steadily to reach practical cut-off at not more than 5 degrees outside the prescribed sectors.

(b) All-round lights shall be so located as not to be obscured by masts, topmasts or structures within angular sectors of more than 6 degrees, except anchor lights prescribed in Rule 30, which need not be placed at an impracticable height above the hull.

(b) All-round lights shall be so located as not to be obscured by masts, topmasts or structures within angular sectors of more than 6 degrees, except anchor lights prescribed in Rule 30, which need not be placed at an impracticable height above the hull, and the all-round white light described in Rule 23(d), which may not be obscured at all.

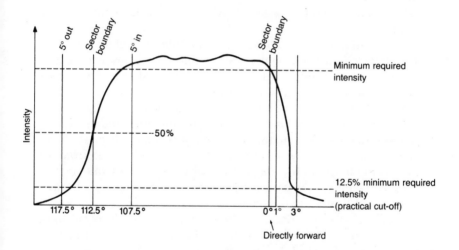

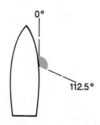

Figure 22—Horizontal sector angles for a sidelight.

A "horizontal sector," defined earlier, refers to the arc around the horizon through which each navigation light is supposed to shine. The sectors are described as being part of a circle divided into 360 degrees and having reference points directly ahead, directly aft, and abeam on each side. The theoretical sectors through which each navigation light is to be seen are given in Rule 21. The actual sectors and corresponding intensities are given here in Annex I. The best way to see how a navigation light conforms to horizontal sector requirements is to plot the light intensity against sector angle. "Practical cut-off" is defined for vessels twenty meters or longer in the first section of the Inland Annex I. The United States uses the same definition for International Rule navigation lights it approves, but other countries define the term in other ways.

All-round lights do not have sector boundaries, but may in some cases have part of their light cut off by interfering masts, topmasts, or structures. All-round lights, such as those that indicate a vessel engaged in fishing or a vessel restricted in ability to maneuver, may be obscured for up to a total of 6 degrees. Anchor lights may be mounted relatively low (especially the after one) and be hidden by the vessel's superstructure through more than 6 degrees of arc. At least one of the two anchor lights should be visible from all around the horizon. If a smaller vessel displays only one anchor light, you should take care to minimize obscuration, even though you are not limited to 6 degrees.

Small vessels are now permitted to display an all-round light in lieu of masthead light and sternlight. If this all-round light is used, it must be mounted where it will not be obscured at all. This latter requirement is implicit in the International version; the masthead light and sternlight the all-round light replaces may not be obscured. (The International Rules before 1983 did not permit the all-round light, and when the Rules were amended, the corresponding Annex I clarifications were overlooked.)

INTERNATIONAL	INLAND
10. Vertical sectors	**§ 84.19 Vertical sectors**
(a) The vertical sectors of electric lights as fitted, with the exception	(a) The vertical sectors of electric lights as fitted, with the exception

of lights on sailing vessels underway shall ensure that:

(i) at least the required minimum intensity is maintained at all angles from 5 degrees above to 5 degrees below the horizontal;
(ii) at least 60 percent of the required minimum intensity is maintained from 7.5 degrees above to 7.5 degrees below the horizontal.
(b) In the case of sailing vessels underway the vertical sectors of electric lights as fitted shall ensure that:
(i) at least the required minimum intensity is maintained at all angles from 5 degrees above to 5 degrees below the horizontal;
(ii) at least 50 percent of the required minimum intensity is maintained from 25 degrees above to 25 degrees below the horizontal.

(c) In the case of lights other than electric these specifications shall be met as closely as possible.

of lights on sailing vessels underway and on unmanned barges, shall ensure that:

(1) At least the required minimum intensity is maintained at all angles from 5 degrees above to 5 degrees below the horizontal;
(2) At least 60 percent of the required minimum intensity is maintained from 7.5 degrees above to 7.5 degrees below the horizontal.
(b) In the case of sailing vessels underway the vertical sectors of electric lights as fitted shall ensure that:
(1) At least the required minimum intensity is maintained at all angles from 5 degrees above to 5 degrees below the horizontal;
(2) At least 50 percent of the required minimum intensity is maintained from 25 degrees above to 25 degrees below the horizontal.
(c) In the case of unmanned barges the minimum required intensity of electric lights as fitted shall be maintained on the horizontal.
(d) In the case of lights other than electric these specifications shall be met as closely as possible.

It is possible to design the lens of a navigation light so that all of the light is focused into a narrow band shining out in a horizontal plane. This would be very efficient and effective as long as the navigation light (and attached vessel) stay level. As soon as the vessel heels or pitches, however, the narrow light beam would shine up into the sky on one side and down into the water on the other. For observers on nearby vessels, the light would disappear.

Navigation lights must therefore shine above and below the horizontal. Sailboats normally heel more than power-driven vessels, so lights for sailing vessels have a greater vertical-dispersion requirement. This special requirement does not, however, apply to sailing vessels that are anchored, for instance; the paragraph (b) technical specifications for sailing vessels apply only to those lights displayed while *underway* (Rule 25 lights).

While power-driven vessels do not normally heel as much as sailing vessels, they often pitch up from their at-rest attitude when moving. If, for example, the masthead light is mounted parallel to the deck and the deck is angled 15 degrees up from horizontal at an operating speed, the light may be pointing too high to comply with the vertical sector requirement. Care must therefore be taken to mount the navigation lights with respect to what is horizontal at operating trim rather than what is horizontal at the dock.

Barges on inland waterways do not normally heel at all, and if unmanned they carry battery-powered navigation lights. So that unwieldy battery packs are not needed, this special class of vessel may use navigation lights with special, very efficient lenses that concentrate the light in a narrow beam around the horizon.

INTERNATIONAL	INLAND
11. Intensity of non-electric lights Non-electric lights shall so far as practicable comply with the minimum intensities, as specified in the Table given in Section 8 of this Annex.	**§ 84.21 Intensity of non-electric lights** Non-electric lights shall so far as practicable comply with the minimum intensities, as specified in the Table given in § 84.15.

Lanterns using oil, kerosene, and such for their light source do not have to meet the intensity requirements of Annex I if not "practicable." Operators must adjust the flame to an optimal level, however, and keep the lenses clean.

INTERNATIONAL	INLAND
12. Maneuvering light Notwithstanding the provisions of paragraph 2(f) of this Annex the maneuvering light described in Rule 34(b) shall be placed in the	**§ 84.23 Maneuvering light** Notwithstanding the provisions of § 84.03(f), the maneuvering light described in Rule 34(b) shall be placed approximately in the same

same fore and aft vertical plane as the masthead light or lights and, where practicable, at a minimum height of 2 meters vertically above the forward masthead light, provided that it shall be carried not less than 2 meters vertically above or below the after masthead light. On a vessel where only one masthead light is carried the maneuvering light, if fitted, shall be carried where it can best be seen, not less than 2 meters vertically apart from the masthead light.

fore and aft vertical plane as the masthead light or lights and, where practicable, at a minimum height of one-half meter vertically above the forward masthead light, provided that it shall be carried not less than one-half meter vertically above or below the after masthead light. On a vessel where only one masthead light is carried the maneuvering light, if fitted, shall be carried where it can best be seen, not less than one-half meter vertically apart from the masthead light.

The maneuvering light is optional and is used to supplement the maneuvering and warning whistle signals of Rule 34. The maneuvering light is an all-round white light (yellow is optional under Inland Rules) having a minimum range of five miles (International) or two miles (Inland). See Rule 34(b)(iii).

INTERNATIONAL

13. Approval
The construction of lights and shapes and the installation of lights on board the vessel shall be to the satisfaction of the appropriate authority of the State whose flag the vessel is entitled to fly.

INLAND

§ 84.25 Approval
[Reserved]

The "appropriate authority" in the United States is the U.S. Coast Guard. The Coast Guard approves navigation lights for use on inspected vessels twenty meters or more in length. For other vessels, the owner/operator is responsible for displaying navigation lights that conform to Annex I requirements.

ANNEX II

Additional Signals for Fishing Vessels Fishing in Close Proximity

1. General

The lights mentioned herein shall, if exhibited in pursuance of Rule 26(d), be placed where they can best be seen. They shall be at least 0.9 meter apart but at a lower level than lights prescribed in Rule 26(b)(i) and (c)(i). The lights shall be visible all around the horizon at a distance of at least 1 mile but at a lesser distance than the lights prescribed by these Rules for fishing vessels.

2. Signals for trawlers

(a) Vessels when engaged in trawling, whether using demersal or pelagic gear, may exhibit:

(i) when shooting their nets: two white lights in a vertical line;

§ 85.1 General

The lights mentioned herein shall, if exhibited in pursuance of Rule 26(d), be placed where they can best be seen. They shall be at least 0.9 meter apart but at a lower level than lights prescribed in Rule 26(b)(i) and (c)(i) contained in the Inland Navigational Rules Act of 1980. The lights shall be visible all around the horizon at a distance of at least 1 mile but at a lesser distance than the lights prescribed by these Rules for fishing vessels.

§ 85.3 Signals for trawlers

(a) Vessels when engaged in trawling, whether using demersal or pelagic gear, may exhibit:

(1) When shooting their nets: two white lights in a vertical line;

(ii) when hauling their nets: one white light over one red light in a vertical line;

INTERNATIONAL

(iii) when the net has come fast upon an obstruction: two red lights in a vertical line.

(b) Each vessel engaged in pair trawling may exhibit:

(i) by night, a searchlight directed forward and in the direction of the other vessel of the pair;

(ii) when shooting or hauling their nets or when their nets have come fast upon an obstruction, the lights prescribed in 2(a) above.

3. Signals for purse seiners

Vessels engaged in fishing with purse seine gear may exhibit two yellow lights in a vertical line. These lights shall flash alternately every second and with equal light and occultation duration. These lights may be exhibited only when the vessel is hampered by its fishing gear.

(2) When hauling their nets: one white light over one red light in a vertical line;

INLAND

(3) When the net has come fast upon an obstruction: two red lights in a vertical line.

(b) Each vessel engaged in pair trawling may exhibit:

(1) By night, a searchlight directed forward and in the direction of the other vessel of the pair;

(2) When shooting or hauling their nets or when their nets have come fast upon an obstruction, the lights prescribed in paragraph (a) above.

§ 85.5 Signals for purse seiners

Vessels engaged in fishing with purse seine gear may exhibit two yellow lights in a vertical line. These lights shall flash alternately every second and with equal light and occultation duration. These lights may be exhibited only when the vessel is hampered by its fishing gear.

The Rule 26 special lights for vessels engaged in fishing are green-over-white all-round lights for trawling and red-over-white for other types of fishing. The lights described in this annex may be used (the display of these lights is voluntary) by vessels fishing in a group or fleet. A vessel engaged in fishing on its own or not near other fishing vessels must *not* use Annex II lights.

The Annex II lights are not intended to prevent collisions between vessels. If they were, they would be described in Rule 26. They are, instead, intended to give more information to those on other fishing vessels so that actions can be coordinated. Depending on the situation, others can assist in the operation, act to avoid interfering with the vessel's nets and lines, or take steps to prevent damage to their own nets and lines.

Annex II lights may not interfere with the visibility or dominance of the Rule 26 navigation lights. They must be lower and not as bright, or else operators of vessels approaching from a distance might see the Annex II lights first and become confused. Under those circumstances, the fishing vessel could conceivably be mistaken for a towing vessel, a pilot vessel, or a vessel aground or not under command.

ANNEX III

Technical Details of Sound Signal Appliances

Annex III is of primary concern to manufacturers of sound-signal appliances and to those who select and install such appliances on vessels. Most mariners will be content to know only that Annex III says big ships have low-pitched whistles and small vessels have high-pitched whistles.

The International Annex III became effective in 1977, and the Inland Annex III was developed in 1981. The Inland version attempts to correct the deficiencies of the International version while retaining the basic format.

Most of Annex III deals with whistles, and much of that concerns sound frequencies and intensity. As was done in Annex I for light, the requirements for sound are given in terms of intensity rather than range of audibility. Sound intensity can be measured accurately and repeatably in a laboratory, while the range of audibility may vary depending on wind, humidity, and other variables, not least of which is the sensitivity of the listener's ear.

1. Whistles

(a) Frequencies and range of audibility

The fundamental frequency of the

Subpart A—Whistles

§ 86.01 Frequencies and range of audibility

The fundamental frequency of the

signal shall lie within the range 70–700 Hz.

The range of audibility of the signal from a whistle shall be determined by those frequencies, which may include the fundamental and/or one or more higher frequencies, which lie within the range 180–700 Hz (± 1 percent) and which provide the sound pressure levels specified in paragraph 1(c) below.

signal shall lie within the range 70–525 Hz. The range of audibility of the signal from a whistle shall be determined by those frequencies, which may include the fundamental and/or one or more higher frequencies, which lie within the frequency ranges and provide the sound pressure levels specified in § 86.05.

By "fundamental frequencies," we refer to the frequency underlying all other frequencies in a note, for sounds are made up of a series of tones superimposed on each other. What a person hears as one note is really a tone of one frequency, plus a tone of two times that frequency, plus a tone of three times that frequency, and so on. The first frequency, the lowest one and the one that determines the overall tone of the sound, is called the fundamental frequency. The higher frequencies, multiples of the fundamental frequency, are called harmonics. The intensity of each harmonic frequency will vary depending on the physical qualities of the whistle (or instrument) producing the note, and this variation determines the *quality* of the note (how "rich" it sounds, how pleasant to the ear).

INTERNATIONAL

(b) Limits of fundamental frequencies

To ensure a wide variety of whistle characteristics, the fundamental frequency of a whistle shall be between the following limits:

(i) 70–200 Hz, for a vessel 200 meters or more in length;

(ii) 130–350 Hz, for a vessel 75 meters but less than 200 meters in length;

INLAND

§ 86.03 Limits of fundamental frequencies

To ensure a wide variety of whistle characteristics, the fundamental frequency of a whistle shall be between the following limits:

(a) 70–200 Hz, for a vessel 200 meters or more in length;

(b) 130–350 Hz, for a vessel 75 meters but less than 200 meters in length;

(iii) 250–700 Hz, for a vessel less than 75 meters in length.

(c) 250–525 Hz, for a vessel less than 75 meters in length.

Baritone whistles belong on large ships and high-pitched whistles belong on small vessels. Annex III divides vessels into three size ranges and gives each a range of fundamental frequencies, although the ranges overlap. Vessels smaller than twelve meters are not covered by Annex III and so they may be considered a fourth size and range, but their whistles (if carried) may have any fundamental frequency. The upper frequency limit for vessels less than seventy-five meters long is 700 Hertz (Hz, that is, cycles per second) for the International Rules and 525 Hz for the Inland Rules. The U.S. Coast Guard thought that whistles with fundamental frequencies higher than 525 Hz were too squeaky for vessels twelve meters or longer. The standard hand-portable "freon" air horn has a fundamental frequency between 500 and 525 Hz. The tiny air horns having higher fundamental frequencies are usually sold to people to scare away robbers and other assorted assailants, but even these may be used on vessels less than twelve meters in length.

INTERNATIONAL

(c) Sound signal intensity and range of audibility

A whistle fitted in a vessel shall provide, in the direction of maximum intensity of the whistle and at a distance of 1 meter from it, a sound pressure level in at least one ⅓-octave band within the range of frequencies 180–700 Hz (± 1 percent) of not less than the appropriate figure given in the table below.

INLAND

§ 86.05 Sound signal intensity and range of audibility

A whistle on a vessel shall provide, in the direction of the forward axis of the whistle and at a distance of 1 meter from it, a sound pressure level in at least one ⅓-octave band of not less than the appropriate figure given in Table 86.05 within the following frequency ranges (± 1 percent):

(a) 130–1200 Hz, for a vessel 75 meters or more in length;

INTERNATIONAL

INLAND

(b) 250–1600 Hz, for a vessel 20 meters but less than 75 meters in length;

(c) 250–2100 Hz, for a vessel 12 meters but less than 20 meters in length.

The range of audibility in the table below is for information and is approximately the range at which a whistle may be heard on its forward axis with 90 percent probability in conditions of still air on board a vessel having average background noise level at the listening posts (taken to be 68 dB in the octave band centered on 250 Hz and 63 dB in the octave band centered on 500 Hz).

In practice the range at which a whistle may be heard is extremely variable and depends critically on weather conditions; the values given can be regarded as typical but under conditions of strong wind or high ambient noise level at the listening post the range may be much reduced.

NOTE. The range of audibility in the table below is for information and is approximately the range at which a whistle may usually be heard on its forward axis in conditions of still air on board a vessel having average background noise level at the listening posts (taken to be 68 dB in the octave band centered on 250 Hz and 63 dB in the octave band centered on 500 Hz).

In practice the range at which a whistle may be heard is extremely variable and depends critically on weather conditions; the values given can be regarded as typical but under conditions of strong wind or high ambient noise level at the listening post the range may be much reduced.

INTERNATIONAL

Length of vessel in meters	$\frac{1}{3}$ octave band level at 1 meter in dB referred to $2 \times 10^{-5} N/m^2$	Audibility range in nautical miles
200 or more	143	2
75 but less than 200	138	1.5
20 but less than 75	130	1
Less than 20	120	0.5

INLAND Table 86.05

Length of vessel in meters	Fundamental frequency range (Hz)	For measured frequencies (Hz)	⅓ octave band level at 1 meter in dB referred to 2×10^{-5} N/m²	Audibility range in nautical miles
200 or more	70–200	130–180 180–250 250–1200	140 143 140	2
75 but less than 200	130–350	130–180 180–250 250–1200	140 138 134	1.5
20 but less than 75	250–525	250–450 450–800 800–1600	130 125 121	1.0
12 but less than 20	250–525	250–450 450–800 800–2100	120 115 111	0.5

The paragraph specifying sound-signal intensity for whistles is the heart of Annex III. The intensities presented in the table of this paragraph are the minimum intensities aimed in the direction of travel—forward. The International version says "in the direction of maximum intensity of the whistle," which in the case of a whistle with one horn will be directly forward. If the whistle has two or more horns, however, the maximum intensity may very well be off to one side or to both sides. The intensity directly forward may be less than the maximum and even less than the minimum specified while still meeting the letter of the requirement.

The Inland version says "in the direction of the forward axis of the whistle." The forward axis is specified by the whistle manufacturer, and the whistle must be mounted on the vessel with the forward axis (as described or indicated by the manufacturer) aligned parallel to the centerline of the vessel and horizontal.

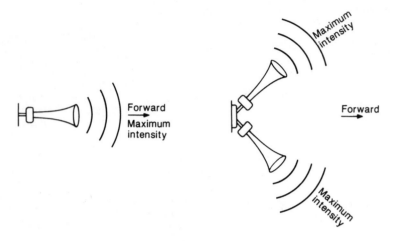

Figure 23—Sound-signal direction of maximum intensity.

Incidentally, the sound pressure level of a whistle is not measured literally "at a distance of one meter from it," but from a farther distance. The sound pressure level at one meter is then calculated.

Sounds are composed of a number of individual elements, each having a different frequency and "loudness." To determine the range of audibility of a whistle, a laboratory measures the separate sound pressure levels of the individual harmonic components of the total sound. How far away a sound can be heard is dependent upon the one harmonic component having the greatest range of audibility. Sound waves of different frequencies, like water waves of different frequencies (or wavelengths), travel independently of one another. The "⅓ octave band level" method used in Annex III separates out all of the individual frequency components.

Imagine a group of people, each representing a sound harmonic (or component) and all lined up at the end of a football field and each holding a baseball. You are out in the field, about as far away as you think is safe. At a signal, each throws his or her baseball at you. If you chose your position wisely, only one ball—that of the strongest thrower—will make it as far as your position, tapping you gently on your foot. You would be at the maximum range of audibility of the "sound" represented by the throwers. The greatest distance thrown, and not the total number of balls or the total energy expended, is what counts. The same effect would have been reached if only the strongest thrower (sound component) had been participating.

Aligned with this illustration are the new fog signals on buoys that emit a "pure" tone—that is, a tone of a single frequency having no harmonics. These signals are extremely energy-efficient because they do not waste energy on sound components that won't go as far as the primary component.

Why does Annex III have different sound pressure levels for different frequency ranges? It does this because the human ear is more sensitive to the higher frequencies (hence for a given pressure level they are more audible), and because lower frequencies travel farther. At closer distances higher frequencies may be more efficient, but when greater audibility ranges are required, lower frequencies are more efficient. The relationship among the variables of frequency, sound pressure level, and audibility range can be graphically represented by a series of curved lines. The International Annex III simplifies these curves down to a single sound pressure level and frequency range for each vessel size group. In doing this it makes substantial compromises. The Inland version follows the curves more closely by using three sets of numbers for each vessel size range. This permits the whistle manufacturer more flexibility and permits a whistle to have the same minimum range of audibility as one meeting International Annex III requirements but at a lower sound pressure level. This is important because high sound pressure levels can impair the hearing of people near the whistle.

INTERNATIONAL

(d) Directional properties
The sound pressure level of a directional whistle shall be not more than 4 dB below the prescribed sound pressure level on the axis at any direction in the horizontal plane within ± 45 degrees of the

INLAND

§ 86.07 Directional properties
The sound pressure level of a directional whistle shall be not more than 4 dB below the sound pressure level specified in § 86.05 in any direction in the horizontal plane within ± 45 degress of the forward

axis. The sound pressure level at any other direction in the horizontal plane shall be not more than 10 dB below the prescribed sound pressure level on the axis, so that the range in any direction will be at least half the range on the forward axis. The sound pressure level shall be measured in that one-third octave band which determines the audibility range.

axis. The sound pressure level of the whistle at any other direction in the horizontal plane shall not be more than 10 dB less than the sound pressure level specified for the forward axis, so that the range of audibility in any direction will be at least half the range required on the forward axis. The sound pressure level shall be measured in that one-third octave band which determines the audibility range.

While it seems all well and good that a whistle measures out just fine in the forward direction, what about crossing vessels? What about overtaking vessels? Annex III provides for audibility in all directions very roughly in proportion to the speed of approach: full intensity directly ahead (meeting head-on), reduced 4 decibels out to 45 degrees (crossing), and reduced 10 decibels everywhere else (lowest rate of approach).

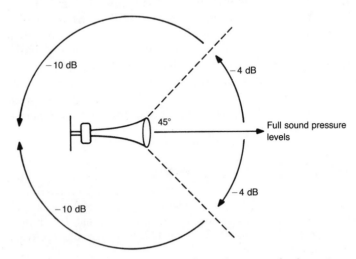

Figure 24—Sound pressure levels in horizontal plane (at 1 meter reference distance).

INTERNATIONAL

(e) Positioning of whistles

When a directional whistle is to be used as the only whistle on a vessel, it shall be installed with its maximum intensity directed straight ahead.

A whistle shall be placed as high as practicable on a vessel, in order to reduce interception of the emitted sound by obstructions and also to minimize hearing damage risk to personnel. The sound pressure level of the vessel's own signal at listening posts shall not exceed 110 dB (A) and so far as practicable should not exceed 100 dB (A).

INLAND

§ 86.09 Positioning of whistles

(a) When a directional whistle is to be used as the only whistle on the vessel and is permanently installed, it shall be installed with its forward axis directed forward.

(b) A whistle shall be placed as high as practicable on a vessel, in order to reduce interception of the emitted sound by obstructions and also to minimize hearing damage risk to personnel. The sound pressure level of the vessel's own signal at listening posts shall not exceed 110 dB (A) and so far as practicable should not exceed 100 dB (A).

Most whistles used on vessels are directional; that is, the sound they emit is not the same intensity in every direction. They are usually loudest in the direction you "point" them. These whistles must be mounted so that their forward axis is aimed directly ahead. Omnidirectional whistles emit sound equally all around the horizontal; it doesn't matter in which direction they are mounted, as long as they are level.

The second part of this section concerns the protection of your hearing so that you can hear the signals from other vessels (as well as what your friends are saying). The measurements for this requirement are made in terms of dB(A), which means all of the energy of all of the harmonic components are measured together. To continue our ball-throwing example, if you unwisely decided to stand on the five-yard line when the signal to throw was given, you would suddenly be concerned with the energy of *all* of the balls thrown, and not with the one ball thrown farthest. That is why we use dB(A) units to measure sound when we're concerned with the person standing next to the whistle, and use $\frac{1}{3}$ octave band dB when we're concerned with the person far away from the whistle.

INTERNATIONAL

(f) Fitting of more than one whistle

If whistles are fitted at a distance apart of more than 100 meters, it shall be so arranged that they are not sounded simultaneously.

INLAND

§ 86.11 Fitting of more than one whistle

If whistles are fitted at a distance apart of more than 100 meters, they shall not be sounded simultaneously.

The speed of sound is approximately 335 meters per second. Many ships are 335 meters long. If whistles were sounded at each end of such a vessel simultaneously, a person listening from in front of (or behind) the ship would likely hear not one signal, but rather two signals separated by about a second in time, the time it takes sound to travel from one end of the ship to the other end. Therefore, a one-half-second-blast would be heard as two separate blasts. When the whistles are separated by 100 meters or less, the delay will be less than one-third of a second and will not likely cause confusion.

INTERNATIONAL

(g) Combined whistle systems

If due to the presence of obstructions the sound field of a single whistle or of one of the whistles referred to in paragraph 1(f) above is likely to have a zone of greatly reduced signal level, it is recommended that a combined whistle system be fitted so as to overcome

INLAND

§ 86.13 Combined whistle systems

(a) A combined whistle system is a number of whistles (sound emitting sources) operated together. For the purposes of the Rules a combined whistle system is to be regarded as a single whistle.

(b) The whistles of a combined system shall—

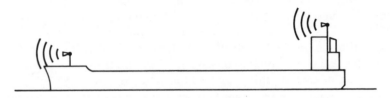

Figure 25—More than one whistle.

this reduction. For the purposes of the Rules a combined whistle system is to be regarded as a single whistle. The whistles of a combined system shall be located at a distance apart of not more than 100 meters and arranged to be sounded simultaneously. The frequency of any one whistle shall differ from those of the others by at least 10 Hz.

(1) Be located at a distance apart of not more than 100 meters,

(2) Be sounded simultaneously,

(3) Each have a fundamental frequency different from those of the others by at least 10 Hz, and

(4) Have a tonal characteristic appropriate for the length of vessel which shall be evidenced by at least two-thirds of the whistles in the combined system having fundamental frequencies falling within the limits prescribed in § 86.03, or if there are only two whistles in the combined system, by the higher fundamental frequency falling within the limits prescribed in § 86.03.

NOTE: If due to the presence of obstructions the sound field of a single whistle or of one of the whistles referred to in § 86.11 is likely to have a zone of greatly reduced signal level, a combined whistle system should be fitted so as to overcome this reduction.

Some people install combined whistle systems when the sound from a single whistle would be obstructed in some direction (resulting in a sound "hole"). Others install them because the com-

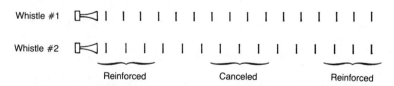

Figure 26—Sound wave interference.

bined sound produced by a number of whistles is music to their ears, and they're willing to pay for it.

The fundamental frequency of each whistle must be at least 10 Hz different from the rest because if the frequencies of two whistles are the same or very close together, the sound waves from each will substantially cancel each other out. If the frequencies are just a little different, a sound phenomenon called "beats" will be produced, yielding alternately high and low levels of sound as the sound waves alternately reinforce and cancel each other. The 10 Hz prohibition reduces these aberrations to an acceptable level.

If only one whistle is installed, it of course has to be the proper tone for the size of the vessel. If two or more whistles are installed in a combined system, however, one (or more than one if there are at least six whistles in the system!) may have a fundamental frequency outside of the range specified for that particular size ship. The conditions this section imposes ensure that the overall sound tone will be appropriate for the vessel.

INLAND

§ 86.15 Towing vessel whistles

A power-driven vessel normally engaged in pushing ahead or towing alongside may, at all times, use a whistle whose characteristic falls within the limits prescribed by § 86.03 for the longest customary composite length of the vessel and its tow.

This provision is only in the Inland Rules Annex III. It permits certain towing vessels to use a whistle whose tone is lower than normally required for vessels of that length. They may instead use a whistle whose fundamental frequency is right for a vessel the same length as the towing vessel and normal tow combined. The towing vessel may continue to use that whistle even after dropping off its barges.

2. Bell or gong

(a) Intensity of signal

A bell or gong, or other device having similar sound characteristics shall produce a sound pressure level of not less than 110 dB at a distance of 1 meter from it.

(b) Construction

Bells and gongs shall be made of corrosion-resistant material and designed to give a clear tone. The diameter of the mouth of the bell shall be not less than 300 mm for vessels of 20 meters or more in length, and shall be not less than 200 mm for vessels of 12 meters or more but of less than 20 meters in length. Where practicable, a power-driven bell striker is recommended to ensure constant force but manual operation shall be possible. The mass of the striker shall be not less than 3 percent of the mass of the bell.

Subpart B—Bell or gong

§ 86.21 Intensity of signal

A bell or gong, or other device having similar sound characteristics shall produce a sound pressure level of not less than 110 dB at 1 meter.

§ 86.23 Construction

Bells and gongs shall be made of corrosion-resistant material and designed to give a clear tone. The diameter of the mouth of the bell shall be not less than 300 mm for vessels of more than 20 meters in length, and shall be not less than 200 mm for vessels of 12 to 20 meters in length. The mass of the striker shall be not less than 3 percent of the mass of the bell. The striker shall be capable of manual operation.

NOTE: When practicable, a power-driven bell striker is recommended to ensure constant force.

Rule 35 requires that vessels anchored or aground in or near restricted visibility give a signal using bell and gong (the gong is needed only on vessels one hundred meters or longer). Normally a power-driven striker will be used or perhaps an electronic sound synthesizer to reproduce and amplify the bell and gong signals. In either case, you must also be able to give the signals manually. If you normally use an electronic bell, you must still have a real one on board.

For the purpose of calculating the required mass of the striker, the "mass of the bell" does not include the mass of the striker or the mass of any supporting structure.

INTERNATIONAL

INLAND

3. Approval

The construction of sound signal appliances, their performance and their installation on board the vessel shall be to the satisfaction of the appropriate authority of the State whose flag the vessel is entitled to fly.

Subpart C—Approval

§ 86.31 Approval [Reserved]

In the United States, the Coast Guard approves sound-signal appliances for use on inspected vessels. For uninspected vessels, compliance of bell, gong, and whistle with Annex III is up to the operator.

ANNEX IV

Distress Signals

1. Need of assistance

The following signals, used or exhibited either together or separately, indicate distress and need of assistance:

(a) a gun or other explosive signal fired at intervals of about a minute;

(b) a continuous sounding with any fog-signaling apparatus;

(c) rockets or shells, throwing red stars fired one at a time at short intervals;

(d) a signal made by radiotelegraphy or by any other signaling method consisting of the group $\cdots --- \cdots$ (SOS) in the Morse Code;

(e) a signal sent by radiotelephony consisting of the spoken word "Mayday;"

(f) the International Code Signal of distress indicated by N.C.;

§ 87.1 Need of assistance

The following signals, used or exhibited either together or separately, indicate distress and need of assistance:

(a) A gun or other explosive signal fired at intervals of about a minute;

(b) A continuous sounding with any fog-signaling apparatus;

(c) Rockets or shells, throwing red stars fired one at a time at short intervals;

(d) A signal made by radiotelegraphy or by any other signaling method consisting of the group $\cdots --- \cdots$ (SOS) in the Morse Code;

(e) A signal sent by radiotelephony consisting of the spoken word "Mayday;"

(f) The International Code Signal of distress indicated by N.C.;

INTERNATIONAL

(g) a signal consisting of a square flag having above or below it a ball or anything resembling a ball;

(h) flames on the vessel (as from a burning tar barrel, oil barrel, etc.);

(i) a rocket parachute flare or a hand flare showing a red light;

(j) a smoke signal giving off orange-colored smoke;

(k) slowly and repeatedly raising and lowering arms outstretched at each side;

(l) the radiotelegraph alarm signal;

(m) the radiotelephone alarm signal;

(n) signals transmitted by emergency position-indicating radio beacons;

(o) approved signals transmitted by radiocommunication systems.

2.

The use or exhibition of any of the foregoing signals except for the purpose of indicating distress and need of assistance and the use of other signals which may be confused with any of the above signals is prohibited.

3.

Attention is drawn to the relevant sections of the International Code of Signals, the Merchant Ship Search and Rescue Manual and the following signals:

(a) a piece of orange-colored canvas with either a black square and

INLAND

(g) A signal consisting of a square flag having above or below it a ball or anything resembling a ball;

(h) Flames on the vessel (as from a burning tar barrel, oil barrel, etc.);

(i) A rocket parachute flare or a hand flare showing a red light;

(j) A smoke signal giving off orange-colored smoke;

(k) Slowly and repeatedly raising and lowering arms outstretched at each side;

(l) The radiotelegraph alarm signal;

(m) The radiotelephone alarm signal;

(n) Signals transmitted by emergency position-indicating radio beacons;

(o) Signals transmitted by radiocommunication systems;

(p) A high intensity white light flashing at regular intervals from 50 to 70 times per minute.

§ 87.3 Exclusive use

The use or exhibition of any of the foregoing signals except for the purpose of indicating distress and need of assistance and the use of other signals which may be confused with any of the above signals is prohibited.

§ 87.5 Supplemental signals

Attention is drawn to the relevant sections of the International Code of Signals, the Merchant Ship Search and Rescue Manual, the International Telecommunication Union Radio Regulations and the following signals:

circle or other appropriate symbol (for identification from the air); (b) a dye marker.

(a) a piece of orange-colored canvas with either a black square and circle or other appropriate symbol (for identification from the air); (b) a dye marker.

Annex IV should be read in conjunction with Rule 37 (Distress Signals). Because the purpose of the Rules is to prevent collisions, information about distress signals alone was put in Annex IV. The short Rule 37 statement referring mariners to Annex IV was a concession to the importance of the subject.

There are two differences between the International and Inland versions of Annex IV. The first (and minor) difference is in paragraph (o), which accommodates distress messages sent by satellite EPIRB or other satellite voice/data communications equipment. The International version refers to "approved" signals; the Inland version recognizes that any effective plain-language message will do just fine in a distress situation. The second difference is more substantial; paragraph (p) in the Inland Rules authorizes the use of "strobe" lights. Strobe lights are also frequently attached to life preservers to help locate persons who have fallen overboard.

Even if you never intend to be in distress, you should be thoroughly familiar with the signals listed here so that you do not use them (or similar signals) for any other purpose.

ANNEX V

Pilot Rules

Annex V is in the Inland Rules only. They are navigation rules that do not fit conveniently into the International Rules format (which was adopted for the Inland Rules in 1980). These regulations apply everywhere the Inland Rules do.

INLAND

§ 88.01 Purpose and applicability
This part applies to all vessels operating on United States inland waters and to United States vessels operating on the Canadian waters of the Great Lakes to the extent there is no conflict with Canadian law.

§ 88.03 Definitions
The terms used in this part have the same meaning as defined in the Inland Navigational Rules Act of 1980.

§ 88.05 Copy of Rules
After January 1, 1983, the operator of each self-propelled vessel 12 meters or more in length shall carry

on board and maintain for ready
reference a copy of the Inland Navigation Rules.

All self-propelled vessels, twelve meters or longer, operating on
Inland Rule waters must carry a copy of the Inland navigation
rules on board. Any copy will do, including an annotated version
(such as this book). You do not need an "official" publication.
You do need an up-to-date version of the Rules. Remember that
the Rules are amended from time to time. Make sure your version
is current or, if not, that you have a copy of the amendments along
with your older version of the Rules (sort of like keeping your
charts current).

INLAND

§ 88.09 Temporary exemption from light and shape requirements when operating under bridges

A vessel's navigation lights and
shapes may be lowered if necessary
to pass under a bridge.

§ 88.11 Law enforcement vessels

(a) Law enforcement vessels may
display a flashing blue light when
engaged in direct law enforcement
activities. This light shall be located so that it does not interfere
with the visibility of the vessel's
navigation lights.

(b) The blue light described in this
section may be displayed by law
enforcement vessels of the United
States and the States and their po-
litical subdivisions.

§ 88.13 Lights on barges at bank or dock

(a) The following barges shall display at night and, if practicable, in

periods of restricted visibility the lights described in paragraph (b) of this section—

(1) Every barge projecting into a buoyed or restricted channel.

(2) Every barge so moored that it reduces the available navigable width of any channel to less than 80 meters.

(3) Barges moored in groups more than two barges wide or to a maximum width of over 25 meters.

(4) Every barge not moored parallel to the bank or dock.

(b) Barges described in paragraph (a) shall carry two unobstructed white lights of an intensity to be visible for at least one mile on a clear dark night, and arranged as follows:

(1) On a single moored barge, lights shall be placed on the two corners farthest from the bank or dock.

(2) On barges moored in group formation, a light shall be placed on each of the upstream and downstream ends of the group, on the corners farthest from the bank or dock.

(3) Any barge in a group, projecting from the main body of the group toward the channel, shall be lighted as a single barge.

(c) Barges moored in any slip or slough which is used primarily for mooring purposes are exempt from the lighting requirements of this section.

(d) Barges moored in well-illuminated areas are exempt from the

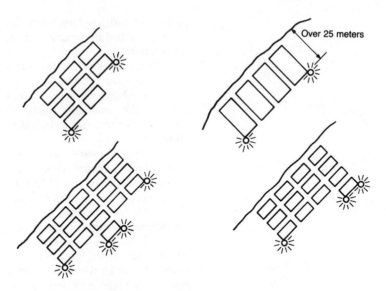

Figure 27—Lights on barges at bank or dock.

INLAND

lighting requirements of this section. These areas are as follows:

Chicago Sanitary Ship Canal
(1) Mile 293.2 to 293.9
(3) Mile 295.2 to 296.1
(5) Mile 297.5 to 297.8
(7) Mile 298 to 298.2
(9) Mile 298.6 to 298.8
(11) Mile 299.3 to 299.4
(13) Mile 299.8 to 300.5
(15) Mile 303 to 303.2
(17) Mile 303.7 to 303.9
(19) Mile 305.7 to 305.8
(21) Mile 310.7 to 310.9
(23) Mile 311 to 311.2
(25) Mile 312.5 to 312.6
(27) Mile 313.8 to 314.2

(29) Mile 314.6

(31) Mile 314.8 to 315.3

(33) Mile 315.7 to 316

(35) Mile 316.8

(37) Mile 316.85 to 317.05

(39) Mile 317.5

(41) Mile 318.4 to 318.9

(43) Mile 318.7 to 318.8

(45) Mile 320 to 320.3

(47) Mile 320.6

(49) Mile 322.3 to 322.4

(51) Mile 322.8

(53) Mile 322.9 to 327.2

Calumet Sag Channel

(61) Mile 316.5

Little Calumet River

(71) Mile 321.2

(73) Mile 322.3

Calumet River

(81) Mile 328.5 to 328.7

(83) Mile 329.2 to 329.4

(85) Mile 330, west bank to 330.2

(87) Mile 331.4 to 331.6

(89) Mile 332.2 to 332.4

(91) Mile 332.6 to 332.8

Cumberland River

(101) Mile 126.8

(103) Mile 191

§ 88.15 Lights on dredge pipelines

Dredge pipelines that are floating or supported on trestles shall display the following lights at night and in periods of restricted visibility.

(a) One row of yellow lights. The lights must be—

(1) Flashing 50 to 70 times per minute,

(2) Visible all around the horizon,

INLAND

(3) Visible for at least 2 miles on a clear dark night,

(4) Not less than 1 and not more than 3.5 meters above the water,

(5) Approximately equally spaced, and

(6) Not more than 10 meters apart where the pipeline crosses a navigable channel. Where the pipeline does not cross a navigable channel the lights must be sufficient in number to clearly show the pipeline's length and course.

(b) Two red lights at each end of the pipeline, including the ends in a channel where the pipeline is separated to allow vessels to pass (whether open or closed). The lights must be—

(1) Visible all around the horizon, and

(2) Visible for at least 2 miles on a clear dark night, and

(3) One meter apart in a vertical line with the lower light at the same height above the water as the flashing yellow light.

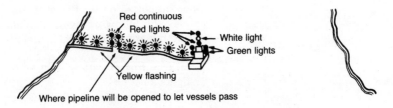

Figure 28—Lights on dredge pipelines.

APPENDIX I

Implementing Rules (Title 33, Code of Federal Regulations)

Exemptions

81.20 Lights and sound signal appliances.

Appendix A—Proclamation of January 19, 1977 and 72 COLREGS

AUTHORITY: 33 U.S.C. 180, 30 Stat. 98; 49 CFR 1.46(c)(2); 28 Stat. 647, 33 U.S.C. 258; 49 CFR 1.46(c)(3); sec. 4233 R.S., 33 U.S.C. 322.

SOURCE: CGD 76–130, 42 FR 17111, Mar. 31, 1977, unless otherwise noted. Redesignated by CGD 81–017, 46 FR 28154, May 26, 1981.

§ *81.1 Definitions*

As used in this part:

"72 COLREGS" refers to the International Regulations for Preventing Collisions at Sea, 1972, done at London, October 20, 1972, as rectified by the Proces-Verbal of December 1, 1973, as amended.

"A vessel of special construction or purpose" means a vessel designed or modified to perform a special function and whose arrangement is thereby made relatively inflexible.

"Interference with the special function of the vessel" occurs when installation or use of lights, shapes, or sound-signaling appliances under 72 COLREGS prevents or significantly hinders the operation in which the vessel is usually engaged.

[CGD 77–136, 47 FR 13799, Apr. 1, 1982]

Subpart B—Waters Upon Which Certain Inland Navigation Rules Apply

89.21 Purpose.

89.23 Definitions.

89.25 Waters upon which inland Rules 9(a)(ii), 14(d), 15(b), and 24(i) apply.

AUTHORITY: Sec. 3, Pub. L. 96–591, 33 U.S.C. 2071; 49 CFR 1.46(n)(14).

Subpart A—Certificate of Alternative Compliance

§ *89.1 Definitions*

As used in this Subpart:

"Inland Rules" refers to the Inland Navigation Rules contained in the Inland Navigational Rules Act of 1980 (Public Law 96–591) and the technical annexes established under that act.

"A vessel of special construction or purpose" means a vessel designed or modified to perform a special function and whose arrangement is thereby made relatively inflexible.

"Interference with the special function of the vessel" occurs when installation or use of lights, shapes, or sound-signaling appliance under the Inland Rules prevents or significantly hinders the operation in which the vessel is usually engaged.

§ 81.3 General

Vessels of special construction or purpose which cannot fully comply with the light, shape, and sound signal provisions of 72 COLREGS without interfering with their special function may instead meet alternative requirements. The Chief of the Marine Safety Division in each Coast Guard District Office makes this determination and requires that alternative compliance be as close as possible with the 72 COLREGS. These regulations set out the procedure by which a vessel may be certified for alternative compliance. The information collection and recordkeeping requirements in §§ 81.5 and 81.18 have been approved by the Office of Management and Budget under OMB control No. 2115–0073.

[CGD 77–136, 47 FR 13799, Apr. 1, 1982]

§ 89.3 General

Vessels of special construction or purpose which cannot fully comply with the light, shape, and sound signal provisions of the Inland Rules without interfering with their special function may instead meet alternative requirements. The Chief of the Marine Safety Division in each Coast Guard District Office makes this determination and requires that alternative compliance be as close as possible with the Inland Rules. These regulations set out the procedure by which a vessel may be certified for alternative compliance. The information collection and recordkeeping requirements in §§ 89.5 and 89.18 have been approved by the Office of Management and Budget under OMB control number 2115–0074.

Alternative Compliance

§ 81.5 Application for a Certificate of Alternative Compliance

(a) The owner, builder, operator, or agent of a vessel of special construction or purpose who believes the vessel cannot fully comply with the 72 COLREGS light, shape, or sound signal provisions without interference with its special function may apply for a determination that alternative compliance is justified. The application must be in writing, submitted to the Chief of the Marine Safety Division of the Coast Guard District in which the

§ 89.5 Application for a Certificate of Alternative Compliance

(a) The owner, builder, operator, or agent of a vessel of special construction or purpose who believes the vessel cannot fully comply with the Inland Rules light, shape, or sound signal provisions without interference with its special function may apply for a determination that alternative compliance is justified. The application must be in writing, submitted to the Chief of the Marine Safety Division of the Coast Guard District in which the vessel is being built or operated, and include the following information:

(1) The name, address, and telephone number of the applicant.

(2) The identification of the vessel by its—

(i) Official number;

(ii) Shipyard hull number;

(iii) Hull identification number; or

(iv) State number, if the vessel does not have an official number or hull identification number.

(3) Vessel name and home port, if known.

(4) A description of the vessel's area of operation.

(5) A description of the provision for which the Certificate of Alternative Compliance is sought, including:

(i) The 72 COLREGS Rule or Annex section number for which the Certificate of Alternative Compliance is sought;

(ii) A description of the special function of the vessel that would be interfered with by full compliance with the provision of that Rule or Annex section; and

(iii) A statement of how full compliance would interfere with the special function of the vessel.

(6) A description of the alternative installation that is in closest possible compliance with the applicable 72 COLREGS Rule or Annex section.

vessel is being built or operated, and include the following information:

(1) The name, address, and telephone number of the applicant.

(2) The identification of the vessel by its—

(i) Official number;

(ii) Shipyard hull number;

(iii) Hull identification number; or

(iv) State number, if the vessel does not have an official number or hull identification number.

(3) Vessel name and home port, if known.

(4) A description of the vessel's area of operation.

(5) A description of the provision for which the Certificate of Alternative Compliance is sought, including:

(i) The Inland Rules Rule or Annex section number for which the Certificate of Alternative Compliance is sought;

(ii) A description of the special function of the vessel that would be interfered with by full compliance with the provision of that Rule or Annex section; and

(iii) A statement of how full compliance would interfere with the special function of the vessel.

(6) A description of the alternative installation that is in closest possible compliance with the applicable Inland Navigation Rules Rule or Annex section.

(7) A copy of the vessel's plans or an accurate scale drawing that clearly shows:

(i) The required installation of the equipment under the 72 COL-REGS,

(ii) The proposed installation of the equipment for which certification is being sought, and

(iii) Any obstructions that may interfere with the equipment when installed in:

(a) The required location; and

(b) The proposed location.

(b) The Coast Guard may request from the applicant additional information concerning the application.

OMB CONTROL NO.: 2115–0073. (47 FR 13799, Apr. 1, 1982)

[47 FR 13799, Apr. 1, 1982]

§ 81.9 Certificate of Alternative Compliance: Contents

The Chief of the Marine Safety Division issues the Certificate of Alternative Compliance to the vessel based on a determination that it cannot comply fully with 72 COL-REGS light, shape, and sound signal provisions without interference with its special function. This Certificate includes—

(a) Identification of the vessel as supplied in the application under § 81.5(a)(2);

(b) The provision of the 72 COL-REGS for which the Certificate authorizes alternative compliance;

(c) A certification that the vessel is unable to comply fully with the 72 COLREGS lights, shape, and sound

(7) A copy of the vessel's plans or an accurate scale drawing that clearly shows:

(i) The required installation of the equipment under the Inland Rules,

(ii) The proposed installation of the equipment for which certification is being sought, and

(iii) Any obstructions that may interfere with the equipment when installed in:

(a) The required location; and

(b) The proposed location.

(b) The Coast Guard may request from the applicant additional information concerning the application.

[CGD 80–157, 47 FR 13801, Apr. 1, 1982; 47 FR 18332, Apr. 29, 1982]

§ 89.9 Certificate of Alternative Compliance: Contents

The Chief of the Marine Safety Division issues the Certificate of Alternative Compliance to the vessel based on a determination that it cannot comply fully with Inland Rules light, shape, and sound signal provisions without interference with its special function. This Certificate includes—

(a) Identification of the vessel as supplied in the application under § 89.5(a)(2);

(b) The provision of the Inland Rules for which the Certificate authorizes alternative compliance;

(c) A certification that the vessel is unable to comply fully with the Inland Rules light, shape, and sound

INTERNATIONAL

signal requirements without interference with its special function;

(d) A statement of why full compliance would interfere with the special function of the vessel;

(e) The required alternative installation;

(f) A statement that the required alternative installation is in the closest possible compliance with the 72 COLREGS without interfering with the special function of the vessel;

(g) The date of issuance;

(h) A statement that the Certificate of Alternative Compliance terminates when the vessel ceases to be usually engaged in the operation for which the certificate is issued.

[CGD 77–136, 47 FR 13800, Apr. 1, 1982]

§ 81.17 Certificate of Alternative Compliance: Termination

The Certificate of Alternative Compliance terminates if the information supplied under § 81.5(a) or the Certificate issued under § 81.9 is no longer applicable to the vessel.

[CGD 77–136, 47 FR 13800, Apr. 1, 1982]

§ 81.18 Notice and record of certification of vessels of special construction or purpose.

(a) In accordance with 33 U.S.C. 1605(c), a notice is published in the FEDERAL REGISTER of the following:

(1) Each Certificate of Alternative Compliance issued under § 81.9; and

INLAND

signal requirements without interference with its special functions;

(d) A statement of why full compliance would interfere with the special function of the vessel;

(e) The required alternative installation;

(f) A statement that the required alternative installation is in the closest possible compliance with the Inland Rules without interfering with the special function of the vessel;

(g) The date of issuance;

(h) A statement that the Certificate of Alternative Compliance terminates when the vessel ceases to be usually engaged in the operation for which the certificate is issued.

§ 89.17 Certificate of Alternative Compliance: Termination

The Certificate of Alternative Compliance terminates if the information supplied under § 89.5(a) or the Certificate issued under § 89.9 is no longer applicable to the vessel.

§ 89.18 Record of certification of vessels of special construction or purpose

(2) Each Coast Guard vessel determined by the Commandant to be a vessel of special construction or purpose.

(b) Copies of Certificate of Alternative Compliance and documentation concerning Coast Guard vessels are available for inspection at Coast Guard Headquarters, Office of Navigation, 2100 Second Street S.W., Washington, D.C. 20593.

(c) The owner or operator of a vessel issued a Certificate shall ensure that the vessel does not operate unless the Certificate of Alternative Compliance or a certified copy of that Certificate is on board the vessel and available for inspection by Coast Guard personnel.

OMB CONTROL NO.: 2115–0073. (47 FR 13800, Apr. 1, 1982)
[CGD 77–136, 47 FR 13800, Apr. 1, 1982]

Exemptions

§ 81.20 *Lights and sound signal appliances*

Each vessel under the 72 COLREGS, except the vessels of the Navy, is exempt from the requirements of the 72 COLREGS to the limitation for the period of time stated in Rule 38 (a), (b), (c), (d), (e), (f), and (g) if—

(a) Her keel is laid or is at a corresponding stage of construction before July 15, 1977; and

(b) She meets the International Regulations for Preventing Collisions at Sea, 1960 (77 Stat. 194, 33 U.S.C. 1051–1094).

(a) Copies of Certificates of Alternative Compliance and documentation concerning Coast Guard vessels are available for inspection at Coast Guard Headquarters, Office of Navigation, 2100 Second Street S.W., Washington, D.C. 20593.

(b) The owner or operator of a vessel issued a Certificate shall ensure that the vessel does not operate unless the Certificate of Alternative Compliance or a certified copy of that Certificate is on board the vessel and available for inspection by Coast Guard personnel.

Subpart B—Waters Upon Which Certain Inland Navigation Rules Apply

§ 89.21 *Purpose*

Inland Navigation Rules 9(a)(ii), 14(d), and 15(b) apply to the Great Lakes, and along with 24(i), apply on the "Western Rivers" as defined in Rule 3(l), and to additional specifically designated waters. The purpose of this Subpart is to specify those additional waters upon which Inland Navigation Rules 9(a)(ii), 14(d), 15(b), and 24(i) apply.

§ 89.23 *Definitions*

As used in this subpart:

"Inland Rules" refers to the Inland Navigation Rules contained in the Inland Navigational Rules Act

NOTE: Appendix A of this part contains the 72 COLREGS.

[CGD 76–133, 42 FR 35792, July 11, 1977. Redesignated at CGD 81–017, 46 FR 28154, May 26, 1981]

of 1980 (Pub. L. 96–591, 33 U.S.C. 2001 et seq.) and the technical annexes established under that act.

§ 89.25 Waters upon which Inland Rules 9(a)(ii), 14(d), 15(b), and 24(i) apply

Inland Rules 9(a)(ii), 14(d), and 15(b) apply on the Great Lakes, and along with 24(i), apply on the Western Rivers and the following specified waters:

(a) Tennessee–Tombigbee Waterway;

(b) Tombigbee River;

(c) Black Warrior River;

(d) Alabama River;

(e) Coosa River;

(f) Mobile River above the Cochrane Bridge at St. Louis Point;

(g) Flint River;

(h) Chattachoochee River; and

(i) The Apalachicola River above its confluence with the Jackson River.

APPENDIX II

Interpretative Rules (Title 33, Code of Federal Regulations)

Part 82—72 COLREGS: Interpretative Rules

Sec.

82.1 Purpose.

82.3 Pushing vessel and vessel being pushed: Composite unit.

AUTHORITY: 33 U.S.C. 180, 30 Stat. 98; 49 CFR 1.46(c)(2); 28 Stat. 647, 33 U.S.C. 258; 49 CRF 1.46(c)(3); sec. 4233 R.S., 33 U.S.C. 322.

§ 82.1 Purpose

This part contains the interpretative rules concerning the 72 COLREGS that are adopted by the Coast Guard for the guidance of the public.

[CGD 76–133, 42 FR 35792, July 11, 1977. Redesignated by CGD 81–017, 46 FR 28154, May 26, 1981]

Part 90—Inland Rules: Interpretative Rules

Sec.

90.1 Purpose.

90.3 Pushing vessel and vessel being pushed: Composite unit.

AUTHORITY: 33 U.S.C. 2071; 49 CFR 1.46(n)(14).

SOURCE: CGD 83–011, 48, FR 51622, Nov. 10, 1983, unless otherwise noted.

§ 90.1 Purpose

This part contains the interpretative rules for the Inland Rules. These interpretative rules are intended as a guide to assist the public and promote compliance with the Inland Rules.

§ 82.3 Pushing vessel and vessel being pushed: Composite unit
Rule 24(b) of the 72 COLREGS states that when a pushing vessel

INTERNATIONAL

and a vessel being pushed ahead are rigidly connected in a composite unit, they are regarded as a power-driven vessel and must exhibit the lights under Rule 23. A "composite unit" is interpreted to be a pushing vessel that is rigidly connected by mechanical means to a vessel being pushed so they react to sea and swell as one vessel. "Mechanical means" does not include the following:
   (a) Lines.
   (b) Hawsers.
   (c) Wires.
   (d) Chains.
[CGD 76–133, 42 FR 35792, July 11, 1977. Redesignated by CGD 81–017, 46 FR 28154, May 26, 1981]

§ 90.3 Pushing vessel and vessel being pushed: Composite unit
Rule 24(b) of the Inland Rules states that when a pushing vessel and a

INLAND

vessel being pushed ahead are rigidly connected in a composite unit, they are regarded as a power-driven vessel and must exhibit the lights prescribed in Rule 23. A "composite unit" is interpreted to be the combination of a pushing vessel and a vessel being pushed ahead that are rigidly connected by mechanical means so they react to sea and swell as one vessel. Mechanical means does not include lines, wires, hawsers, or chains.

APPENDIX III

Summary of Vessel Traffic Service Regulations (Part 161 [Subpart B], Title 33, Code of Federal Regulations)

In 1990, as the second edition of this book was being readied for publication, there were two developments in the status of the vessel traffic service (VTS) regulations. First, the Coast Guard was preparing to propose that the individual sets of regulations applying to each of the several VTS locations be consolidated into one comprehensive set of regulations, which would apply to all existing and new VTSs. The amendments were intended to change only the form of the regulations, not the substance.

Second, in August 1990, immediately prior to the release of the Coast Guard's planned consolidation proposal, the U.S. Congress passed the Oil Pollution Act of 1990 (amending the Ports and Waterways Safety Act). This new legislation was enacted in response to the rash of vessel oil spills during the spring and summer of 1990, and it contained a number of provisions directly affecting the operation of VTSs. The Coast Guard therefore delayed the release of its Notice of Proposed Rulemaking until the new substantive and more stringent requirements could be incorporated into their proposal, reflecting and implementing the legislative mandates contained in the Oil Pollution Act of 1990.

In general, the expected changes to the VTS regulations as a result of the Oil Pollution Act are (1) to make all VTS areas mandatory (some are now voluntary) and (2) to perhaps expand their applicability to smaller vessels. At the time of this writing, the revised proposal was expected to be released early in 1991.

The summary of the existing (pre-1991) VTS regulations presented here is only intended to be a general explanation of the types of requirements imposed in VTS areas. Anyone who expects to be operating a vessel in a VTS should of course contact the Coast Guard for a copy of the latest requirements.

The stated purposes of the vessel operation rules are to prevent collisions and groundings and minimize the associated risk of property damage and environmental harm. Some parts of the rules apply to all vessels (usually general rules); other parts (generally communications requirements) apply to certain classes of vessels. Depending on the particular VTS area, the rules are applicable to: vessels 300 gross tons or more propelled by machinery; vessels 100 gross tons or more carrying one or more passengers for hire; commercial towing vessels 26 feet/8 meters or more in length; dredges and floating plants; small vessels carrying more than six passengers for hire; and vessels 30 meters or more in length. Other vessels may be covered in certain specific places or situations.

The regulations contain an extensive list of definitions for terms used, from "vessel" to "Cooperative Vessel Traffic Management Area."

During conditions of vessel congestion, adverse weather, reduced visibility, full or partial channel obstructions, heavy ice, strong currents, or other hazardous circumstances in the VTS area, shore-based vessel traffic centers may issue directions to control and supervise traffic and may specify times when vessels may enter, move within or through, or depart VTS waters. If a specific vessel is operating in an unsafe manner or with improperly functioning equipment (for example, broken VHF radio or radar), the vessel traffic center may direct the vessel's movement, possibly directing it to anchor or moor.

Many vessels that operate in a VTS area are required to carry on board a copy of the VTS regulations that apply to that area. The Coast Guard provides free of charge copies of VTS *User's Manuals* (also called *Operating Manuals*), which contain the regulations, navigation information, and guidelines for the efficient operation of vessels in VTS areas.

The regulations state that nothing in the VTS regulations is intended to relieve any person from complying with any other applicable laws or regulations. Although the VTS operators are watching and perhaps directing traffic, vessel operators should not assume that they can relinquish complete control. They are still fully responsible for tracking other traffic and avoiding collisions and for complying with all of the navigation rules. The vessel traffic center is there to help operators of vessels in the VTS with those tasks.

The VTS regulations include a provision on emergencies, which states that the operator of a vessel in a VTS may deviate from specific VTS regulations to the extent necessary to avoid endangering persons, property, or the environment. Vessel operators are still required, however, to report any such deviation to the vessel traffic center as soon as possible.

There are other provisions in the VTS regulations that permit a deviation under nonemergency circumstances. Alternate operational procedures may be authorized by the Coast Guard upon written request if they determine that the alternate procedure gives a level of safety equivalent to that provided by the regulations.

VTS operations are extremely dependent on reliable and timely communications from vessels in the system. The communications rules in the VTS regulations are therefore quite comprehensive.

The regulations require the vessel operator to maintain a radio listening watch on the appropriate frequency when underway and also in some situations or locations when anchored or moored in the VTS (the regulations are specific about classes of vessel and circumstances for which compliance is required). The listening watch is to be maintained from the vessel's bridge; when the vessel is anchored or moored, some other location is also acceptable. The primary frequency is normally channel 14 (VHF-FM); the secondary frequency is usually channel 13. Some VTS areas use other frequencies and some areas are divided into several zones, each having different primary and secondary frequencies. Transmissions are to be at low power unless there is no response.

Just as in the air-traffic-control system, vessels in VTS systems are required to make a number of reports, normally over their VHF radiotelephones. This includes a report of a radio failure, as soon as possible, using whatever means.

Most of the reports concern vessel movements. There are local harbor reports, initial reports, underway or movement reports, reports from "permanent reporting points" and from "seasonal reporting points," calling-in-point and zone boundary reports, and final reports. There are special reports for ferry vessels, reports of impairment to the operation of the vessel, and miscellaneous reports.

A typical report would include the name and type of vessel, the vessel's position, time (24-hour clock), destination and estimated time of arrival, vessel speed in knots, and a general description of the operation to be performed. Depending on the specific type of report, other information required is whether use of a traffic separation scheme (TSS) is planned, whether there is a dangerous cargo on board, and so forth.

The VTS regulations also contain specific rules for vessel movements where unique geographic or other conditions exist. Some examples of these special requirements are TSS rules, one-way traffic, passing, winter navigation, anchorage rules, speed rules, high-water towing limitations, and rules for vessel movements under a particular bridge.

Finally, the regulations contain detailed descriptions and geographic coordinates for all of the VTS areas.

Index

About the Authors

Christopher B. Llana, a former U.S. Coast Guard officer with advanced degrees in marine affairs and law, drafted the annexes to the Inland Navigation Rules as a civilian navigation rules expert in the Coast Guard's Waterways Safety Branch. He is currently a writer of fiction and nonfiction and a consultant on maritime regulations and mobile satellite communications. He lives in Warwick, New York.

George P. Wisneskey is a graduate of the U.S. Coast Guard Academy who holds a master's degree in education from George Washington University. As chief of the Coast Guard's Rules of the Road Branch before his retirement in 1982, he oversaw the drafting of the Inland Navigational Rules Act of 1980. He is presently a senior instructor with a large defense contractor in the Washington, D.C., area.

THE NAVAL INSTITUTE PRESS
HANDBOOK OF THE NAUTICAL RULES OF THE ROAD
Second Edition
Designed by Karen L. White

Set in Eurostyle and Melior
by NK Graphics, Inc.
Baltimore, Maryland

Printed on 50-lb. Penntech Clarion Book Blue-White
and bound
by R.R. Donnelley & Sons Company
Crawfordsville, Indiana